Wall Street
and the
Stock
Markets

A CHRONOLOGY

(1644-1971)

Wall Street and the Stock Markets

A CHRONOLOGY
(1644-1971)

PETER WYCKOFF

CHILTON BOOK COMPANY

Philadelphia   New York   London

Published in Philadelphia by Chilton Book Company
and simultaneously in Ontario, Canada,
by Thomas Nelson & Sons, Ltd.

Designed by Ann Churchman
Manufactured in the United States of America

Library of Congress Cataloging in Publication Data

Wyckoff, Peter.
  Wall Street and the stock markets.

  Bibliography: p.
  1. Wall Street. 2. Stocks—United States—
Tables, etc. I. Title.
HG4572.W87   332.6′42′0973   72-8277
ISBN 0-8019-5708-7

To Molly

Foreword

Much has been written about Wall Street and the markets. It fills a large space in the newspapers. It has inspired the plots for plays, the backgrounds for novels, the ideas for magazine articles. The mechanism of the Exchange and its history have been described in print. Formulas for "beating the market" have been revealed. Certain financial nabobs have "told all" to publishers, and books about trading, investing, selling short, analyzing securities, dealing in options, and other techniques have appeared.

Yet no one has undertaken to outline, in regular sequence, the development of the stock market since "buttonwood" days, to present in terms of price and time elapsed its performance linked with specific events and its many records achieved in 180 years of operation.

Sportscasters can find out instantly who kicked the longest field goal, or how many times a certain boxer was knocked out. But comparable records, showing the longest consecutive daily advance by the Dow Industrials, or how many times the discount rate was boosted in 1966, for example, have only just now been made easy to find.

This book is divided into four sections dealing, respectively, with "A Chronology (1644–1971)," "The Exchanges," "The Averages," "Market Influences."

Section One covers important historical incidents and items of market interest. Annual tables are included from 1900 through 1971, giving the total number of trading days, the number of advancing, declining, and unchanged sessions, plus annual and monthly net gains or losses for the Dow Jones Averages.

Section Two of the volume gives the history of seat prices, share turnover, odd-lots, listing requirements, short sales, the short position, fails, block transactions, and more.

Section Three analyzes the market averages: Dow Jones, Standard & Poor's, New York Stock Exchange, American Stock Exchange.

Section Four reviews some factors responsible for price movements: wars, presidential elections, the Federal Reserve, together with theories that what has happened may very well recur.

Private and institutional investors, corporate managers, libraries, universities, schools, and interested professional or amateur market operators can now quickly find certain previously obscure data which, hopefully, will assist a research effort, or refresh faded memories about the reaction of the world's greatest auction center to some specific event.

From the author's standpoint this book will have accomplished a basic purpose if it contributes toward a better understanding of Wall Street and the markets, by bringing to the surface some hitherto buried facts of financial history; not skeletons from the closets of Broad and Wall, but irrefutable records of what has happened. In this way the impartial student or trained professional may examine them, form his own conclusions, and possibly mold them into an accurate trading or investment decision.

Acknowledgments

The author expresses thanks and appreciation to the American Stock Exchange, Inc., for permission to use material from their "Amex Databook 1971," and to the New York Stock Exchange, Inc., for permission to use material from their "Fact Book." Also, to the Federal Reserve Bank of New York and to Standard & Poor's Corporation for providing certain data from their records.

Contents

xi

SECTION 1

A Chronology

(1644-1971)

1644

March 31: Notice was posted which located Wall Street: "Resolved . . . that a fence or park shall be made beginning at the Great Bouwery, and extending to Emanuel's plantation, and every one . . . is warned to repair thither on Monday, being the 4th. of April, at 7 o'clock, with tools to aid in constructing said fence. . . ."

1653

Peter Stuyvesant built palisade on line of modern Wall Street to protect the settled area south of it from attack by Indians or by English.

1685

December 16: Wall Street surveyed and established.

1688

Term "stock jobber" first used in England.

1690

First government paper to circulate as money in the U.S. issued by colony of Massachusetts, to pay soldiers returning from unsuccessful expedition against Canada.

3

1694
Bank of England established.

1697
Britain's Parliament enacted law to curb speculation and provided system for licensing brokers.

1720
South Sea Company collapsed. Shares had climbed from 120 in April to above 1,000 in July.

1726
Paris Bourse founded. (Change de Paris from which it evolved went back to 1304.)

1730
Pirates and slave traders infested Wall-Water Streets. Captain William Kidd resided at 56 William Street.

1734
Sir John Barnard's Act passed in England; first serious attempt to regulate securities speculation by law.

1746
Groundwork for Philadelphia-Baltimore-Washington Stock Exchange prepared when Philadelphia's mayor appropriated 150 pounds to establish common market place.

1754
Brokers and merchants—nucleus of Philadelphia Stock Exchange— met in London Coffee House, Philadelphia.

1759
First U.S. insurance policy, written this year, was an annuity.

1761
First book about a stock exchange, "Every Man His Own Broker, or A Guide to Exchange Alley," written in London by J. Mortimer.

1764

Whipping post, stocks, cage, and pillory removed from Wall Street.

1768

Chamber of Commerce of New York organized at Fraunce's Tavern.

1773

July 5: London Stock Exchange formed.

1775

June: First paper money proposed in Continental Congress.

1776

July 16: Declaration of Independence read from City Hall steps in New York.

September 21: The Wall demolished by great fire that destroyed 500 houses, about one eighth of the city. It had cost taxpayers a present-day equivalent of about $1,265.

1781

December: Bank of North America, first in the U.S., incorporated in Philadelphia. It was planned and put in operation by Robert Morris, Superintendent of Finance of the Revolution, to give financial support to Washington's army.

1782

December 4: Washington bade farewell to officers at Fraunce's Tavern.

1784

June 9: Alexander Hamilton founded Bank of New York.

1786

First authenticated strike in one trade in U.S. Minimum weekly wage of $6 won by Philadelphia printers.

1789

March 4: First U.S. Congress called at Federal Hall, New York; authorized issue of $80 million in stocks to help pay for Revolutionary War.

April 30: Washington inaugurated at Federal Hall, New York.
September: Department of the Treasury established.

1790

First American turnpike built.

Matthew McConnell elected first president of Philadelphia Board of Brokers, later the Philadelphia Stock Exchange.

Last of thirteen original states ratified Constitution.

1791

May: First recorded strike in building trades. Philadelphia carpenters struck unsuccessfully for 10-hour day, plus overtime.

December: First Bank of the United States, devised by Alexander Hamilton, began operations.

First recognizable Wall Street pool organized to corner stock of U.S. Bank.

1792

April: Trade conditions and tight money led to Wall Street's first serious reaction. The failure for $3 million of Colonel William Duer, who tried to corner "when issued" U.S. Bank stock in 1791, helped this along. Treasury Secretary Hamilton bought government bonds to relieve situation.

May 17: Twenty-four gentlemen met beneath buttonwood tree (sycamore) in front of what is now 68 Wall Street; declared themselves "Brokers for the purchase and sale of public stocks." Organization was forerunner of New York Stock Exchange. They signed agreement to charge commission of not less than ¼ percent. Exchange opened with following quotations:

U.S. Government 6 percents	. . . .	22 shillings.
U.S. Government 3 percents	. . . .	12s, 8d.
U.S. Government Deferred	. . . .	13s, 2d.
U.S. Government Indents.	. . . .	12s, 6d.
Final Settlements	. . . .	50% premium.
Shares Bank of North America	. . . .	.15% premium.

Philadelphia shoemakers organized first local craft union for collective bargaining. It disbanded within a year.

1793

Adopting new rules, "buttonwood" brokers transferred operations indoors to Tontine Coffee House at Wall and Water Streets, which merchants-brokers had chartered by subscribing $200 each.

1794

Insurance Company of North America chartered in Philadelphia.

1796

First U.S. depression.

1798

American bond yields first recorded.

1802

New York Post began quoting prices on 4 government bonds, 3 bank stocks, 3 insurance companies.

1807

First U.S. railroad built. Steam navigation inaugurated on Hudson River.

August 11: Robert Fulton's "Clermont" traveled from New York to Albany and back, opening an era of steamboat building, new areas of commerce and trade.

1808

Bank, insurance stocks, and government loans monopolized trading list, consisting of merely 15 issues as published by newspapers.

1812

War of 1812 gave speculation its first genuine impetus.

Heavy speculation in "shin plasters" caused New York State Legislature to enact law designed to prevent short selling. (It was rescinded in 1858.)

Trading list expanded to 30 securities, mostly bank and insurance stocks. Exchange had 28 members.

1814

Exports fell to $7 million this year of crisis. Hundreds of businesses failed.

August 24: British captured Washington; parts of city leveled by fire. Banks in Baltimore, Philadelphia, New York suspended specie payments.

1815
New York Manufacturing Co. became first issue admitted to trading list, other than federal, state loans and bank or insurance stocks.

1816
Second Bank of the United States established at insistence of President Madison, to end currency disorders resulting from War of 1812.
December: Provident Institution for Savings, the first U.S. savings bank, established in Boston, Mass.

1817
March 18: Eight firms and 19 brokers trading as individuals formed New York Stock & Exchange Board. First formal constitution adopted. President was Anthony Stockholm. Initiation fee was $25.
Erie Canal was started.

1818
Massachusetts Hospital Life Insurance Co., one of first U.S. trust companies, established in Boston, Mass.

1819
Depression of past 5 years ended.

1820
The New York Stock & Exchange Board revised their constitution; initiated daily meetings, a regular "call" of stocks. Tontine Coffee House was abandoned as a meeting place. Subsequent meetings were held in the office of Samuel Beebe at 47 Wall Street, a room at Leonard Bleecker's, office of the *Courier and Journal,* and, principally, in old Merchants' Exchange Building. Beebe and Bleecker were founding members of "buttonwood" group. Most active speculators were John Ward and Nathaniel Prime.
Securities traded on the Board belonged to either the Regular List or the Free List. Former were called in sequence by vice-president in the chair; latter were subject to call at discretion of any broker. Most impor-

tant was the Regular List, including the main body of stocks, the market leaders. Brokers waited until stock in which they were interested was called. Then they would leap into trading arena with bids or offers. Regular List was called first.

July: Period of great financial distress, caused by excessive imports, a deranged currency.

1822

Board memberships cost $100. Newspapers began devoting more space to Wall Street.

1824

Stock market continued to expand. Companies with total capital of $52 million organized in New York alone.

1825

October: Opening of Erie Canal created a craze for speculation.
First regular stock market report appeared in London.

1826

March 7: Granite City Railroad Co. of Massachusetts—the first railroad in the U.S.—began to operate.

Extensive public-works building and high employment characterized early part of year. But U.S. had gone ahead too fast on wings of speculation. Banks could not accommodate all demands. Money contracted, new ventures halted, panic ensued.

1827

Stock & Exchange Board moved into new Merchants' Exchange at Wall and Hanover Streets. Trading confined to 42 issues: 12 bank stocks, 8 public bonds, 19 fire and marine insurance companies, Delaware & Hudson Canal, New York Gas Light (first public utility), and Merchants' Exchange stock.

February 12: Baltimore & Ohio Railroad organized.

1828

July 4: Construction began on B&O Railroad, first passenger line in U.S.

1829

August 8: "Stourbridge Lion," first locomotive, placed on American rails.

1830

March 16: Dullest day in Exchange history. Transactions totaled 31 shares, valued at $3,470.25: 5 shares of Morris Canal & Banking Co. (75¼), 26 shares of U.S. Bank (119).

May: First regular passenger service on a U.S. railroad instituted between Baltimore and Ellicott's Mills. Horse-drawn cars traveled the 13 miles in 1¼ hours.

August: Mohawk & Hudson, first rail stock, admitted to trading on Stock & Exchange Board.

August 28: "Tom Thumb," tiny engine designed by Peter Cooper, pulled one-car train with B&O officials from Baltimore to Ellicott's Mills and back.

1831

Rush of foreign goods turning tide of gold outward helped depression to end.

1834

Boston Stock Exchange established as market for New England rail stocks.

Although it failed in Panic of 1837, National Trades Union (formed in New York City, 1834) was first attempt toward a national labor federation in U.S.

1835

January: Jumping from almost nothing to $185 a share, Morris Canal was object of first corner; engineered by Jacob Little, who generally is credited with inventing short selling as applied to securities.

May 11: First article about money appeared in New York newspaper.

May 14: Stock sales were first reported.

December 16–17: Nearly everything south of Wall Street and east of Broadway destroyed by fire. Merchants' Exchange was gutted; the Board was homeless. However, by the following day it was ready for business in a hall above John Warren's Reading Room. (Subsequent meetings held in various locations until 1842.)

1836

Credit almost at breaking point early this year.

April 10: Second U.S. Bank lost government charter, but continued under Pennsylvania charter a few more years.

July 11: Government curbed land speculation by its "Specie Circular," which permitted federal land agents to accept payment only in gold or silver. This caused land prices to fall and was greatly responsible for 1837 panic.

A rival organization, the Bourse or New Board, formed to compete with New York Stock & Exchange Board.

Committee from Exchange went to Albany to protest bill that would ban stock trading that was not done publicly.

October 23: Small panic hit Wall Street; coming events cast their shadows.

1837

First panic of any importance. Generally regarded as "land panic," but other factors were included: overexpansion of banking and credit, real estate speculation, mania for canal building. New York real estate values dropped more than $40 million in six months. Three hundred large failures in New York, 168 in Boston.

Daily trading volume was only 4,000 shares several times this year.

May 10: New York banks suspended specie payments; banks around the country followed.

1838

May: New York and New England banks resumed specie payments, after suspending them in 1837 because of the panic. Philadelphia banks resumed in August; most other banks in January, 1839.

1840

March 31: President Van Buren issued order establishing 10-hour day for federal employees on public works without reduction in pay.

July: Bill organizing U.S. Sub-Treasury became law. (It was repealed in 1841, but re-enacted in 1846.)

Rails occupied speculative limelight on Exchange. Stocks traded mostly in 50-share lots.

1841

June 30: Erie Railroad's first passenger train began operation.

First mercantile credit agency formed by Louis Tappan. (Became R. S. Dun & Co. in 1859. Bradstreet Co., a similar firm, formed in 1849.)

1842

Stock & Exchange Board leased "the large hall over the Reading Room" and moved to the rebuilt Merchants' Exchange Building. The rival New Board with 20 members followed.

October 18: First submarine telegraph cable laid between Governor's Island and Battery.

1843

Depression ended.

Foreign commerce yielded net balance of $40,392,000 in favor of U.S.—best showing to date.

1844

January: First U.S. telegraph line erected between Washington and Baltimore.

May 24: Samuel Morse tapped out message "What hath God wrought" over new telegraph. Scarcely anything added more to Wall Street's influence.

Iron rails first used by railroads.

1846

Jacob Little, inventor of short selling, experienced first failure.

Seventeen states added to Union.

War with Mexico (1846–1848) had little influence on nation or stock market.

1847

New Hampshire passed first law establishing 10-hour legal workday.

1848

January 2: John Marshall discovered gold at Sutter's Sawmill, El Dorado County, California.

Chicago Board of Trade established, providing market place for commodity trading.

The rival organization formed in 1836 to compete with Stock & Exchange Board went out of business.

1850

U.S. wealth was about $7 billion.

First national union (printers') formed.

1851

August 13: Depression reached a peak. It stemmed from bad credit system, lower-than-expected trade with California, unfavorable export-import balance, declining European commodities. Following brief leveling-off period, there was panic in October over value of state money. Market dived; four banks in the country folded before order was restored.

1852

Typographical Union, first national organization to endure to present, formed.

1853

The Crimean War.

July: The New York State Legislature decreed that banks publish weekly statements of condition in *The New York Times.* Brief panic followed when banks called in majority of loans preparatory to making this statement.

Stock & Exchange Board moved from Merchants' Exchange to Commercial Exchange Bank Building, corner of Beaver and William Streets. All principal railroads included in trading list.

Bank Clearing House organized at 14 Wall Street.

Between 1851 and 1853 twenty-seven new banks were reorganized in New York.

Exchange memberships cost $400 in 1853–1854. There were 209 "regular brokers"; curbstone brokers were more numerous.

1854

January: California defaulted interest payments; heavy failures followed in February.

July: Market collapsed. Many suspensions in New York, Boston, and Philadelphia, resulting from fraud and deception by government officials.

August: New York Clearing House formed.

Curbstone brokers gathered at Wall and William Streets during the 1850's. Their speculative activities, coupled with widespread fraud and forgery, prompted uproar against stock gamblers.

1855

September: Financial panic in San Francisco caused by many failures of prominent bankers.

1856

April 21: First train crossed Mississippi River from Illinois to Iowa.

November 24: Banker's Magazine reported: "Aggregate transactions during the past four weeks were exceedingly large . . . nearly one million shares" on Exchange and on the Curb.

December 5: Jacob Little, first great manipulator, failed for $10 million and for last time by selling short too soon in rising market.

Market reached highest level in December, then sagged for several months, but real panic was deferred until August, 1857.

Railroad building totaled 3,600 miles in 1856, versus 2,452 miles in 1853, 1,656 miles in 1850.

1857

January: Bull market topped out. Erie touched 64; New York Central, 95. By October they had dropped to 18 and 53, respectively.

April: B&O freight men struck. Militia called out; many killed and wounded.

August 24: Fostered by widespread speculation and overextension of credit, so-called Banking Panic, or "Western Blizzard," cracked the market wide open. Touched off mainly by failure of Ohio Life Insurance & Trust Co., which had $7 million of liabilities. Trading volume hit new daily peak of 70,000 shares. Until then 8,000 to 9,000 shares was a good day's business. Crash due also to influx of gold from California, which caused vast expansion of banking system, a bad crop year, and rapid construction of railroads on borrowed capital. Suspension of specie payments by banks lasted for 59 days. Business generally was prostrated for 6 to 7 months. During this panic Jay Cooke made famous remark:

"Money is not tight, it is not to be had at all." Banks had reached limit of their ability to finance merchants and speculators.

First Mining Board opened at 29 William Street. The "call" included North Carolina Gold, Tennessee and Maryland Copper, New York and Pennsylvania Lead Mines.

During 1857–1864 curbstone brokers' headquarters were on William Street between Beaver Street and Exchange Place.

Stock & Exchange Board's headquarters between 1857 and 1865 were in Dan Lord's Building, in a room overlooking Lord's Court. It formed the center of a block bounded by Exchange Place, William, Beaver, and Broad Streets. Commissions were $\frac{1}{8}$ of 1% for buying and selling. Cost of membership, including initiation fee, was about $500. Speculators often offered $100 a week for privilege of listening at a keyhole during the "calls."

1858

May: Exchange initiation fees increased to $1,000, although brokers' clerks of three years' standing could be charged only $500.

August 13: President Buchanan and Queen Victoria exchanged messages via trans-Atlantic cable.

December: News of gold discoveries around Pikes Peak caused rush to Colorado by those seeking to recoup losses from Panic of 1857.

Ban against short selling, instigated in 1812 in New York State, was annulled and method was legalized. "No contract, written or verbal, hereafter made for the sale of any share in the stock of any incorporated company shall be voidable because the vendor, at the time of making such contract, is not the owner of such share."

1859

August 27: Edwin L. Drake struck oil (formerly known as "Kier's Medicine") at Titusville, Pa. Well produced 20 barrels daily.

New Mining Board inaugurated at 25 William Street. But it gradually faded and for next 3 to 4 years regular Stock Exchange was scene of most mining share activity. Big favorites were Copake Iron and Mariposa.

1860

May: South threatened to secede if Republican president was elected in fall.

July: Congress authorized war loan of $250 million. National debt was $64,640,838. (It reached $2,756,431,571 by 1885.)

August: Congress authorized treasury notes in amount of $50 million.

November: Lincoln elected. Situation became acute. Stocks declined 7 to 16 points in month's time.

November 23: For first time in history New York Clearing House was forced to issue loan certificates for $7,375,000 to carry banks over crisis.

December 12: Southern banks suspended specie payments.

Also: Sir John Barnard's Act, which became effective in England in 1734, was repealed. This was frank admission of government's failure to regulate speculation in securities by law, especially short selling.

Henry Varnum Poor published America's first financial reference, *History of Railroads and Canals in the U.S.,* later retitled *Poor's Manual of Railroads.*

1861

February 9: Government of Confederate States of America formed at Montgomery, Alabama. Jefferson Davis named president.

March 4: Abraham Lincoln took office.

April: U.S. bonds reached lowest price of war years.

April 7: Stock & Exchange Board passed resolution signifying allegiance to Union.

April 12–13: Cannonading began at Fort Sumter, South Carolina. Semipanic greeted the news. Money unobtainable, distrust everywhere.

August 5: Congress authorized 3% tax on excess of all incomes over $800.

December: Treasury Secretary Chase recommended national bank system.

Also: Jay Gould (25 years old) arrived in Wall Street. Gold more or less ceased to circulate as money.

Exchange seats sold for $460. Trading list had 22 stocks, including 16 Rails.

Adjoining Stock Exchange board room was an annex (Goodwin's Room) where certain operators did their own speculating. A delegate perched on high stool listened at keyhole to Exchange next door and shouted quotations to his associates so they could trade. When business was dull, they played "Crack-loo"—throwing half dollars at cracks in floor. A third market was conducted on William Street between Exchange Place and Beaver Street.

1862

January 1: About 1,496 banks in U.S.

January: Premium on gold first became noticeable. Successful speculators in stocks turned suddenly to gold, which caused it to be heavily traded.

February: First issue of Greenbacks (government scrip) released when Congress passed Legal Tender Act, which authorized Government to issue $150 million of irredeemable paper currency. This nearly doubled nation's money circulation and sparked wave of unprecedented speculation.

April 12: Gold price first quoted at a premium.

May: Leading brokers and operators devised plans to get news from war front. They gave those who transmitted it an interest in stocks, so they would be repaid in form of early news. Telegraph lines were sometimes subsidized and large advance payments made for war information. Wall Street operators employed politicians, soldiers, government officials to keep them informed.

July: Increase in Greenback issue by $300 million authorized.

September 8: San Francisco Stock & Exchange Board formed.

Also: Gold Exchange formed in fall of year. Annual membership: $100.

Brokers met in halls and reading rooms of Fifth Avenue Hotel after regular Exchange hours. Business grew; daily volume approximated 10,000 shares. A favorite spot was "Coal Hole," a redecorated cellar at 17 William Street. Curbstone brokers speculated there in rails. Then gold brokers took over, but later moved to Gilpin's News Room (corner of William Street and Exchange Place).

Rival exchange called Public Board, and later the Open Board of Brokers was formed. First sessions held in "Coal Hole." They offered to do business for $\frac{1}{32}$ brokerage, i.e., $3.12 for 100 shares. Old Board then lowered commissions to $\frac{1}{8}\%$ from $\frac{1}{4}\%$ and passed rule that any members who dealt with rival board would be expelled.

1863

January 13: First gold sales recorded.

January 29: New York Stock & Exchange Board changed name to New York Stock Exchange.

January 30: NYSE Building Co. organized.

February: Congress tried unsuccessfully to curb gold gamblers.

February 25: National bank system established. A main objective was to set up market for government bonds. Under National Banking Act banks had to buy government bonds amounting to ⅓ of their capital stock.

June 21: Bill passed by Congress in March went into effect, affixing severe penalties to practice of dealing in gold by contract for future purchases and delivery. It was intended to suppress gold speculation, but traders thought this a confession by Government that war would be long. Those short of gold got frightened and covered, which caused wild price gyrations and worse confusion. Law soon repealed.

October 6: NYSE Building Co. bought first property at 13 Wall and 4 New Street.

Also: Uniform currency first became available.

Brotherhood of Locomotive Engineers formed.

Second Open Board of Brokers established, with headquarters in "Coal Hole." It continued all day and night in corridors and rooms of Fifth Avenue Hotel; later at an Evening Exchange. Commissions reduced from ¼ to ⅛ of 1% to encourage business.

1864

February: Wild speculation in stocks.

March 21: Forty-one gentlemen formed nucleus of Mining Board of New York. Admission: $250. First sessions held in old quarters of Gold Board.

March: Gold advanced rapidly.

April 18: Semipanic on stock exchange, caused largely by failure of Anthony W. Morse, leading speculator.

June: National currency of $300 million authorized by Congress.

June 8: Government prohibited private coining of gold, which put many coin manufacturers out of business, although they were not counterfeiters, nor did they initiate designs of U.S. coins.

June 30: U.S. Treasury stopped issuing Greenbacks; $431 million worth were then outstanding.

August: Gold touched new high of 261¾.

October 14: Gold brokers formed definite organization and moved to quarters of old Stock Board, 24 Beaver Street.

Also: NYSE initiation fee raised to $3,000, but for members' clerks of three years' standing fee was $1,500.

Commodore Vanderbilt began securing control of New York Central.

Federal Government enacted law to prevent short selling (later repealed).

Treasury Secretary Chase's efforts to help Greenbacks by selling gold failed. Gold reached 285 on July 11.

An exchange called Government Bond Department formed to deal only in government securities.

Public Board moved to 16 Broad Street, changing name to Open Board of Brokers. Members were individuals who could not secure admission to old Board; they formed competing organization.

A notable factor in sharp rises by rail stocks was their small capitalizations. Moneyed interests could buy entire floating supply of any stock and push it to unheard-of figures, far above investment values. Long declines and panics were inevitable.

Vanderbilt and John Tobin boomed Harlem Railroad stock from 90 to 285 in five months.

Gilpin's Reading Room on southeast corner of William Street and Exchange Place became separate room for those wanting to speculate in gold. Annual dues: $25.

In spring and summer stocks were bulled to levels not duplicated for many years. But excessive loans at New York banks, plus scarcity and premium on gold, contributed to sharp declines in fall, carrying well into October.

1865

April 9: Lee surrendered at Appomattox; the Confederacy was ended.

April 14: Lincoln shot at Ford's Theater.

April 15: Lincoln died. *The New York Times* columned in black; the NYSE adjourned. Andrew Johnson became President.

July: NYSE ruled that any members attending Gallagher's uptown night exchange would be expelled.

August 8: Railroads taken over by Government during war were returned to owners.

October: Tight money checked rise in stocks.

October 31: Petroleum Board formed. First meeting held at 16 Broad Street. Trading began with 11 stocks, but soon expanded to 35. Buchanan Farm, Germania (the Erie of oil), and Titus were prominent. Big favorite was Excelsior Shade River.

November: Famous corner in Prairie du Chien Railroad ("Prairie Dog").

December 9: New Stock Exchange building opened at 10–12 Broad Street.

Also: Standard Oil Co., a Cleveland firm, organized with capital of $100,000.

Trading days so short in winter and spring of 1864–1865 that operators crowded Fifth Avenue Hotel to trade at dusk. Gallagher's Exchange had opened in back room, where admission cost fifty cents. However, after Ketchum Son & Co. failed, it sank into oblivion.

Gilpin's Reading Room members moved into Gold Room on New Street. Admission dues went up as gold speculation increased—to $1,000 and, finally, to $10,000 for a seat.

1866

January 1: Mining-oil brokers joined forces to become Petroleum & Mining Board. Many new members admitted; fee raised to $1,000.

February 20: Market verged on panic. Everyone wanted to borrow money; nobody would lend. People worried about course of Government in selling upward of $12 million in gold.

March: D.L.&W. Railroad replied to NYSE request for information: "The Delaware, Lackawanna and Western RR. Co. make no reports and publish no statements—and have not done anything of the kind for the past five years" (A. C. Odell, Treasurer).

April: Big corner in Michigan Southern ("Old Sow").

May 11: Short panic caused by failure of Overend, Gurney & Co., London bankers.

May 18: Daniel Drew marketed Erie Railroad. Stock dropped from 74½ to 60½ on May 31.

July 27: Atlantic cable successfully laid, opened for operation.

August: London market prices first quoted in New York by Atlantic cable.

November: Wild speculation until Treasury, for its own purposes, withdrew $15 million from circulation. Stocks dropped 10 points on average. Money very tight.

December: N.Y. Gold Exchange Bank organized to facilitate business rising from buying, selling, delivering gold. A clearing house for gold, it performed work similar to that done by Bank Clearing House for banks.

(Exchange continued until 1877, but all speculation in gold ceased when specie payments resumed in 1879.)

Also: The "Erie Wars" started.

Arbitrage was inaugurated.

National Labor Congress organized in Baltimore—the first significant nationwide labor movement.

Napoleon Oil scandal occurred when stock ballooned from 2 to 34.

1867

January 18: Stocks broke badly; many failures; money tied up by bear operators.

March 30: Alaska bought from Russia for two cents an acre.

May: Pool in Erie smashed by large selling of English holdings.

October: Drew expelled from Erie; stock recovered 10 points.

November 15: Stock tickers introduced.

December: Vanderbilt got final control of New York Central.

Also: First stock clearing system successfully established in Frankfurt, Germany.

Half the brokers on Petroleum Mining Board resigned. Stocks so badly mangled by corners, they had been bled white and business dropped off.

Government Bond Department established at NYSE.

1868

January: Corner in Rock Island broken when directors threw 49,000 shares on market.

March 5: President Johnson's impeachment trial began; lasted until May 26 and failed.

March 10: Erie cornered and opened at 80. At 83, a clique composed of James Fisk, Jr., Jay Gould, and Daniel Drew dumped 50,000 shares of bogus stock, manufactured by printing press. Vanderbilt failed to support the price. Erie fell to 78 and closed at 71, as panic raged on Exchange.

March 11: "Erie Robbers" fled to Jersey City with printing press and several million Vanderbilt dollars.

June: Winston Churchill's grandfather, Leonard Jerome, tried unsuccessfully to corner Pacific Mail.

July: Jay Gould installed as president of Erie.

October: Money tight owing to withdrawal of funds from New York for the West. Bears tried to raid market, but bulls acquired time loans running to year-end and thus stabilized prices.

October 23: NYSE memberships first made salable.

November: Localized panic on Exchange as Erie was cornered again. Drew caught short of 70,000 shares.

Also: Only about 400 stock brokers did any considerable business. First Governing Committee of NYSE elected.

Official sales on "call" at Regular and Open Boards totaled 19,713,402 shares of stock; $245,245,240 par value of bonds.

Massachusetts established first State Labor Bureau.

Congress passed first federal 8-hour-day law, but it applied only to laborers, workmen, and mechanics employed by or on behalf of Government.

Practice of dealing in active stocks at specific locations on trading floor first started.

1869

February 1: NYSE required registration of securities by listed companies to prevent overissuance, such as the Erie clique accomplished with printing press in 1868.

May 1: Government Bond Board members were offered full membership privileges on NYSE for $1,000.

May 8: Government Board, Open Board of Brokers, and NYSE joined under one management. Headquarters were at 16 Broad Street. Revised constitution and bylaws were passed. NYSE had 533 members, Open Board 354, Government Board 173. New Exchange thus had 1,060 members and $750,000 in treasury. Annual dues were $50. There were 40 members of the Governing Committee. Real unit of trading was 10 shares; anything less was an odd-lot.

May 10: After five years of labor, gold and silver spikes were driven at Promontory Point, Utah (where first locomotives from Atlantic and Pacific coasts faced each other) to celebrate meeting of Union Pacific and Central Pacific Railroads.

May 15: Transcontinental rail service inaugurated.

June: Jay Gould secretly began buying quantities of gold.

July: Heavy speculation in Vanderbilt stocks. N.Y. Central crossed 217. Money became scarce.

September 24: "Black Friday"—day of panic—when gold price in terms of currency reached 160. Intended corner, engineered by Fisk and Gould, broke when U.S. Treasury put $4 million in gold on the market to buy bonds and caused gold price to collapse to 133 in minutes.

September 30: Another day of panic.

October 2: Gould and Fisk dumped $50 million of gold.

November 17: Suez Canal opened.

Also: Rockefeller, Flagler, and Andrews merged interests into Standard Oil Co.

Government held about $75 million of gold; floating supply for trading purposes was about $20 million.

Vanderbilt got an act passed enabling the Harlem, the Hudson, and the New York Central to merge. Representative stocks climbed sharply on announcement.

Morning sessions on Exchange were from 10:30 to 12 o'clock; afternoon sessions from 1 to 2 o'clock. Government, state, and municipal bonds, plus rail, bank, insurance, and miscellaneous issues with market value of about $4 billion were bought and sold.

Noble Order of the Knights of Labor organized in Philadelphia. It maintained extreme secrecy until 1878, then began organizing workers openly. By winning strikes against Jay Gould's lines and advancing 8-hour day, Knights won many followers. However, the organization declined rapidly after 1886, when AFL emerged.

1870

January 20: First all-female brokerage firm, Woodhull, Claflin & Co., opened at 44 Broad Street.

April: Cliques who bought stocks on "Black Friday" decline started a bull movement. When public turned bullish at peak of the rise, cliques turned bearish. Pushing prices so low that margins were wiped out and inducing further selling, they soon covered short positions at bottom and bought long again for an advance—a practice known as "shearing the lambs."

June: A broker carrying 40,000 shares of stock and $5 million of gold failed. Market started to break, but was supported by cliques.

July: Act of Congress added $54 million to national currency.

July 29: First written contract signed between coal miners and operators. Sliding pay scale was provided, based on price of coal.

Also: There were 54,435 miles of railroads in U.S.

Only about 70 stocks actively traded on Exchange.

Franco-Prussian War began.

Philadelphia Board of Brokers (now Philadelphia-Baltimore-Washington Exchange) instituted first successful clearing system.

Curb brokers' commissions were $\frac{1}{32}$ or $3.12 for buying or selling 100 shares, versus anything up to $12.50 in 1857.

1871

April: Period of heavy speculation.

July: Big corner in Rock Island. Stock climbed to $130\frac{7}{8}$ from $114\frac{1}{2}$, then back to 110.

September: Continuous markets in stocks established, although old "call" system was not officially discarded until 1882 for stocks, March 1902 for bonds.

October: Chicago fire, involving loss of $196 million, clipped 4 to 10 points from leading issues. Further unsettlement caused by banks' contracting loans to raise money for crop purposes. Near panic in London when French payments to Germany for war settlements sparked rise in Bank of England rate from 3% to 5%.

November 1: Constitution & By-Laws (NYSE): "Any member of the Exchange dealing with a person not a member, in the rooms of the Exchange, shall be subject to the penalty of suspension for not less than 60 days, nor more than 12 months."

December: Stocks well supported despite failures of Union Square Bank, Ocean National Bank, Eighth National Bank.

Also: Tweed Ring had charter for incorporation of the Stock Exchange passed and signed by governor of New York; then demanded $100,000 for services. But charter was refused and the demand repudiated.

1872

March: Upheaval in Erie. Directorate overthrown. Jay Gould resigned presidency, succeeded by General Dix. Market very active; money became tight.

May 22: NYSE bought all outstanding stock of Stock Exchange Building Co.

September: Erie cornered. Gould-Smith clique were bears; German brokers and Daniel Drew were bulls. Gould and Henry Smith tried to "lock up" money and thereby compel Erie holders to liquidate. Action of two banks refusing to pay out legal tender on certified checks scuttled the plan. This halted manipulation going on in money and averted panic. Many failures occurred.

September 17: "Day of three corners," i.e., three stocks were cornered.

November: Gould arrested on criminal charges, based on bad conduct during management of Erie. Undaunted, he surrendered securities with face value of $9 million; then engineered a corner in Northwestern with Horace F. Clark and Augustus Schell. Stock opened at 83¾ on November 20 and closed at 95. Next day it carried to 100; following day it was 200 bid at close. Then it lofted to 230. Drew and Smith were victims of the corner, one of most profitable ever made.

November 11: Great Boston fire. Stocks dived. They rallied in December, but bull market was over.

Also: NYSE trading list included 50 rails.

Index of rail stock prices fell about 60% between 1872 and 1878.

1873

January 6: James Fisk, Jr., shot and killed.

April: Stocks nervous; there was a small panic. The Atlantic Bank failed. Tighter European market for U.S. securities was a major bearish factor.

April 13: "Gratuity Fund" system adopted: $10,000 to be paid to families of deceased NYSE members. (This was raised to $20,000 on March 28, 1930.)

May: Pacific Mail broke badly. Congress prohibited further retirement of Greenbacks.

August: Fraud discovered in certain bond issues of New York Central and Hudson River Railroads.

September: Numerous failures: On the 8th, New York Warehouse and Security Co.; on the 13th, Daniel Drew's firm, Kenyon Cox & Co.; Jay Cooke & Co. on the 18th; Fisk & Hatch on the 19th. Many individuals also "went to the wall." Bank of the Commonwealth closed its doors. There were runs on Fourth National Bank and Union Trust Co. Secretary of the latter defaulted for $500,000. Such panic prevailed that

Western Union dropped 10 points in as many minutes. First panic where public really suffered.

September 18: NYSE closed at noon because of panic. Only trading thereafter was by curbstone brokers.

September 30: Exchange reopened. Between September 18 and year-end there were 57 Exchange failures. In all of 1873, 79 members failed.

November 17: General Sherman's telegram saying he was opposed to war and inflation caused big sell off in market.

December 1: Regular trading hours of 10 A.M. to 3 P.M. established. Saturdays: 10 A.M. to noon.

December: Crédit Mobilier organized to build Union Pacific. Composed of railroad company shareholders, it had a credit of $3,750,000. The stock (UP) was quoted at $400. So that the company might win favor, certain Congressmen were given stock at par on their personal notes. For accepting bribes, Oakes Ames (Mass.) and James Brooks (N.Y.) were expelled from House.

Also: Death and panic wiped out the Old Guard: Drew, Henry Smith, Jay Cooke. Only Jay Gould survived. Major cause of panic was the collapse of rail speculation. Lack of capital virtually halted all rail building in U.S.

Business boomed while stocks declined. Example: iron and steel business topped all prior records.

Brotherhood of Locomotive Firemen and Enginemen organized.

Ticker first began printing full names and prices of stocks on two lines.

1874

February: Exchange received letters from Wabash Railroad and Western Union announcing that stock increases had been approved by their directorates. Market dropped 3 points before discovery that letters were forged.

April: Heavy bear raid on market when President Grant vetoed anti-inflation bill.

Also: Public confidence low from 1873 panic.

Agriculture pulled U.S. out of doldrums.

Arrangements first made to trade in odd-lots. Certain NYSE members set themselves up as odd-lot dealers to service brokers who had buy or sell orders for less than 100 shares.

1875

February: Wabash Railroad in receivership.

August: Bank of California failed.

Also: Board of Brokers established in Philadelphia (1790) changed name to Philadelphia Stock Exchange.

Reports of Dun & Co., issued quarterly for first time after 1875, showed that bankruptcies doubled from 5,183 in 1873 to 10,479 in 1878.

Stock Exchange records of complete transactions started. Previously only sales on "calls" were reported.

Only 163 stock issues on NYSE.

1876

March 10: Alexander Graham Bell's sentence to Thomas Watson, "Mr. Watson, come here, I want you," opened telephone era.

April: National Bank of the State of New York failed.

October 26: 191,000 shares traded on NYSE.

Also: All financial fundamentals were bearish. Rail rate wars, dividend reductions, rail foreclosures and receiverships, small crops, poor business, heavy gold exports, and tighter money in fall followed one after the other.

1877

January 4: Vanderbilt died, leaving about $95 million, one of world's biggest fortunes.

February: Jersey Central Railroad in receivership.

July: Rail strikes and rioting in Baltimore-Pittsburgh caused losses of $10 million; over 100,000 workers were involved.

Also: First major labor dispute occurred—a railroad strike.

Market trended unmistakably downward, but repeated bear raiding finally drove prices to 20-year low in the spring. Final down drive in June marked bottom, but all gains since 1861 were wiped out.

1878

January: Michigan Central, Lake Shore, and Canada Southern included in Vanderbilt railroad combination.

February 2: New England Tel. & Tel. became first commercial telephone company in U.S.

February 28: Bland-Allison Act, providing for coinage of limited amount of silver, became law. During 12 years that that law endured, 378,160,000 silver dollars were coined.

May: Congress passed Resumption Act.

November 13: Telegraph and telephone lines installed at NYSE.

December 17: Gold Exchange closed. Premium on gold had gradually disappeared; Exchange members had nothing to do.

Also: Total labor union membership estimated at 50,000.

Bankruptcy Act repealed. U.S. had no subsequent bankruptcy legislation until 1898.

Railroads grew from 2,665 miles in 1875 to 11,569 in 1882, as lines completed building of main lines interrupted by Panic of 1873.

Stocks began rising in spring. Strong bull year with good crops, large rail earnings.

1879

January 1: Return to gold standard revived confidence.

April: Cyrus Field and Jay Gould caused merger of the St. Louis, Kansas City & Northern, and Wabash Railways. Union Pacific and Kansas Pacific were already controlled by Gould, who later acquired also Denver & Rio Grande and Missouri Pacific.

August: Stocks in big retreat.

September 18: Daniel Drew died, leaving a Bible, sealskin coat, watch and chain, and stock ticker.

October: Bull market topped out, followed by big drop in November.

October 22: NYSE bought adjacent property south of Exchange, 24 feet on Broad Street and 68 feet on New Street.

November 12: Forty new Exchange seats authorized to pay for enlarging NYSE building. Membership then became 1,100.

Also: Net rail earnings increased for first time since 1873.

Good crops pushed general trade revival; enriched U.S. Treasury by $120 million.

Iron and steel industries expanded capacity to meet rail demands.

1880

January: Steel rails were worth $71 a ton. (Value dropped to $33–$35 by December, 1883, and to $20 in January, 1884.)

May: Failure of Philadelphia Reading Railway and Coal & Iron Co. caused irregular and nervous market.

Also: Stock dividends exceeded $40 million.

Foreign trade balance was favorable.

Gould controlled about 10,000 miles of rail trackage.

Net rail earnings increased to $39 million. Chicago Rock Island & Pacific declared 100% in stock and still paid 7% in dividends; Louisville & Nashville paid 6% in stock. Chicago, Burlington & Quincy paid 8% after 20% stock bonus.

Reading Railroad's receivership caused upheaval, but market trended upward. Immense crops, record rail earnings, high gold imports, booming business, rail consolidations, and high dividends all helped to lift stocks. But money was dear, due to activity of business and speculation, and this sparked break in December.

1881

January: Western Union, American Union, and Atlantic & Pacific merged.

January 29: Electric annunciator boards for paging members installed on trading floor.

May: Gould's southwestern railway system consolidated.

Gould, Russell Sage, and Cyrus Field raided the "L" (Manhattan Elevated). Driving the stock from 55 to 15½, they covered shorts, then bought long and won control. By November, stock was selling at 55 again.

June: Boom in market culminated.

July 2: President Garfield shot. Market fell abruptly. Panic averted only by intervention of Sunday and Monday's July 4 holiday.

September 19: Garfield died as a result of shooting. Chester Arthur became President.

October 1: Enlargement of NYSE building completed.

November: Federation of Organized Trades and Labor Unions (FOTLU), which later became American Federation of Labor, organized in Pittsburgh.

Also: Corners investigated by a legislative committee.

U.S. Treasury showed a $101 million surplus.

London subscribed 20 million pounds sterling to new American rail issues in first half year.

1881 volume: 117 million shares.

1882

February 23: Market bottomed out after drop from January high.

March 13: To offset reports that he was in financial trouble, Jay Gould displayed some wealth on this day. From a tin box he took $23 million worth of Western Union, $12 million of Missouri Pacific, $6 million of Manhattan Elevated, $2 million of Wabash Railroad common, and $10 million of bonds of Metropolitan, N.Y. Elevated, and Wabash preferred. He offered to produce $30 million worth of other rail securities, but the doubters had seen enough.

September 18: San Francisco Stock Exchange founded. Meeting hours were 11 A.M. and 2 P.M. weekdays; 2 P.M. on Saturdays.

Also: Depression of 1882–1885 began.

Market's downtrend accelerated in fall. Many stocks reached lowest levels in over a year. Difficulty of raising capital for railroads became very pronounced.

Peter J. McGuire, New York City carpenter, suggested setting aside one day each year to honor labor. First annual Labor Day celebration held in New York.

Railway war in Northwest lasted from September to mid-December. When accord was reached, it improved confidence and stocks closed year on strength.

1883

March 3: Revised tariff law upset iron, textile industries. General business slackened. Commodities fell.

July: National Petroleum Exchange and New York Mining Stock Exchange consolidated.

Western Union operators struck for more pay, but month-long strike failed.

Also: Brotherhood of Railroad Trainmen organized.

Rail mileage totaled 106,938.

Brooklyn Bridge opened to foot passengers.

Market speculators suffered huge losses. Business worsened steadily. Gradual transition from prosperity to depression was completed this year. Rail construction lagged, causing job cancellations in related industries. Rail stocks weak. Banks reluctant to make new loans.

1884

January: Surplus reserve of N.Y. national banks wiped out.

May 6: Grant & Ward failed, involving prestige of General Grant and dragging Marine Bank down with it. This accelerated downswing already underway and carried to June 27.

May 11: N.Y. Clearing House lent strong support to financial community by sixth issue of $24.9 million of loan certificates.

May 13: Second National Bank "went to the wall" after president stole $3 million.

May 14: Metropolitan Bank closed because of a run. Stocks dived; panic ensued. Confidence damaged by Government's silver policy. A. S. Hatch, NYSE president, failed during panic. But panic was short-lived and did not upset fundamentally sound business conditions.

June 27: Market rallied from deeply oversold position, but public stayed aloof.

July 3: Dow Jones & Co. began publishing average closing prices of active representative stocks. First average closing price was 69.93. Nine of the eleven stocks listed were rails. The original list:

Chicago & North Western	Northern Pacific Pfd.
D., L. & Western	Pacific Mail
Lake Shore	St. Paul
Louisville & Nashville	Union Pacific
Missouri Pacific	Western Union
New York Central	

Also: U.S. had record corn crop, estimated at 1.8 billion bushels.

Market declined into December, as Cleveland's election sparked apprehension about tariff.

Bureau of Labor, established in Department of the Interior, later became independent—a department of labor without cabinet rank. It then was absorbed into new Department of Commerce and Labor, where it remained until present Department of Labor was established in 1913.

1884 volume: 96 million shares.

1885

January 15: J. J. Cisco & Co. failed when Hetty Green called in $25 million of securities and $475,000 in cash.

January–June: Period marred by rail rate wars. New York Central tried to crush competing West Shore road.

March 7: Cincinnati Stock Exchange organized.

March 25: NYSE established an "Unlisted Department," dealing mostly in rails and a few mining issues. It dissolved in 1910.

April: Market reached low following 1884 panic.

June–December: Period of market strength. Building was prosperous; rail industry, harmonious.

December 8: William H. Vanderbilt died. To offset possible panic a $12 million pool was formed to support leading stocks, but only a mild setback occurred.

Also: Railroad mileage totaled 123,320.

   Coffee Exchange was incorporated by special charter.

   National debt at record high: $2,756,431,571.

   Much agitation for securities market regulation.

   NYSE seat sold at new high—$34,000.

   1885 volume: 93 million shares.

1886

January: Henry N. Smith, noted bear and partner in Smith, Gould & Martin (Jay Gould's firm) failed, dragging William Heath & Co. with him. His explanation to governing committee of the Exchange illustrates the precarious speculation going on at the time: "On January 1, 1885, I was worth $1,400,000. I had $1,100,000 in money and the balance in good real estate. On the following January 1, I had lost the whole amount and was $1,200,000 in debt, a million of which I owed William Heath & Co."

March 7: Unsuccessful attempt to strike the Gould system of railroads.

April 1: New high for labor strikes depressed business and market. Under initiative of Federation of Organized Trades and Labor Unions, labor demanded 8-hour day. But Chicago Haymarket riot (May 4) aroused public opinion against unionism and radicalism and stopped the 8-hour movement for several years.

December 8: American Federation of Labor established. Samuel Gompers, first president.

December 15: First million-share day (1,200,000), with stocks on toboggan. Money tight; low-priced issues hit especially hard.

December: Interstate Commerce bill introduced in Congress.

Also: Consolidated Stock & Petroleum Exchange of N.Y. introduced system said to have been "the first system to clear both stocks and money for a Board of brokers," although Philadelphia Stock Exchange had taken previous steps along same line.

1887

January: European war rumors prompted foreign selling and a decline on NYSE, which soon recovered.

Also: Interstate Commerce Act passed, which prohibited pools or rebates among railroads. It also established Interstate Commerce Commission.

Railroad building reached high-water mark of 12,876 miles.

1888

March 11–14: Big blizzard. Only 32 brokers on trading floor. Volume dropped to 15,250 shares.

September 13: St. Paul passed dividend; market dived.

October: Atchison cut dividend.

Also: Sugar Trust combined 18 refineries, closed 11 others. Distillery Trust combined 80 distillers, closing all but 12.

Salt Lake Stock Exchange formed.

First federal labor relations law enacted.

Unfavorable rail traffic and rate wars retarded market. Worried rail managements, cutting rates incessantly to buoy business, thus impaired stock values. Harrison election insured continuation of protective tariff and market advanced moderately. But too much silver legislation prompted downside reversal in December.

1889

January 10: J. P. Morgan effected "gentlemen's agreement" between rail and trunk-line officials as to rates. Market responded bullishly.

Also: Bucket shops infested Wall Street. NYSE banned all stock tickers in effort to drive them out. Exchange Alley called "Tinpot Alley."

1890

July: Exchange volume dropped to average of 83,400 shares daily.

July 14: Congress passed Sherman Act for issue of an indefinite amount of legal tender notes to buy silver bullion. President Harrison approved it same day.

November: Baring crisis in London caused steep decline on LSE; thirty Exchange houses announced inability to meet obligations. British began liquidating American securities.

December: NYSE in strong recovery after November selling smash.

Also: Sherman Antitrust Act passed, as result of public resentment against large business combinations.

Stocks at new record highs.

National Park Bank, New York's biggest, had $45 million deposits.

Electricity was actually applied for first time to industrial use.

First investment trust, United Electric Securities Co., organized.

First published coverage of industrial stocks: "Poor's Handbook of Investment Securities."

1890 volume: 71,282,885 shares.

1891

December 4: Unsuccessful attempt to assassinate Russell Sage, father of puts and calls in U.S.

Also: Money flurry in fall caused market decline, but gradual return of money to banks sparked recovery. Stocks ended year around highest levels.

1891 volume: 69,031,689 shares.

1892

February 11: Day's volume of 1,446,915 set record that remained almost 7 years.

May 17: One-hundredth anniversary of "buttonwood" agreement. Exchange had 1,100 members, $18.3 billion of listed securities. NYSE clearing plan introduced; only 4 stocks were cleared at start.

July 6: Carnegie Steel strike at Homestead, Pa., caused fight between

Pinkerton men and strikers; 18 killed, many wounded. National Guard restored order (July 12); strike failed.

December 2: Jay Gould died.

Also: Method of doing business at "posts" on Exchange trading floor adopted. Special groups of stocks were assigned to specific posts.

General Electric formed.

First automobile appeared on American streets.

Stocks generally trended lower.

Harmony in rail industry; earnings were largest ever. McKinley tariff law (1890) helped business. But there was partial crop failure; Northern Pacific passed dividend; several railroads went into receivership. Money stringency in fall and gold exports discouraged traders. Cleveland re-election insured an eventual attack on McKinley tariff law. Market declined until January.

1892 volume: 85,875,092 shares.

1893

January: Market topped out, declined during winter. Spring rally followed by further drop carried to year's low in July, where prices stabilized until recovery began in fourth quarter.

February 20: Philadelphia & Reading in receivership.

May 4: National Cordage in receivership.

July 25: Erie Railroad in receivership.

August 16: Northern Pacific in receivership.

October 13: Union Pacific in receivership.

December 23: Atchison in receivership.

December 27: N.Y. & N.Eng. Railroad in receivership.

November 1: Sherman Act repealed. During 3 years law was in force, $155.9 million treasury notes were issued.

Also: Bad agricultural conditions, lack of confidence in monetary system, unfavorable trade balance, overspeculation, and overcapitalization contributed to market unsettlement.

Aggregate liabilities of business failures were almost $350 million, over 20% greater than 1892. New rail building halted completely; unemployment and labor troubles increased.

First investment trust in U.S. formed—Boston Personal Property Trust.

1893 volume: 80,977,839 shares.

1894

May–September: Strike at Pullman Palace Car Co. in Chicago defeated by injunctions and federal troops.

June 30: Volume for week ended this day—576,000 shares.

July 3: Seats lost value, pessimism increased, when daily turnover fell to 60,200 shares.

July 25: Sino-Japanese War began.

Also: Large amount of money idle in banks. Dividends totaled $83 million, versus $93 million in 1893. Coxey's Army marched to Washington and there were several big strikes. Improved rail earnings did not offset many depressing factors. Two $50 million bond issues to replenish Treasury's gold reserve contributed further to bearishness.

1894 volume: 49,075,062 shares.

1895

January: Gold standard in danger. Virtual run on Treasury began. Banks and citizens hoarded gold.

February: Banking syndicate arranged with President Cleveland to provide Treasury with gold equal to $65 million, and that syndicate determined to "exert all financial influence and make all legitimate efforts to protect the Treasury of the U.S. against the withdrawals of gold." This boosted confidence everywhere.

December 17: Cleveland sent Congress message on Venezuelan affairs which seemed to contain threat of war with Great Britain under certain circumstances. Public was shocked and market went into tailspin that canceled all gains scored earlier.

Also: 1895 volume: 66,583,232 shares.

1896

May 27: Share turnover fell to 65,700.

July: Big decline known as "Silver Panic."

August: Market at 10-year low. Thereafter, bumper crops, wheat exports, and McKinley's election (decisive defeat for free-silver advocates) sparked strong recovery.

Also: 1896 volume: 54,654,096 shares.

1897

January: Dow Jones Averages separated into two sections—Industrials and Rails. Twelve stocks comprised Industrials:

American Cotton Oil	Laclede Gas
American Spirits Mfg.	National Lead
American Sugar	Pacific Mail
American Tobacco	Standard Rope & Twine
Chicago Gas	Tennessee Coal & Iron
General Electric	U.S. Leather Pfd.

Twenty stocks comprised Rails:

Atchison	Mo., Kansas & Texas Pfd.
Burlington	Missouri Pacific
C., C., C. & St. Louis	New York Central
Chesapeake & Ohio	Northern Pacific Pfd.
Chicago & North Western	New York, Ontario & West.
Erie	Reading
Jersey Central	Rock Island
Lake Shore	St. Paul
Louisville & Nashville	Southern Railway Pfd.
Manhattan Elevated	Wabash Pfd.

Dow Industrials gained 8.67 and Rails 10.58 in 302 market sessions during year.

Closing high Industrials: 55.82 (9/10); closing low: 38.49 (4/23).

Closing high Rails: 67.23 (9/17); closing low: 48.12 (4/19).

January 18: Spokane Stock Exchange opened during mining boom in British Columbia.

July 24: McKinley signed Dingley Tariff Bill, sparking strength in stocks.

Also: Klondike Gold Rush.

Stocks regained virtually all ground lost since 1893.

1897 volume: 77,324,172 shares.

1898

February 15: Battleship "Maine" blown up in Havana harbor.

April 25: Congress passed bill declaring "war exists between the United States and the Kingdom of Spain."

May: Dewey victorious at Manila Bay.

July 3: Spanish fleet destroyed near Santiago, Cuba.

August 26: Honolulu Stock Exchange organized.

December 10: Treaty of Paris ended war with Spain.

Also: Gold discoveries in Alaska.

Trusts with capitalization of $916 million formed.

AVERAGE PRICE ACTION OF TEN LEADING STOCKS (1860 to 1907)

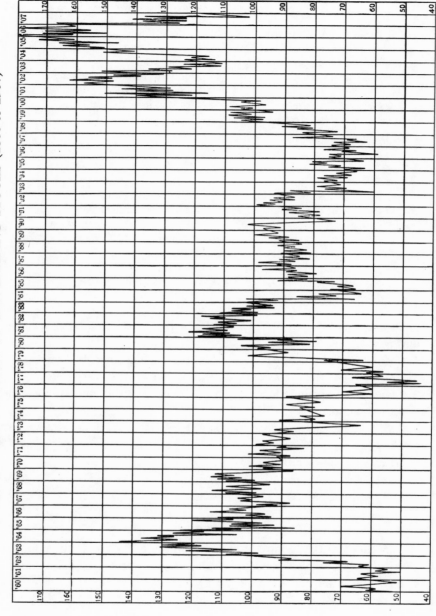

Tendency toward centralization in rail industry first shown by merger of Lake Shore with New York Central.

Dow Industrials gained 11.11 and Rails 12.70 in 298 market sessions during year.

Closing high Industrials: 60.97 (8/26); closing low: 42.00 (3/25).

Closing high Rails: 74.99 (12/30); closing low: 55.89 (4/21).

1898 volume: 90,468,213 shares.

1899

April: Amalgamated Copper Corp. formed—a creation of Standard Oil magnates. It had large interests in over 30 companies, headed by Anaconda of Montana.

Also: Los Angeles Stock Exchange founded.

Carnegie Steel partners netted $21 million; in 1900, $40 million.

Many important industrial concerns were born—Allis-Chalmers, Republic Steel, United Fruit, American Smelting—representing consolidations of numerous scattered interests in their respective fields.

Market climbed steadily until August, when it faced rising interest rates and falling surplus deposits. British military reverses in South Africa and tight money caused setback in December. But overall business was good and drop merely interrupted the basic upward trend.

Dow Industrials gained 5.56 and Rails 2.74 in 296 market sessions during year.

Closing high Industrials: 77.61 (9/5); closing low: 58.27 (12/18).

Closing high Rails: 87.04 (4/3); closing low: 72.48 (12/22).

1899 volume: 173,912,086 shares.**

The chart reproduced here from the book "How Money Is Made in Security Investments," written in 1908 by Henry Hall, portrays the average price movements of ten leading stocks from 1860 through 1907.

The stocks used were: until 1870 inclusive, C.C.C. & St. L.; * Central of New Jersey; Cleveland & Pittsburgh; Erie; Delaware & Hudson; Illinois Central; New York Central; Reading; Rock Island; Chicago, Milwaukee & St. Paul.

Chicago & Northwestern and Union Pacific were substituted for Erie and Cleveland & Pittsburgh in 1871. From 1873 to 1879, both inclusive, Reading was dropped in favor of Chicago & Alton. Alton was omitted in 1880. Pennsylvania was exchanged for Rock Island in 1899.

Rail issues dominated the trading list in the very early days. Industrials were virtually unknown; utilities were unheard of. As the "Streaks of Rust" went, so went the rest of the market; they piped the tune for other stocks to follow.

* Cleveland, Cincinnati, Chicago & St. Louis Railway Co.
** For volume in subsequent years, see Section Two.

1900

Trading Sessions: 300

			Monthly Record		
Advances	DJI:	151		*Inds.*	*Rails*
Declines	DJI:	144			
Unchanged	DJI:	5	J	Plus .05	Plus .35
			F	Plus 3.23	Plus .70
Advances	DJR:	163	M	Plus 2.06	Plus 3.62
Declines	DJR:	134	A	Minus 4.69	Minus 2.89
Unchanged	DJR:	3	M	Minus 2.23	Minus .36
			J	Minus 4.17	Minus 4.66
Closing High DJI:		71.04 (12/27)	J	Plus 1.87	Plus 1.46
Closing Low DJI:		52.96 (9/24)	A	Plus 1.01	Plus 1.18
Closing High DJR:		94.99 (12/31)	S	Minus 3.54	Minus 1.78
Closing Low DJR:		72.99 (6/23)	O	Plus 4.77	Plus 4.20
			N	Plus 7.55	Plus 9.33
Change from 1899			D	Plus 4.12	Plus 6.11

Dow Industrials: Plus   4.63
Dow Rails: Plus 17.26

March 14: Gold standard officially adopted when President McKinley signed Gold Standard Act.

August 22: Volume only 86,000 shares. Daily average for August: about 150,000.

November: McKinley's re-election set off another bull upsurge.

Also: Money plentiful; interest rates low. Rail earnings set records. Business excellent, prompted by Dingley Tariff passed in 1897.

Market leaders after 1900: John W. "Bet a Million" Gates, J. P. Morgan, Edward H. Harriman.

Passage of currency bill in March and McKinley's re-election helped increase Europe's faith in U.S. monetary stability.

Security analyst, John Moody, became first to rate investment quality and character of bonds.

Stock tickers in use: 837.

1901

January 7: First 2-million-share day.

January 10: Lucas Well (Beaumont, Texas) struck oil, starting new era in oil business.

February 26: First sales of U.S. Steel "when issued" began at 39

Trading Sessions: 293

Advances	DJI:	149
Declines	DJI:	141
Unchanged	DJI:	3
Advances	DJR:	167
Declines	DJR:	121
Unchanged	DJR:	5

Closing High DJI:	78.26	(6/17)
Closing Low DJI:	61.52	(12/24)
Closing High DJR:	117.86	(5/1)
Closing Low DJR:	92.66	(1/3)

Change from 1900

Dow Industrials:	Minus	6.15
Dow Rails:	Plus	19.86

Monthly Record

	Inds.		Rails	
J	Minus	3.90	Plus	2.17
F	Plus	.19	Plus	.18
M	Plus	2.92	Plus	7.69
A	Plus	5.88	Plus	11.32
M	Minus	.03	Minus	4.20
J	Plus	2.17	Plus	5.06
J	Minus	6.31	Minus	9.82
A	Plus	1.84	Plus	4.15
S	Minus	6.81	Minus	3.33
O	Minus	2.21	Plus	2.58
N	Plus	.56	Plus	3.41
D	Minus	.45	Plus	.65

(common) and 84 (preferred). Company, formed by J. P. Morgan & Co., had capitalization of $1.4 billion.

March: E. H. Harriman and Jacob Schiff began buying Northern Pacific Railroad stock.

April 24: 662,000 shares of Union Pacific—two thirds of entire issue—were traded.

April 30: Volume equaled 3,234,339; first 3-million-share day. Nine stocks accounted for 2,150,000 shares of this turnover.

NYSE moved temporarily to Produce Building while new quarters were being built.

May 6: Northern Pacific opened at 149¾.

May 9: Day of "Nipper Panic," when Northern Pacific was cornered and vaulted to $1,000 a share (against 45¾ in fall of 1900). NP opened at 170, up 10 from previous close; by 10:20 A.M. it reached 205. Rest of market dropped 50 to 75 points. Day's volume was 3,336,-695—a record not broken until 1925.

May 10: Morgan and Kuhn, Loeb settled with NP shorts at 150 and panic ended.

September 6: President McKinley shot.

September 9: Cornerstone laid for new NYSE building.

September 14: McKinley died from wounds. T. Roosevelt became President.

September 30: 4,221 national banks in existence.

October 1: New bear market got underway.

November 23: Henry Ford Automobile Co. formed with capital of $38,000.

Also: All previous records for bank clearings, securities transactions, exports, manufactured goods, volume of trade were broken.

NYSE had 119 out-of-town member firms, including 26 in Philadelphia, 26 in Chicago, 25 in Boston. There were 246 branch offices maintained by member firms.

Many wildcat securities collapsed. McKinley's assassination and the "Nipper Panic" made the market wild and irregular.

Total value of Exchange seats: $88,000,000.

1902

Trading Sessions:	298

			Monthly Record			
Advances	DJI:	155		*Inds.*		*Rails*
Declines	DJI:	137	J	Plus .39	Minus	.66
Unchanged	DJI:	6	F	Minus .14	Minus	.54
Advances	DJR:	163	M	Plus 2.38	Plus	2.43
Declines	DJR:	132	A	Minus .18	Plus	5.18
Unchanged	DJR:	3	M	Minus .59	Minus	1.94
			J	Minus 2.12	Plus	1.06
Closing High DJI:	68.44	(4/24)	J	Plus 1.51	Plus	5.47
Closing Low DJI:	59.57	(12/15)	A	Plus .46	Plus	1.38
Closing High DJR:	129.36	(9/9)	S	Minus .13	Minus	2.45
Closing Low DJR:	111.73	(1/14)	O	Minus .09	Minus	3.10
			N	Minus 4.01	Minus	4.20
Change from 1901			D	Plus 2.24	Plus	1.50

Dow Industrials:	Minus	.27
Dow Rails:	Plus	4.13

March: Government began action, under Sherman Antitrust Act of 1890, against Northern Securities Co., a $400 million holding company controlled by E. H. Harriman, J. P. Morgan, Jacob Schiff.

April 15: 877,000 shares of the total 1,200,000 issued of Southern Railway were traded.

May 12: 145,000 coal miners struck in Pennsylvania.

August–September: Money very tight. Banking capital overtaxed; resources of all financial institutions stretched to breaking point. In New

York five brokerage firms alone borrowed in excess of $100 million. Call loans rose to 25% and 30% in October.

October 21: United Mine Workers of America ended 5-month strike against anthracite operators, agreeing to arbitration by presidential commission.

Also: Market value of all listed stocks was $7 billion.

American Tel. & Tel. had 10,742 stockholders; Standard Oil of New Jersey, 4,197.

E.I. du Pont de Nemours opened first laboratory.

Agricultural Implement Trust was formed.

9,000 passenger cars and 700 trucks were manufactured.

1903

Trading Sessions: 298

Advances	DJI:	139
Declines	DJI:	158
Unchanged	DJI:	1

Advances	DJR:	137
Declines	DJR:	159
Unchanged	DJR:	2

| Closing High | DJI: | 67.70 | (2/16) |
| Closing Low | DJI: | 42.15 | (11/9) |

| Closing High | DJR: | 121.28 | (1/9) |
| Closing Low | DJR: | 88.80 | (9/28) |

Change from 1902

| Dow Industrials: | Minus 15.18 |
| Dow Rails: | Minus 20.65 |

Monthly Record

	Inds.		Rails	
J	Plus	.89	Plus	.08
F	Plus	1.01	Minus	3.87
M	Minus	2.55	Minus	5.21
A	Plus	.14	Minus	1.12
M	Minus	3.51	Minus	5.08
J	Minus	1.19	Minus	.11
J	Minus	8.32	Minus	7.19
A	Plus	2.43	Plus	1.57
S	Minus	7.39	Minus	8.30
O	Minus	.67	Plus	3.06
N	Minus	.80	Plus	.99
D	Plus	4.78	Plus	4.53

February: Roosevelt hinted he would call extra sessions of Congress, unless it did something against trusts.

February 14: Department of Commerce and Labor created by act of Congress; its Secretary became member of the Cabinet.

April 23: New NYSE building opened at 18 Broad Street.

April: U.S. Circuit Court of Appeals unanimously declared Northern Securities merger illegal. This threatened harmony in railroad world.

May 23–August 1: Automobile crossed U.S. from San Francisco to New York.

June: "Rich Man's Panic" in full swing—the result of country's inability to digest more securities.

October: Various banks suspended. Iron and steel industries very depressed.

November 9: Low point of panic with Dow Industrials at 42.15. Other panic lows: Allis-Chalmers, 7; American Can, 2⅜; American Smelting, 36¾; International Paper, 9; National Lead, 10½; Republic Iron & Steel, 5⅝.

December 17: Airplane age opened. Orville and Wilbur Wright made world's first successful flight at Kitty Hawk, N.C.

Also: Chicago World's Fair increased rail passenger traffic above normal.

Banking situation bad all year. Loans exceeded deposits every month, except January and February. High interest rates. Rails pulled back on equipment purchases. James J. Hill: "The crest of the wave of prosperity is passed."

Buick Motor Co. produced 16 cars valued at $1,200.

1904

Trading Sessions:	300		

Monthly Record

			Inds.		Rails	
Advances	DJI:	173				
Declines	DJI:	124				
Unchanged	DJI:	3	J	Minus .20	Minus .43	
			F	Minus 1.38	Minus 5.62	
Advances	DJR:	173	M	Plus 1.59	Plus 4.21	
Declines	DJR:	122	A	Minus .32	Minus .45	
Unchanged	DJR:	5	M	Minus .62	Minus 1.68	
			J	Plus 1.07	Plus 2.96	
Closing High	DJI:	73.23 (12/5)	J	Plus 2.88	Plus 3.20	
Closing Low	DJI:	46.41 (3/12)	A	Plus 2.44	Plus 4.70	
			S	Plus 3.02	Plus 3.56	
Closing High	DJR:	119.46 (12/3)	O	Plus 5.44	Plus 4.58	
Closing Low	DJR:	91.31 (3/14)	N	Plus 8.99	Plus 5.57	
			D	Minus 2.41	Minus 1.50	

Change from 1903

Dow Industrials:	Plus	20.50
Dow Rails:	Plus	19.10

March 4: Supreme Court ordered Northern Securities dissolved.

March 10: Lowest volume day in 8 years: 73,188 shares.

May: U.S. Steel sold at all-time low of 8⅜. By 1909 it reached 94⅞, yielded 4%.

November: Roosevelt re-elected. Market continued recovery from 1903 panic. Money abundant and cheap. Crops large; rails did well. Market bulls had everything their way after Northern Securities decision.

Also: "Undigested Securities" of 1902–1903 quickly absorbed.

Per capita wealth in U.S. reached $1,310, versus $307 in 1850.

War between Greece and Turkey created heavy European demand for American products.

Big fire in Baltimore depressed market in spring.

Russo-Japanese War began.

An estimated 318 industrial trusts with capital of $7,246 million, representing consolidations of nearly 5,300 distinct plants existed in U.S. Of this amount, over ⅓ was controlled by seven giant corporations.

1905

Trading Sessions:		301	

Monthly Record

				Inds.		Rails	
Advances	DJI:	171	J	Plus	1.72	Plus	3.62
Declines	DJI:	127	F	Plus	3.82	Plus	2.73
Unchanged	DJI:	3	M	Plus	4.87	Plus	1.11
Advances	DJR:	167	A	Minus	3.94	Minus	7.08
Declines	DJR:	134	M	Minus	1.76	Plus	1.49
Unchanged	DJR:	0	J	Plus	2.55	Plus	3.27
Closing High	DJI:	96.56 (12/29)	J	Plus	4.83	Plus	3.71
Closing Low	DJI:	68.76 (1/25)	A	Minus	1.07	Plus	3.29
Closing High	DJR:	133.54 (12/29)	S	Plus	1.27	Plus	2.29
Closing Low	DJR:	114.52 (5/22)	O	Plus	1.87	Plus	.47
			N	Plus	6.12	Minus	.99
			D	Plus	6.31	Plus	1.92

Change from 1904

Dow Industrials:	Plus	26.59
Dow Rails:	Plus	15.83

June 17: NYSE volume for week ended this day only about 1.8 million shares.

Also: Rail dividends totaled $238 million, against $222 million in 1904, $197 million in 1903. Despite depression, only 10 rails cut payments, versus 39 increases.

1906

Trading Sessions:		304

Monthly Record

Advances	DJI:	157
Declines	DJI:	147
Unchanged	DJI:	0
Advances	DJR:	155
Declines	DJR:	148
Unchanged	DJR:	1

	Inds.			*Rails*	
J	Plus	4.49	Plus	2.08	
F	Minus	6.75	Minus	5.78	
M	Plus	3.01	Plus	3.17	
A	Minus	6.42	Minus	8.67	
M	Plus	3.22	Plus	4.55	
J	Minus	6.74	Minus	5.30	
J	Plus	5.40	Plus	5.80	
A	Plus	1.60	Plus	6.09	
S	Plus	.83	Plus	.72	
O	Minus	1.93	Minus	4.55	
N	Plus	2.21	Plus	4.64	
D	Minus	.77	Minus	6.21	

Closing High	DJI:	103.00	(1/19)
Closing Low	DJI:	85.18	(7/13)
Closing High	DJR:	138.36	(1/22)
Closing Low	DJR:	120.30	(5/3)

Change from 1905

Dow Industrials:	Minus	1.85
Dow Rails:	Minus	3.46

January 12: Dow Industrials closed above 100 for first time.

April 18–19: San Francisco earthquake and fire.

May 28: San Francisco Stock Exchange reopened after being closed since April 18 on account of earthquake-fire.

August: E. H. Harriman began buying about $56 million of New York Central, Baltimore & Ohio, Atchison.

Also: U.S. Steel paid 2%; its preferred stock paid 7%.

Practice of "stock pyramiding" was born.

U.S. began antitrust suits against Standard Oil Co. of New Jersey and American Tobacco on grounds that they represented combinations of restraint of trade.

International Typographical Union (AFL) struck unsuccessfully in book and job printing establishments for 8-hour day, paving way for extension of shorter hours in printing trades.

Standard Statistics was founded.

Tickers in use: 1,278.

1907

January 7: Dow Industrials reached annual high, as year of panic began—a credit crisis arising from inflation. From January 7 to November 15 the Dow dropped 45%, wiping out three years of advance.

Trading Sessions: 301

				Monthly Record		

Advances   DJI: 129

Declines   DJI: 171

Unchanged DJI: 1

Advances   DJR: 134

Declines   DJR: 164

Unchanged DJR: 3

Closing High DJI: 96.37   (1/7)

Closing Low   DJI: 53.00   (11/15)

Closing High DJR: 131.95   (1/5)

Closing Low   DJR: 81.41   (11/21)

Change from 1906

Dow Industrials: Minus 35.60

Dow Rails: Minus 41.03

	Inds.		*Rails*	
J	Minus	2.65	Minus	7.55
F	Minus	1.16	Minus	3.57
M	Minus	10.39	Minus	12.83
A	Plus	4.15	Plus	4.12
M	Minus	6.20	Minus	9.05
J	Plus	2.26	Plus	4.14
J	Minus	1.49	Plus	.20
A	Minus	6.59	Minus	7.43
S	Minus	4.56	Plus	.52
O	Minus	10.02	Minus	14.33
N	Plus	.71	Plus	3.11
D	Plus	.34	Plus	1.64

October: Westinghouse Manufacturing in receivership. Knickerbocker Trust depositors staged an $8 million run on bank. Pittsburgh Stock Exchange closed.

October 23: Call money loaned at record high (125%). Clearing House later issued $100 million of "Clearing House Certificates" to ease money market.

October 24: J. P. Morgan & Co. helped to avert national financial disaster by assembling $25 million to sustain solvency of certain New York banks.

Also: Detroit Stock Exchange organized.

NYSE listed securities lost more than $4 billion in value.

Jesse Livermore emerged from 1907 as "Boy Plunger," worth $3 million.

Cash at a premium. Anyone could take $1,000 to a bank and receive $1,040.

Loans topped deposits all year. Money situation tense. By late November 40 leading stocks were selling $52 a share on average below 1906 peaks; specialty issues were down 60–140 points.

1908

February: Federal Government officials denounced Wall Street.

February 13: Dow Industrials hit low (58.62), which held above previous November low (53.00).

Trading Sessions: 301

Advances	DJI:	174
Declines	DJI:	127
Unchanged	DJI:	0
Advances	DJR:	174
Declines	DJR:	127
Unchanged	DJR:	0
Closing High	DJI:	88.38	(11/13)
Closing Low	DJI:	58.62	(2/13)
Closing High	DJR:	120.05	(12/31)
Closing Low	DJR:	86.04	(2/17)

Change from 1907

Dow Industrials:	Plus	27.40
Dow Rails:	Plus	31.28

Monthly Record

	Inds.		Rails	
J	Plus	3.95	Plus	3.42
F	Minus	2.16	Minus	5.67
M	Plus	6.97	Plus	5.48
A	Plus	2.04	Plus	4.95
M	Plus	3.21	Plus	2.19
J	Minus	.17	Plus	.74
J	Plus	7.75	Plus	6.88
A	Plus	4.32	Plus	2.34
S	Minus	4.73	Minus	3.15
O	Plus	2.60	Plus	3.62
N	Plus	4.77	Plus	7.53
D	Minus	1.15	Plus	2.95

May 30: Aldrich-Vreeland Act passed. Helped banks to organize National Currency Associations; also, to deposit commercial paper and industrial and municipal bonds as security for currency.

December 14: Charles Evans Hughes, governor of New York, appointed a commission headed by Horace White to ascertain "what changes, if any, are advisable in the laws of the State bearing upon speculation in securities and commodities, or relating to the protection of investors, or with regard to the instrumentalities and organizations used in dealings in securities and commodities which are the subject of speculation."

1909

January 1: Trading in bonds "and interest" inaugurated.

June 7: Hughes Committee (appointed to investigate NYSE after 1907 panic) released its report on securities market. Horace White, chairman, said the study showed "conclusively that speculation on the Stock Exchange was not the chief contributor to the collapse of 1907, but that speculation on a much wider scale, through the length and breadth of the land, was the exciting cause."

Also: Seats reached new high: $94,000.

W. C. Durant, General Motors magnate, had chance to buy Ford Motor Co. for $8 million.

Trading Sessions:	296

Trading Sessions: 296

Advances DJI: 163
Declines DJI: 128
Unchanged DJI: 5

Advances DJR: 158
Declines DJR: 134
Unchanged DJR: 4

Closing High DJI: 100.53 (11/19)
Closing Low DJI: 79.91 (2/23)

Closing High DJR: 134.46 (8/14)
Closing Low DJR: 113.90 (2/23)

Change from 1908

Dow Industrials: Plus 12.90
Dow Rails: Plus 10.36

Monthly Record

	Inds.		Rails	
J	Minus	2.06	Minus	3.12
F	Minus	2.24	Minus	.57
M	Plus	4.27	Plus	5.28
A	Plus	2.17	Plus	1.81
M	Plus	3.89	Plus	2.06
J	Plus	.10	Plus	1.64
J	Plus	4.51	Plus	4.09
A	Plus	1.11	Minus	.54
S	Plus	1.65	Plus	1.61
O	Minus	.48	Minus	2.70
N	Minus	3.05	Minus	3.56
D	Plus	3.03	Plus	4.36

When E. H. Harriman died, he was on directorates of 27 railroads covering 39,354 miles of track.

1909–1913 were years of comparative calm for business and the market.

Annual auto output reached 100,000 vehicles.

1910

Trading Sessions: 297

Advances DJI: 156
Declines DJI: 139
Unchanged DJI: 2

Advances DJR: 149
Declines DJR: 144
Unchanged DJR: 4

Closing High DJI: 98.34 (1/3)
Closing Low DJI: 73.62 (7/26)

Closing High DJR: 129.90 (1/4)
Closing Low DJR: 105.59 (7/26)

Change from 1909

Dow Industrials: Minus 17.69
Dow Rails: Minus 16.35

Monthly Record

	Inds.		Rails	
J	Minus	7.14	Minus	7.68
F	Minus	.57	Plus	.82
M	Minus	1.63	Minus	1.72
A	Minus	3.51	Minus	3.54
M	Plus	.12	Plus	1.33
J	Minus	5.14	Minus	7.99
J	Minus	4.70	Minus	2.44
A	Plus	3.20	Plus	2.91
S	Plus	.04	Plus	2.35
O	Plus	5.05	Plus	2.31
N	Minus	2.25	Minus	3.57
D	Minus	1.16	Plus	.87

March 31: NYSE Department of Unlisted Securities abolished: it helped to promote speculation. Department had existed since 1885 to enlarge opportunities for brokerage transactions. Industrial stocks with unlisted privileges were automatically admitted to regular listing.

June: Postal Savings Act passed. It provided that individuals could deposit up to $500 in U.S. Post Offices and get 2% interest. Designed to encourage economy and thrift.

1911

Trading Sessions:		298			*Monthly Record*			
Advances	DJI:	143			*Inds.*		*Rails*	
Declines	DJI:	153		J	Plus	3.57	Plus	4.76
Unchanged	DJI:	2		F	Plus	.09	Minus	1.48
Advances	DJR:	147		M	Minus	1.75	Plus	.37
Declines	DJR:	146		A	Plus	.38	Plus	.54
Unchanged	DJR:	5		M	Plus	1.90	Plus	2.30
				J	Plus	.43	Plus	2.22
Closing High	DJI:	87.06	(6/19)	J	Plus	.04	Plus	.23
Closing Low	DJI:	72.94	(9/25)	A	Minus	6.77	Minus	10.09
				S	Minus	2.94	Minus	1.63
Closing High	DJR:	123.86	(7/21)	O	Minus	.52	Plus	3.18
Closing Low	DJR:	109.80	(9/27)	N	Plus	5.18	Plus	2.78
				D	Plus	.71	Minus	.41

Change from 1910

Dow Industrials: Plus   .32
Dow Rails: Plus 2.77

March 15: Troops sent to Mexico under General Pershing because of Francisco Villa's raids.

March: Listing Department for New York Curb Market Agency (formed 1906) organized; trading hours coinciding with NYSE established. All trading was out of doors until 1921, when brokers moved inside to own building at 86 Trinity Place. The constitution defined status of curb trading as follows: "The New York Curb Market is open to all who choose to trade there, but no one is obliged to accept any contract which is not acceptable. Strangers or others must be properly identified in justice to themselves and to those they attempt to trade with, and they may be called upon to 'give up' acceptable persons before the contract is closed. This is for the safety of all concerned."

March 31: Further step taken, to insure distinction between securities regularly listed by New York Curb Market Association (founded 1911) and by others that may be traded in by various members without being listed, was by a resolution that "advertising or furnishing of quotations to newspapers . . . of any securities not listed on the New York Curb Market, without stating in such advertisement or quotation lists that they are not listed securities . . . is prohibited."

May 15: Supreme Court ordered Standard Oil combine dissolved.

May 29: Supreme Court ordered American Tobacco dissolved.

September 17: First successful transcontinental airplane flight from New York to Pasadena; completed in November after various landings.

Also: Automobile era began when General Motors voting trust certificates were listed on Exchange.

Kansas became first state to enact "blue-sky" law.

1912

Trading Sessions:	301			Monthly Record				
					Inds.		*Rails*	
Advances	DJI:	163						
Declines	DJI:	136						
Unchanged	DJI:	2		J	Minus	1.49	Minus	1.77
				F	Plus	1.21	Plus	.67
Advances	DJR:	154		M	Plus	6.87	Plus	3.53
Declines	DJR:	145		A	Plus	2.03	Plus	2.32
Unchanged	DJR:	2		M	Minus	2.29	Minus	3.21
				J	Plus	2.91	Plus	1.40
Closing High	DJI:	94.15	(9/30)	J	Minus	1.21	Plus	.90
Closing Low	DJI:	80.15	(2/10)	A	Plus	1.86	Plus	1.57
				S	Plus	2.58	Plus	1.71
Closing High	DJR:	124.35	(10/5)	O	Minus	3.44	Minus	3.57
Closing Low	DJR:	114.92	(2/5)	N	Plus	.69	Plus	.37
				D	Minus	3.53	Minus	3.91

Change from 1911

Dow Industrials:	Plus	6.19
Dow Rails:	Plus	.01

January 30: San Francisco Stock Exchange changed name to San Francisco Stock & Bond Exchange.

April 15: "Titanic" sank after ramming iceberg.

October: Panic on Paris Bourse.

Also: Massachusetts the first state to enact minimum-wage statute.

Pujo Committee organized "to investigate the concentration of control of money and credit." Also called the "Money Trust Investigation."

N.Y. passed first law permitting shares to be issued without par value.

1913

Trading Sessions: 298

Advances   DJI: 130
Declines   DJI: 165
Unchanged   DJI: 3

Advances   DJR: 127
Declines   DJR: 170
Unchanged   DJR: 1

Closing High   DJI: 88.57   (1/9)
Closing Low   DJI: 72.11   (6/11)

Closing High   DJR: 118.10   (1/9)
Closing Low   DJR: 100.50   (6/11)

Change from 1912

Dow Industrials: Minus   9.09
Dow Rails: Minus   13.12

Monthly Record

	Inds.		Rails	
J	Minus	4.15	Minus	1.35
F	Minus	3.40	Minus	4.55
M	Plus	.60	Plus	.75
A	Minus	2.38	Minus	3.94
M	Minus	.16	Minus	.34
J	Minus	3.49	Minus	3.80
J	Plus	3.59	Plus	2.16
A	Plus	3.33	Plus	1.37
S	Minus	1.44	Minus	.13
O	Minus	2.07	Minus	2.96
N	Minus	2.36	Minus	1.02
D	Plus	2.84	Plus	.69

February 5: NYSE declared (in war against manipulation) that "no Stock Exchange member firm, or member of a Stock Exchange firm, shall give, or without knowledge execute, orders for the purchase or sale of securities which would involve no change of ownership."

February 13: NYSE adopted rule which provided that accepting and carrying an account without proper and adequate margin may constitute an act detrimental to the interest and welfare of the Exchange. Committee on Business Conduct was appointed to enforce it.

February 25: Federal income taxes and excess profits taxes became legal under Sixteenth Congressional Amendment.

February 28: Pujo Committee published report on wrongdoings of the "Money Trust." This led to enactment of Federal Reserve Law.

December 23: Federal Reserve System established.

Also: Department of Labor established.

Ford introduced first moving assembly line.

1914

| Trading Sessions: | | 191 | | Monthly Record | | | |

Advances	DJI:	93
Declines	DJI:	95
Unchanged	DJI:	3

Advances	DJR:	86
Declines	DJR:	102
Unchanged	DJR:	3

| Closing High | DJI: | 83.43 | (3/20) |
| Closing Low | DJI: | 53.17 | (12/24) |

| Closing High | DJR: | 109.43 | (1/31) |
| Closing Low | DJR: | 87.40 | (12/24) |

Change from 1913

| Dow Industrials: | Minus 24.20 |
| Dow Rails: | Minus 15.19 |

Monthly Record

	Inds.		Rails	
J	Plus	4.07	Plus	5.71
F	Minus	.59	Minus	3.95
M	Plus	.13	Minus	.73
A	Minus	3.27	Minus	3.52
M	Plus	3.45	Plus	1.88
J	Minus	.91	Minus	.70
J	Minus	9.24	Minus	13.00
A				
S	Market closed on account war			
O				
N				
D	Minus	16.84	Minus	.88

June 28: Archduke Ferdinand, heir to Austrian throne, assassinated. Dow Industrials closed the following session at 80.00, down .11.

July 28: Austria declared war on Serbia.

July 31: (10 A.M.): War in Europe prompted closing of NYSE. Exchange was impotent for first time since 1873. New York Curb Market closed also. Wall Street authorities feared that markets might be avalanched by liquidation for European account, then estimated at $2.4 billion of American securities. Possibility of panic, or bear raiding from domestic sources, was another contributing factor. During previous week U.S. Rubber fell 16 points; General Motors, 39; International Harvester, 26; U.S. Steel and Bethlehem, 12 points each.

August 1: Germany declared war on Russia.

August 3: Germany declared war on France.

August 4: Germany attacked Belgium. England declared war on Germany.

November 16: Federal Reserve System began active operation.

November 28: NYSE reopened for bond trading under restrictions.

December 1: San Francisco Stock & Bond Exchange reopened—first U.S. exchange to do so after outbreak of war.

December 12: Trading resumed on NYSE at pegged prices. Example: U.S. Steel pegged at $48. Dow Industrials declined 16.70 to 54.72.

December 15: Trading in all stocks resumed under restrictions. Dow Industrials then stood 36% below the March level—lowest point in seven years, just slightly above their 1907 panic low.

December 31: Eight state banks and 7,574 national banks belonged to Federal Reserve System.

Also: An outlaw market flourished outside NYSE while it was closed. But war revived industry and stock market from lethargy which had prevailed since Panic of 1907.

Thomas J. Watson, Sr., took over Computer-Tabulating-Recording Co., changed name to International Business Machines.

1915

Trading Sessions:	302			Monthly Record			
Advances	DJI:	181		*Inds.*		*Rails*	
Declines	DJI:	120					
Unchanged	DJI:	1	J	Plus	2.58	Plus	3.07
			F	Minus	1.98	Minus	3.39
Advances	DJR:	151	M	Plus	5.65	Plus	4.61
Declines	DJR:	149	A	Plus	10.95	Plus	4.53
Unchanged	DJR:	2	M	Minus	7.11	Minus	5.29
			J	Plus	5.39	Plus	.90
Closing High	DJI:	99.21 (12/27)	J	Plus	5.28	Minus	.94
Closing Low	DJI:	54.22 (2/24)	A	Plus	5.86	Plus	2.06
Closing High	DJR:	108.28 (11/4)	S	Plus	9.38	Plus	3.85
Closing Low	DJR:	87.85 (2/24)	O	Plus	5.44	Plus	9.11
			N	Plus	.69	Minus	.68
Change from 1914			D	Plus	2.44	Plus	1.69
Dow Industrials:	Plus	44.57					
Dow Rails:	Plus	19.52					

February 18: Effective this date German Government declared: "The waters surrounding Great Britain and Ireland including the whole English Channel are hereby declared to be comprised within the seat of war."

April 1: Normal and unrestricted trading privileges restored on NYSE. Dow Industrials closed at 61.05, their low for month, before advancing sharply.

Dow Jones Bond Averages initiated. First closing price was 90.86.

May 7: "Lusitania" sunk by German submarine.

August 15: Panama Canal opened to shipping.

October 13: NYSE ruled that stocks be quoted-traded on dollar-share basis, versus percentages as formerly.

October 15: At General Motors' board meeting William C. Durant stalemated a banking group when he put down a suitcase full of certificates and proxies and declared: "Gentlemen, I control. You may get your hats as you handed me mine five years ago."

Also: War boom really began in this year.

Income taxes were increased $30 million; in 1916 they went up another $44 million.

Fall of year marked beginning of "lazy money" period.

J. P. Morgan & Co. underwrote a $500 million loan to buy American war materials.

1916

Trading Sessions:	301				

Monthly Record

			Inds.		Rails
Advances	DJI:	154			
Declines	DJI:	143			
Unchanged	DJI:	4	J Minus 8.57	Minus 7.30	
			F Plus .45	Plus .38	
Advances	DJR:	143	M Plus 2.22	Plus .50	
Declines	DJR:	155	A Minus 3.47	Plus .10	
Unchanged	DJR:	3	M Plus 2.02	Plus 4.95	
			J Minus 2.22	Minus .73	
Closing High	DJI:	110.15 (11/21)	J Minus .33	Minus 2.30	
Closing Low	DJI:	84.96 (4/22)	A Plus 3.00	Plus 1.40	
			S Plus 10.65	Plus 5.00	
Closing High	DJR:	112.28 (10/4)	O Plus 1.71	Minus .10	
Closing Low	DJR:	99.11 (4/22)	N Plus 1.36	Minus 2.10	
			D Minus 10.97	Minus 2.70	

Change from 1915

Dow Industrials:	Minus 4.15
Dow Rails:	Minus 2.90

June: Congress approved National Defense Act.

July 30: "Black Tom" explosion in Jersey City attributed to German saboteurs. No effect on market.

September: Basic income tax raised to 2% and the highest surtax to 13%.

November 15: Dow Industrials closed above Rails for first time: 107.72, versus 107.23.

November 21: Dow Industrials reached new high at 110.15 before dropping abruptly on "peace overtures." Scramble to sell featured "War Babies" and extended into 1917. DJI lost about 40%. Trading in "War Babies" was prolific prior to this correction. The 29 millions who bought Liberty and Victory bonds had become educated to ways of Wall Street.

December 27: NYSE adopted resolution that "a Stop Order to buy stock becomes a market order when the stock sells at or above the Stop Price; a Stop Order to sell stock becomes a market order when the stock sells at or below the Stop Price."

Also: Adamson Act, providing a basic 8-hour day on railroads, was enacted to eliminate a threatened nationwide rail tie-up.

1917

Trading Sessions:		298					

Monthly Record

					Inds.		Rails
Advances	DJI:	140					
Declines	DJI:	157	J	Plus	.43	Minus	2.44
Unchanged	DJI:	1	F	Minus	3.87	Minus	5.34
			M	Plus	3.85	Plus	2.96
Advances	DJR:	138	A	Minus	2.18	Minus	3.53
Declines	DJR:	157	M	Plus	4.15	Minus	1.60
Unchanged	DJR:	3	J	Minus	1.51	Minus	1.00
			J	Minus	4.12	Minus	.63
Closing High	DJI:	99.18 (1/3)	A	Minus	8.35	Minus	4.12
Closing Low	DJI:	65.95 (12/19)	S	Plus	.41	Minus	2.90
			O	Minus	9.31	Minus	6.94
Closing High	DJR:	105.76 (1/3)	N	Minus	1.85	Minus	3.81
Closing Low	DJR:	70.75 (12/19)	D	Plus	1.73	Plus	3.93

Change from 1916

Dow Industrials:	Minus 20.62
Dow Rails:	Minus 25.42

February 1-2: Market broke sharply on news of ruptured relations with German Government.

April 2: President Wilson asked Congress to declare state of war.

April 6: United States entered war. DJI continued to drop with few rallies to low for the month of 90.66 on the 24th.

May 17: Selective Service Act became law.

May: First Liberty Loan: $2 billion.

August 4: Sizzling temperatures forced NYSE to close.

November: Second Liberty Loan: $3 billion.

December 28: Railroads taken over by U.S. Railroad Commission under existing federal legislation, which provide for government rail operation in wartime.

Also: President appointed a mediation commission headed by Secretary of Labor to adjust wartime labor difficulties.

World War I Excess Profits Tax was enacted; expired in 1922.

1918

Trading Sessions:	297

Advances	DJI:	145
Declines	DJI:	150
Unchanged	DJI:	2

Advances	DJR:	148
Declines	DJR:	145
Unchanged	DJR:	4

Closing High	DJI:	89.07	(10/18)
Closing Low	DJI:	73.38	(1/15)

Closing High	DJR:	92.91	(11/9)
Closing Low	DJR:	77.21	(1/15)

Change from 1917

Dow Industrials:	Plus 7.82
Dow Rails:	Plus 4.59

Monthly Record

	Inds.		Rails	
J	Plus	5.42	Plus	1.30
F	Plus	.59	Plus	.10
M	Minus	3.67	Minus	1.15
A	Plus	.79	Minus	1.30
M	Plus	.57	Plus	4.20
J	Plus	4.60	Plus	.23
J	Minus	1.45	Minus	.25
A	Plus	1.61	Plus	3.50
S	Plus	1.84	Minus	.86
O	Plus	.83	Plus	2.61
N	Minus	4.38	Minus	1.03
D	Plus	1.07	Minus	2.76

January: NYSE initiated certain Monday closings to conserve electricity for war effort. Also, Fuel Administration, created by Lever Act of 1917, ruled that all factories east of Mississippi, except those engaged in armament work, be closed for five days. Heatless Mondays introduced; lasted for nine consecutive weeks.

March 4: Bernard M. Baruch appointed Chairman of War Industries Board by President Wilson.

April 8: National War Labor Board established to settle labor disputes. Strikes outlawed for duration of war.

May: Third Liberty Loan: $3 billion.

July 18: Marshal Foch launched big offensive.

October: Fourth Liberty Loan: $6 billion.

October 6: Germany asked for peace terms.

November 7: NYSE closed early to celebrate what turned out to be false Armistice report.

November 11: War ended; Armistice signed.

November 29: NYSE Building Co. bought Mortimer Building at corner of Wall and New Streets.

December 26: NYSE passed amendment to its constitution which authorized Governing Committee to organize a corporation for purpose of "performing the duties of the existing Stock Exchange Clearing House and any other functions which the Governing Committee saw fit to assign to it." As a result of amendment, Stock Clearing Corp. was formed in 1920 with capital of $500,000 divided into 5,000 shares, all controlled by the Exchange.

1919

Trading Sessions:	293				

				Monthly Record	
				Inds.	*Rails*
Advances	DJI:	166			
Declines	DJI:	126	J	Minus 1.59	Minus 2.35
Unchanged	DJI:	1	F	Plus 4.20	Plus 2.25
			M	Plus 4.04	Minus .63
Advances	DJR:	138	A	Plus 4.03	Plus 1.44
Declines	DJR:	150	M	Plus 12.62	Plus 6.05
Unchanged	DJR:	5	J	Plus 1.48	Minus 4.52
			J	Plus .18	Minus .06
Closing High	DJI:	119.62 (11/3)	A	Minus 2.41	Minus 5.29
Closing Low	DJI:	79.15 (2/8)	S	Plus 6.67	Minus .59
			O	Plus 7.50	Minus .34
Closing High	DJR:	91.13 (5/26)	N	Minus 5.32	Minus 4.42
Closing Low	DJR:	73.63 (12/12)	D	Plus 3.63	Minus .56

Change from 1918

Dow Industrials:	Plus	25.03
Dow Rails:	Minus	9.02

January: Market hesitated briefly and drifted to closing low of 79.88 (DJI) on the 21st. Thereafter, trend was straight up, fueled by idea of inflation.

January 2: Separate tickers for bonds installed.

April: $4.5 billion Victory Loan oversubscribed by $749,908,308.

June 28: Versailles Treaty signed.

July: Bull market especially violent, despite growing signs of industrial unrest. Speculation rampant; everyone thrived on peacetime boom. Scandals rocked Wall Street, mostly because of corners and attempted corners.

July 31: Communications industries returned to private control by Government.

August: Statement by Federal Reserve Bank about "the speculative tendency of the times" caused heavy liquidation.

September 22: Major steel strike began that lasted until January 20, 1920.

November 1: United Mine Workers struck against bituminous coal operators. In December, union agreed to arbitration by presidential commission.

November 3: DJI closed at 119.62, high of post-Armistice inflationary boom; then started decline that carried to low of 63.90 on August 24, 1920. Decline was sparked by indications of tightening money and credit.

November 5: Banks around the country applied credit brakes. Money rates climbed to highest level since 1907: 20% on November 6; 25% on November 11; 30% on November 12. Three million-share sessions appeared for first time since 1901. General Motors was a downside leader.

Also: NYSE minimum commission rates were readjusted early this year.

1920

January 1: NYSE Building Corp. leased Wilkes Building, at corner of Wall and Broad Streets, for 21 years with three renewal privileges.

January 8: AFL Iron and Steel Organizing Committee concluded an unsuccessful 3½ month strike in steel industry.

January 10: League of Nations organized.

January 17: Prohibition began.

January: Raw material prices very weak.

March 1: Railroads returned to owners after 26 months of government control. ICC subsequently allowed major rail rate increase.

April 26: Establishment of Stock Clearing Corp.

June: Federal Reserve Board raised discount rate from 6% to 7%. Public began a buyers' strike.

Trading Sessions: 299

Advances	DJI:	139
Declines	DJI:	159
Unchanged	DJI:	1

Advances	DJR:	139
Declines	DJR:	157
Unchanged	DJR:	3

Closing High DJI: 109.88 (1/3)
Closing Low   DJI: 66.75 (12/21)

Closing High DJR: 85.37 (11/3)
Closing Low   DJR: 67.83 (2/11)

Change from 1919

Dow Industrials: Minus 35.28
Dow Rails: Plus   .66

Monthly Record

	Inds.		*Rails*	
J	Minus	3.41	Minus	.62
F	Minus	12.51	Plus	.09
M	Plus	11.50	Plus	1.34
A	Minus	9.27	Minus	3.90
M	Minus	1.48	Plus	1.03
J	Minus	1.30	Minus	2.33
J	Minus	3.91	Plus	2.12
A	Minus	.69	Plus	4.47
S	Minus	3.21	Plus	3.83
O	Plus	2.00	Plus	1.29
N	Minus	2.91	Minus	5.07
D	Minus	4.09	Minus	1.59

July 27: A 100,000-share block of General Motors fell suddenly on market. William C. Durant, General Motors president, bought most of it on way down from 28 to 12, and lost nearly $90 million.

September 16: Thirty killed and over 100 injured by explosion on Wall Street outside J. P. Morgan & Co. NYSE closed for rest of day.

December 1: Durant resigned as General Motors' president.

Also: Market mostly in professional hands; stocks had rough going all year. Collapse of prices caused 1920–1921 recession.

J. P. Morgan & Co. paid some $80 million for control of General Motors.

Transportation Act of 1920 governed the issuance of rail securities.

Jesse Livermore ran corner in Piggly Wiggly for Clarence Saunders, who failed to issue 100,000 shares of authorized stock.

Allan A. Ryan lost Stutz Motor in a dramatic corner. Stock was ballooned from 100 to 200 and then above 700. This was last big corner on NYSE. It evoked new rules and set precedent discouraging to such manipulative practices.

Mexican Petroleum Co. became first oil stock on NYSE.

NYSE prices at end of 1920 were 33% below their April average.

1921

March 22: Stock Clearing Corp. began clearance of loans for NYSE members.

Trading Sessions		298
Advances	DJI:	152
Declines	DJI:	145
Unchanged	DJI:	1
Advances	DJR:	147
Declines	DJR:	149
Unchanged	DJR:	2

Closing High	DJI:	81.50	(12/15)
Closing Low	DJI:	63.90	(8/24)
Closing High	DJR:	77.56	(1/15)
Closing Low	DJR:	65.52	(6/20)

Change from 1920

Dow Industrials:	Plus	9.85
Dow Rails:	Minus	1.69

Monthly Record

	Inds.		Rails	
J	Plus	4.18	Plus	.21
F	Minus	1.15	Minus	2.85
M	Plus	.78	Minus	2.54
A	Plus	3.08	Plus	.47
M	Minus	5.40	Plus	.58
J	Minus	4.99	Minus	.79
J	Plus	.41	Plus	2.64
A	Minus	1.75	Minus	1.53
S	Plus	3.97	Plus	2.02
O	Plus	2.13	Minus	1.61
N	Plus	4.09	Plus	3.77
D	Plus	3.80	Minus	2.06

June 20: U.S. Steel sold at 71, lowest since 1915. Dow Rails closed at 65.52, lowest since 1897.

June 27: New York Curb Market moved indoors to 86 Trinity Place. Edward R. McCormick was president. N.Y. streets thus clear of security traders for first time since colonial days.

June 30: Selling pressure abated and market responded slowly to stimulus of expanding bank credit. Farmers prosperous, rails busy moving good crops; their orders for new equipment boosted steel output.

August 24: Postwar bear market terminated when DJI reached low of 63.90. During preceding 21 months the Average had declined 46.6%. At bottom of downward cycle steel industry operated at only 18% of capacity. Many layoffs in Wall Street; many dividends passed.

Also: 1920–1921 was period of subnormal business activity, but no panic, as in 1837, 1873, 1893, 1907.

Radio first appeared as social-economic factor when nationwide hookup carried President Harding's Inaugural Address.

1922

April 26: Questionnaire for regular examination of the financial condition of member firms inaugurated.

June 6: Better Business Bureau of New York established for fighting financial fraud.

Trading Sessions: 300

			Monthly Record			

				Inds.		*Rails*	
Advances	DJI:	165	J	Plus	.20	Plus	.46
Declines	DJI:	133	F	Plus	4.16	Plus	3.93
Unchanged	DJI:	2	M	Plus	3.59	Plus	2.00
Advances	DJR:	162	A	Plus	3.69	Plus	3.77
Declines	DJR:	132	M	Plus	2.89	Plus	1.10
Unchanged	DJR:	6	J	Minus	2.70	Minus	1.08

Advances   DJR: 162
Declines   DJR: 132
Unchanged DJR: 6

Closing High   DJI: 103.45 (10/14)
Closing Low   DJI: 78.59 (1/10)

Closing High   DJR: 93.99 (9/11)
Closing Low   DJR: 73.43 (1/9)

Change from 1921

Dow Industrials: Plus 17.63
Dow Rails: Plus 11.84

	Inds.		Rails	
J	Plus	.20	Plus	.46
F	Plus	4.16	Plus	3.93
M	Plus	3.59	Plus	2.00
A	Plus	3.69	Plus	3.77
M	Plus	2.89	Plus	1.10
J	Minus	2.70	Minus	1.08
J	Plus	4.12	Plus	4.53
A	Plus	3.73	Plus	3.50
S	Minus	4.48	Minus	2.88
O	Minus	.19	Minus	.35
N	Minus	1.46	Minus	4.69
D	Plus	4.08	Plus	1.55

July 1: Unsuccessful 2½ month nationwide strike of railway shopmen against wage reductions began.

October 2: NYSE's 24-story office building at 11 Wall Street formally opened.

Also: Spectacular growth of General Motors really began.

Installment buying came into its own, on wheels of automobile financing.

Sales of radios and accessories topped $60 million.

Florida land boom started.

About 15 million individuals in U.S. owned stocks.

Grain Futures Act enacted by Congress. It limited futures trading to established markets.

Mussolini marched into Rome.

Federal Trade Commission estimated that employees of American corporations owned less than 2% of common stock of major companies.

FTC investigated the grain markets.

Excess Profits Tax, enacted in 1917, expired.

1923

March 22: Basis of trading in government bonds changed from 50ths to 32nds.

Trading Sessions: 300

Advances DJI: 155
Declines DJI: 143
Unchanged DJI: 2

Advances DJR: 157
Declines DJR: 142
Unchanged DJR: 1

Closing High: DJI: 105.38 (3/20)
Closing Low DJI: 85.76 (10/27)

Closing High DJR: 90.63 (3/3)
Closing Low DJR: 76.78 (8/4)

Change from 1922

Dow Industrials: Minus 3.21
Dow Rails: Minus 5.25

Monthly Record

	Inds.		*Rails*	
J	Minus	1.30	Plus	.15
F	Plus	6.47	Plus	3.30
M	Minus	1.10	Minus	2.41
A	Minus	4.37	Minus	2.29
M	Minus	.85	Minus	1.82
J	Minus	9.68	Minus	6.19
J	Minus	.94	Plus	.29
A	Plus	6.55	Plus	3.16
S	Minus	5.57	Minus	1.97
O	Plus	.64	Plus	.49
N	Plus	3.81	Plus	2.27
D	Plus	3.18	Minus	.23

April 9: Clearing house night division organized to clear New York Curb Market securities transactions.

April 25: System of assignable stock transfer receipts by Stock Clearing Corp. was inaugurated, facilitating use of securities in transfer as collateral for loans.

August 2: President Harding died in office.

Also: Market broke badly in January. Foreign news was disturbing: Breakup of Paris Peace Conference, occupation of the Ruhr, et cetera. But on March 20 DJI reached new recovery high (105.38).

Demand for autos was unprecedented. Fisher Body Corp. absorbed by General Motors in transactions involving $200–$300 million.

Frank Bliss handled pool in Piggly Wiggly (a Clarence Saunders project) for Jesse Livermore. Stock soared 52 points in one day.

1924

May: FRB cut discount rate.

July: Public attention first focused on investment trusts. There were then only about 15 in U.S., the oldest being Boston Personal Property Trust.

August: Discount rate cut again, following another cut in June.

October: Radio Corp. listed on NYSE.

Also: Commission rates readjusted from the structure set up in 1919.

Trading Sessions: 302

				Monthly Record		
Advances	DJI:	177		*Inds.*		*Rails*
Declines	DJI:	122				
Unchanged	DJI:	3	J	Plus 5.14	Plus	1.23
			F	Minus 3.44	Minus	1.09
Advances	DJR:	166	M	Minus 4.21	Plus	.26
Declines	DJR:	136	A	Minus 2.38	Minus	.20
Unchanged	DJR:	0	M	Minus .73	Plus	1.23
			J	Plus 6.47	Plus	3.51
Closing High	DJI:	120.51 (12/31)	J	Plus 5.77	Plus	4.28
Closing Low	DJI:	88.33 (5/20)	A	Plus 3.02	Plus	.52
Closing High	DJR:	99.50 (12/18)	S	Minus 2.00	Minus	.40
Closing Low	DJR:	80.23 (2/18)	O	Plus .90	Minus	.92
			N	Plus 7.32	Plus	7.07
	Change from 1923		D	Plus 9.13	Plus	1.98

Dow Industrials: Plus 24.99
Dow Rails: Plus 17.47

Philadelphia Stock Exchange established facilities for night clearing of transactions in odd-lots.

Coolidge bull market began.

Everyone had radio fever. "The craze for the wireless voice was only exceeded by the frenzy for radio stocks" (A. Newton Plummer).

1925

Trading Sessions: 301

				Monthly Record		
Advances	DJI:	178		*Inds.*		*Rails*
Declines	DJI:	123				
Unchanged	DJI:	0	J	Plus 2.71	Plus	.93
			F	Minus .51	Plus	.62
Advances	DJR:	160	M	Minus 5.96	Minus	5.94
Declines	DJR:	136	A	Plus 3.26	Plus	2.21
Unchanged	DJR:	5	M	Plus 9.94	Plus	3.83
			J	Plus 1.06	Minus	1.57
Closing High	DJI:	159.39 (11/6)	J	Plus 2.80	Plus	.33
Closing Low	DJI:	115.00 (3/30)	A	Plus 7.37	Plus	3.21
Closing High	DJR:	112.93 (12/31)	S	Plus 2.28	Plus	.51
Closing Low	DJR:	92.98 (3/30)	O	Plus 13.06	Plus	2.57
			N	Minus 5.44	Plus	2.49
	Change from 1924		D	Plus 5.58	Plus	5.41

Dow Industrials: Plus 36.15
Dow Rails: Plus 14.60

February 5: Special code of listing requirements for foreign government bonds announced.

February 15: San Francisco Stock & Bond Exchange installed ticker service.

April 3: "Black Friday" in the wheat pit.

June 25: Revised NYSE constitution became effective.

Also: Colorado Springs Stock Exchange organized as successor to Colorado Springs Mining Stock Association.

Market's advance virtually undisturbed. Dow Industrials attained record peak by pushing through 1919 high of 119.62.

Jesse Livermore, Mike Meehan, Ben Smith, Tom Bragg were the leading traders.

1926

				Monthly Record				
Trading Sessions:	299							
					Inds.		*Rails*	
Advances	DJI:	167						
Declines	DJI:	132	J	Plus	.78	Minus	1.57	
Unchanged	DJI:	0	F	Minus	2.99	Minus	3.40	
			M	Minus	13.99	Minus	2.43	
Advances	DJR:	153	A	Plus	3.25	Plus	2.76	
Declines	DJR:	142	M	Minus	.28	Plus	1.94	
Unchanged	DJR:	4	J	Plus	9.61	Plus	4.47	
			J	Plus	7.43	Plus	1.82	
Closing High	DJI: 166.64	(8/14)	A	Plus	2.04	Plus	5.04	
Closing Low	DJI: 135.20	(3/30)	S	Minus	4.32	Minus	.33	
			O	Minus	7.81	Minus	3.66	
Closing High	DJR: 123.33	(9/3)	N	Plus	6.17	Plus	.09	
Closing Low	DJR: 102.41	(3/30)	D	Plus	.65	Plus	3.20	

Change from 1925

Dow Industrials: Plus .54
Dow Rails: Plus 7.93

January 19: NYSE initiated monthly reports of the aggregate amount of call and time borrowings by members. FRB made similar statement with respect to loans to brokers by its members.

January 27: NYSE issued statement that "in the future the committee in considering applications for the listing of securities will give careful thought to the matter of voting control."

March 1–3: Heavy selling caused by an ICC decision considered a blow to rail merger program. Dow Rails dropped 4.76 to 103.20. Market sold off 26% in March, but scored new high again in August.

May 3–12: Great Britain idled by general strike.

May 4: Post trading installed on San Francisco Stock & Bond Exchange.

May 13: Pilsudski revolution in Poland, discovery of a Fascist plot and resignation of Luther cabinet in Germany, coupled with decline of more than 30 points by Italian lira, raised many fears about Europe's financial situation. DJI dropped six straight days to May closing low of 137.16.

August 2: Wild trading in General Motors caused by unprecedented remarks of Thomas Cochrané, partner of J. P. Morgan & Co., as he left for Europe: "General business throughout the country is fine, and it should continue so indefinitely. The rise in the price of the stock of General Motors has been very rapid in the past week, but it is more than justified by the earnings, the prospects of the company and its management. I have made a careful analysis of General Motors and am convinced it will earn more than $35 a share for the year. . . . General Motors running at its present rate is cheap at this price, and it should and will sell at least 100 points higher."

Also: Highest production records set since war.

William C. Durant returned to market after his $90 million drubbing in General Motors in 1919.

So-called Western money barons heavy buyers of stocks: J. J. Raskob, the Fisher brothers, A. W. Cutten. Example: Baldwin kited from 92 in 1926 to 261 in August, 1927.

NYSE stopped listing nonvoting stock.

Exchange closed out year with a party. Trading floor took on aspects of Mardi Gras celebration—confetti, toy balloons, and music by The Ipana Troubadors.

1927

January 3: Trading inaugurated in inactive stocks on the basis of a 10-share unit of trading. A special post (Post 30), located at northeast wall of 11 Wall Street building, was designated for "10 share unit" stock issues.

January 6: Marines to Nicaragua to guard U.S. property.

Trading Sessions: 301

Advances   DJI: 183
Declines   DJI: 115
Unchanged   DJI: 3

Advances   DJR: 162
Declines   DJR: 137
Unchanged   DJR: 2

Closing High   DJI: 202.40   (12/31)
Closing Low   DJI: 152.73   (1/25)

Closing High: DJR: 144.82   (10/3)
Closing Low   DJR: 119.29   (1/28)

Change from 1926

Dow Industrials: Plus 45.20
Dow Rails: Plus 19.44

Monthly Record

	Inds.		Rails	
J	Minus	.79	Minus	.03
F	Plus	5.55	Plus	6.93
M	Minus	1.88	Plus	2.55
A	Plus	4.13	Plus	.74
M	Plus	8.75	Plus	6.21
J	Minus	6.73	Minus	3.54
J	Plus	16.38	Plus	7.54
A	Plus	7.18	Minus	2.70
S	Plus	7.80	Plus	3.49
O	Minus	15.86	Minus	7.78
N	Plus	16.48	Plus	6.18
D	Plus	4.19	Minus	.15

February: Discount rate still at 4% since boost on August 13, 1926.

March 24: Marines to China to protect U.S. interests.

May 23: Lindbergh landed in Paris; airplane stocks given a whirl. Wright Aeronautical soared from low 20's close to 100 by year-end.

May: DJI advanced in previously unexplored territory.

May 26: Ford Motor Co. produced its 15 millionth car.

July 13: Dow Rails reached 138.54, highest level in 21 years.

August 3: Big decline at NYSE opening, after Coolidge announced, "I do not choose to run."

October 7: Special requirements for listing of foreign internal shares announced.

December 8: San Francisco Stock & Bond Exchange changed name to San Francisco Stock Exchange.

Also: Stock Clearing Corp. of Philadelphia incorporated under laws of Commonwealth of Pennsylvania.

Sales of new stock issues topped sales of new bond issues for first time.

Offices of brokerage firms flourished on ocean liners: "Leviathan," "Bremen," "Berengaria."

Dividends totaled $6,423 million versus $4,169 million in 1923, but corporate earnings declined despite ballooning stock prices. Mild recession occurred in final months.

Bad news was not only ignored; it seemed to spark new advances.

DJI traveled over a 50-point range for first time. (In 1928 the Average moved over 100 points; in 1929, more than 180 points.)

Advantages of common stocks as long-term investments received their first advertising.

1928

Trading Sessions:		295		*Monthly Record*			
				Inds.		*Rails*	
Advances	DJI:	175					
Declines	DJI:	120					
Unchanged	DJI:	0	J	Minus	3.81	Minus	3.12
			F	Minus	3.81	Minus	2.83
Advances	DJR:	158	M	Plus	18.57	Plus	6.90
Declines	DJR:	136	A	Minus	1.72	Plus	3.30
Unchanged	DJR:	1	M	Plus	8.18	Minus	.45
			J	Minus	9.26	Minus	5.89
Closing High	DJI:	300.00 (12/31)	J	Plus	5.45	Plus	1.62
Closing Low	DJI:	191.33 (2/20)	A	Plus	24.41	Plus	3.32
Closing High	DJR:	152.70 (11/27)	S	Minus	.98	Minus	.54
Closing Low	DJR:	132.60 (2/20)	O	Plus	12.73	Minus	.95
			N	Plus	41.22	Plus	10.12
Change from 1927			D	Plus	6.62	Minus	.64
Dow Industrials:		Plus 97.60					
Dow Rails:		Plus 10.84					

March: Radio Corp. vaulted 61 points in 4 days (caused by technical corner). During year it jumped from 85 to 420.

March 28: DJI sagged to 210.03 when N.Y. Federal Reserve Bank indicated credit tightening. Call money climbed to 20%, but soon dropped again and market forged ahead.

May 14: New Bond Room opened, adding about 6,000 square feet to trading floor.

June 12: First 5-million-share day (5,252,425).

September: Hatry failure in London sparked foreign selling in New York.

October 1: Central quotation system for reporting bid and asked prices initiated on experimental basis at six NYSE trading posts. (Complete service inaugurated at all posts, February 11, 1929.)

November: Hoover bull market began rolling after election. Radio above 400, Montgomery Ward 439⅞, International Harvester 368,

U.S. Steel 179½. Seats sold at $580,000. Five-million-share days prevalent.

November 23: Seven million shares traded. Ticker ran 2½ hours behind floor transactions.

December 5–8: Decline by DJI from 291.30 to 257.33 caused Federal Reserve to issue statement designed to halt reloaning of Reserve funds to brokers.

December 21: Purchase of Commercial Cable and Blair Buildings adjacent to present site of NYSE announced.

December 31: DJI closed year at all-time record peak of 300.

Also: NYSE memberships were increased to 1,375 because of booming business.

Second stage of bull market that started in 1926 ended.

Harry F. Sinclair and Arthur W. Cutten ran pool in Consolidated Oil that netted $12.6 million.

Roger Babson predicted a 60 to 80-point drop. Market dipped on the news, but came back again after Yale Professor Irving Fisher forecast higher dividends.

1929

Trading Sessions:	291

Advances DJI:	155
Declines DJI:	135
Unchanged DJI:	1
Advances DJR:	150
Declines DJR:	138
Unchanged DJR:	3
Advances DJU:	163
Declines DJU:	124
Unchanged DJU:	3
Closing High DJI:	381.17	(9/3)
Closing Low DJI:	198.69	(11/13)
Closing High DJR:	189.11	(9/3)
Closing Low DJR:	128.07	(11/13)
Closing High DJU:	144.61	(9/21)
Closing Low DJU:	64.72	(11/13)

Monthly Record

	Inds.		Rails		Utils.	
J	Plus	17.51	Plus	7.40	Plus	12.28
F	Minus	.10	Minus	3.05	Minus	1.80
M	Minus	8.56	Minus	4.59	Minus	.88
A	Plus	10.44	Plus	1.13	Plus	2.29
M	Minus	21.88	Plus	1.92	Minus	.58
J	Plus	36.38	Plus	7.73	Plus	21.55
J	Plus	13.91	Plus	11.75	Plus	7.62
A	Plus	32.63	Plus	15.33	Plus	14.29
S	Minus	36.88	Minus	14.98	Minus	.80
O	Minus	69.94	Minus	13.96	Minus	44.27
N	Minus	34.56	Minus	13.93	Minus	12.71
D	Plus	9.53	Minus	1.17	Plus	5.64

Change from 1928

Dow Industrials:	Minus	51.52
Dow Rails:	Minus	6.42
Dow Utilities:	Plus	2.63

January 2: Utilities added to Dow Jones Averages. First closing average price was 85.64. Twenty stocks used in the Averages:

American & Foreign Power	American Water Works
American Gas & Electric	Brooklyn Union Gas
American Power & Light	Columbia Gas & Electric
American Tel. & Tel.	Commonwealth & Southern
Consolidated Gas	North American
Electric Power & Light	Pacific Gas & Electric
Engineers Public Service	Public Serv. of New Jersey
International Tel. & Tel.	Southern California Edison
National Power & Light	Standard Gas & Electric
Niagara Hudson. Power	Western Union

January: Third stage of bull market began.

February 2: FRB warned against speculation, but market only tremored. DJI closed at 319.76 before reaching month's high of 322.06 on the 5th.

February 11: Complete quotation service installed at all NYSE trading posts.

February 18: NYSE members voted a 25% dividend in form of "rights." Each member received the rights to ¼ of a new seat, which he could dispose of by sale or transfer within three years. With the transfer of the last of these rights on March 3, 1932, membership was raised to 1,375.

April 18: Stock Clearing Corp. started system of central delivery between corporation members (banks and trust companies) in a limited number of securities. The list was extended until, on May 29, 1929, it included all cleared stocks. Cleared bonds were added later in 1929; noncleared stocks, in 1930; U.S. government bonds, in 1932; noncleared bonds, on January 23, 1933, which brought into the central delivery system all securities listed on Exchange.

May 4: DJI climbed to new high of 327.08, but reacted sharply on profit-taking to 293.42, before resuming uptrend and closing at another new peak of 333.79 on June 29.

June 7: Special, tentative requirements for listing investment trust shares announced. Investment trust idea began sweeping U.S. later in year.

August 9: New York Reserve Bank lifted discount rate from 5% to 6% and DJI dropped 14.11 to 337.99, month's low. This was highest since July 21, 1921, and marked first time the rate was increased a full point in a single move since June 1, 1920.

September 3: Dow Industrials closed at their final bull market top: 381.17.

October 23: Although a Saturday, the DJI fell 9.42. Many rumors that Jesse Livermore headed the bear contingent.

October 23: 2,500,000 shares rained on the bulls in one frantic hour, as DJI dived 20.66. Day's volume: 6 million shares.

October 24: "Banker's Pool" with $250 million failed to absorb the selling. Richard Whitney's dramatic: "205 bid for 10,000 Steel" was wasted. Volume: 12,894,640 shares. Thomas W. Lamont, senior partner J. P. Morgan & Co., observed: "There has been a little distress selling on the Exchange."

October 29: 16,410,030 shares traded. President Whitney said later that turnover was actually 23 million. Volume on New York Curb Exchange was 7,100,000. Volume in October alone was higher than in any full year prior to 1898.

October 30: Variety: "Wall Street Lays an Egg!"

October 30–31: DJI rallied 43 points to 273.51. After close on the 31st, FRB cut discount rate to 5% from 6%.

November 11: Market on toboggan again. DJI dropped 16.14 on way to November low of 198.69 on the 13th.

November 15: Discount rate cut again.

Also: New York Curb Market changed name to New York Curb Exchange.

Forty-five to 75 million people had interest in stocks.

New security listings on NYSE totaled $15.6 million; new subscription rights offerings broke all precedents.

National debt was about $194 billion; national income, about $85 billion.

Shortly before crash C. E. Mitchell, president of National City Bank, denied there was anything fundamentally wrong: "The public is suffering from brokers' loan-itis."

Composite stock yields fell below bond yields for first time in 1928–1929.

Cash and margin customers of NYSE firms totaled 1,371,920; margin accounts numbered 559,934.

1930

Trading Sessions: 298

Advances	DJI:	159
Declines	DJI:	137
Unchanged	DJI:	2
Advances	DJR:	128
Declines	DJR:	169
Unchanged	DJR:	1
Advances	DJU:	154
Declines	DJU:	142
Unchanged	DJU:	2

Closing High DJI:	294.07	(4/17)
Closing Low DJI:	157.51	(12/16)
Closing High DJR:	157.94	(3/29)
Closing Low DJR:	91.65	(12/16)
Closing High DJU:	108.62	(4/12)
Closing Low DJU:	55.14	(12/16)

Monthly Record

	Inds.		Rails		Utils.	
J	Plus	18.66	Plus	4.14	Plus	3.82
F	Plus	3.97	Plus	3.48	Plus	8.41
M	Plus	14.99	Plus	4.94	Plus	5.63
A	Minus	6.87	Minus	12.20	Minus	.98
M	Minus	4.16	Minus	1.22	Minus	2.20
J	Minus	48.73	Minus	5.86	Minus	20.16
J	Plus	7.65	Plus	2.95	Plus	3.67
A	Plus	6.43	Plus	.33	Plus	.30
S	Minus	35.52	Minus	9.61	Minus	10.85
O	Minus	21.55	Minus	9.17	Minus	8.18
N	Plus	.04	Minus	6.96	Minus	3.63
D	Minus	18.81	Minus	8.96	Minus	3.30

Change from 1929

Dow Industrials:	Minus 83.90
Dow Rails:	Minus 48.14
Dow Utilities:	Minus 27.47

January 1: Associated Press began transmitting San Francisco Stock Exchange daily transaction lists to AP's northwest circuits.

April 17: DJI reached 294.07, the peak of a most deceptive recovery, totaling 95.38 points from previous low.

May: Herbert Hoover: "I am convinced we have now passed the worst . . . we shall rapidly recover."

September 2: New high-speed ticker service started.

December 16: Dow Industrials reached new low, well below November, 1929, bottom.

Also: First stage of the Great Depression began about mid-year. It lasted until mid-1931, when Hoover moratorium stirred hope for recovery.

Warner Bros. was star performer in "Baby Bull" market that got underway after crash, but topped out in April.

1931

February 26: Hoover vetoed Bonus Bill, but Congress overrode it; more than $1 billion was released to World War I veterans.

March 21: German-Austrian agreement for a customs union plunged convalescing U.S. into a second, more critical depression phase.

Trading Sessions:	300						

Trading Sessions: 300

Advances DJI: 123
Declines DJI: 177
Unchanged DJI: 0

Advances DJR: 125
Declines DJR: 174
Unchanged DJR: 1

Advances DJU: 130
Declines DJU: 169
Unchanged DJU: 1

Closing High DJI: 194.36 (2/24)
Closing Low DJI: 73.79 (12/17)

Closing High DJR: 111.58 (2/24)
Closing Low DJR: 31.42 (12/17)

Closing High DJU: 73.40 (3/19)
Closing Low DJU: 30.55 (12/28)

Monthly Record

	Inds.		Rails		Utils.	
J	Plus	2.97	Plus	11.60	Plus	1.61
F	Plus	22.11	Plus	1.31	Plus	9.20
M	Minus	17.30	Minus	12.61	Minus	4.07
A	Minus	21.17	Minus	8.74	Minus	7.34
M	Minus	22.73	Minus	16.08	Minus	7.85
J	Plus	21.72	Plus	12.30	Plus	8.02
J	Minus	14.79	Minus	10.92	Minus	4.51
A	Plus	4.02	Minus	5.26	Plus	1.47
S	Minus	42.80	Minus	14.59	Minus	19.42
O	Plus	8.82	Minus	1.40	Plus	2.60
N	Minus	11.56	Minus	11.35	Minus	3.45
D	Minus	15.97	Minus	7.21	Minus	5.65

Change from 1930

Dow Industrials: Minus 86.68
Dow Rails: Minus 62.95
Dow Utilities: Minus 29.39

May 7: Committee on Stock List, with approval of Governing Committee, announced regulations under which member firms were permitted to become associated with fixed-type investment trusts.

May: Richard Whitney elected to NYSE presidency for fourth straight term.

May 25: Circulars first distributed to individuals and member firms requesting information relative to their short position.

June: Market turned stronger when Hoover announced moratorium on intergovernmental debts, but soon gave way to further price weakness.

September 14: New addition to New York Curb Exchange opened for business.

September 18: Japan took over Manchuria.

September 21: Great Britain went off gold standard. Every important stock exchange in Europe, except Paris Bourse, closed temporarily. NYSE suspended short selling.

September 23: NYSE lifted short selling ban.

October 4: Hoover asked 30 financial leaders to meet him at Treasury Secretary Mellon's apartment to discuss ways of meeting crisis.

October 28: Short interest in U.S. Steel was 24% of total shares outstanding.

Also: Average short account was 400 shares.

The bear was Public Enemy No. 1. The Danforth interests and Percy Rockefeller said to be heavily short.

There were 2,290 bank shutdowns. Most spectacular was closing of Bank of the U.S. in New York.

1932

Trading Sessions:		302	

Monthly Record

			Inds.		Rails		Utils.	
Advances	DJI:	139						
Declines	DJI:	163	J	Minus 1.71	Plus 3.39	Minus .80
Unchanged	DJI:	0	F	Plus 5.25	Minus .73	Plus 2.64
			M	Minus 8.16	Minus 6.72	Minus 4.65
Advances	DJR:	133	A	Minus 7.17	Minus 8.13	Minus 4.38
Declines	DJR:	166	M	Minus 11.37	Minus 7.14	Minus 6.48
Unchanged	DJR:	3	J	Minus 1.90	Minus .87	Minus .66
			J	Plus 11.42	Plus 8.31	Plus 5.71
Advances	DJU:	133	A	Plus 18.90	Plus 14.79	Plus 10.31
Declines	DJU:	166	S	Minus 1.60	Minus 1.92	Minus 1.49
Unchanged	DJU:	3	O	Minus 9.66	Minus 6.60	Minus 4.16
			N	Minus 5.55	Minus 2.97	Minus 1.37
Closing High DJI:		88.78 (3/8)	D	Plus 3.58	Plus .86	Plus 1.42
Closing Low DJI:		41.22 (7/8)				

Closing High DJR:	41.30 (1/15)
Closing Low DJR:	13.23 (7/8)

Change from 1931

Closing High DJU:	36.11 (9/7)	Dow Industrials:	Minus 17.97
Closing Low DJU:	16.53 (7/8)	Dow Rails:	Minus 7.73
		Dow Utilities:	Minus 3.91

January 22: Hoover signed bill establishing Reconstruction Finance Corporation—his best effort to halt depression. It enabled the corporation to buy stock of insurance companies, banks, agricultural corporations, to aid in financing public work construction, and to make loans deemed necessary.

February 17: Hoover tried to use influence of office to halt bear raiding. Closing of Exchange was considered. He got Senate Committee on Banking and Currency to investigate short selling activities.

March 1: "The Match King," Ivar Krueger, a suicide.

March 3: Sale of last seat rights brought Exchange membership to 1,375.

April 1: Stock Exchange ruled that written permission must be obtained before stock in account of a margin buyer could be loaned.

April 2: New York Times Index broke triple bottom formed by lows of December 17, 1931, and January 10 and February 5, 1932.

April 9: Richard Whitney summoned to Washington to supply short selling figures for March and first week of April. He denied before Senate Banking Committee that bears were responsible for market's condition.

April 11: Treasury reported deficit of $2 billion—greater than cost of the North's participation in Civil War.

April 27: NYSE ruled that all corporations must notify Exchange of any change in their underlying securities.

April: Steel industry operated at slightly over 20% capacity.

May: NYSE requested a record of puts and calls issued by member firms.

July 8: DJI reached rock bottom, closing low for depression at 41.22. Rails hit 13.23 same day; Utilities, 16.53.

November: Franklin D. Roosevelt elected.

Also: 2,430 banks with deposits exceeding $1,750 million closed.

Rail freight revenues dropped to $2.4 billion from $4.8 billion in 1929.

Bond prices collapsed. Foreign bond defaults increased.

Fifteen million unemployed in U.S.

Wisconsin adopted the first unemployment insurance act.

Gross National Product totaled $58.3 billion, versus $103.8 billion in 1929.

Samuel Insull's utility empire collapsed. George Eastman, president of Eastman Kodak, a suicide.

Value of listed securities was $75 billion in March, against $87 billion in September, 1929, before crash.

Radio Corp. dropped from 101 on September 3, 1929, to 6 on April 1, 1932. New York Central fell from 256⅜ to 25; Westinghouse, from 289⅞ to 23½; Anaconda, from 131½ to 5⅞.

1933

January 6: NYSE announced formal adoption of rule requiring independent audit of statements of listed companies.

January 30: Adolf Hitler became German chancellor.

January–March: Entire U.S. banking system on verge of collapse, despite help from RFC and Federal Reserve.

February: Guardian National Bank of Commerce in Detroit failed, with deposits of over $90 million.

Trading Sessions:	285

Advances	DJI:	146
Declines	DJI:	138
Unchanged	DJI:	1
Advances	DJR:	136
Declines	DJR:	145
Unchanged	DJR:	3
Advances	DJU:	128
Declines	DJU:	154
Unchanged	DJU:	3

	Inds.		*Rails*		*Utils.*	
J	Plus	.97	Plus	3.02	Minus	.81
F	Minus	9.51	Minus	4.84	Minus	5.01
M	Plus	4.01	Plus	1.46	Minus	2.35
A	Plus	22.26	Plus	6.83	Plus	5.76
M	Plus	10.45	Plus	10.05	Plus	4.41
J	Plus	10.03	Plus	6.18	Plus	4.85
J	Minus	7.37	Minus	3.14	Minus	4.36
A	Plus	11.64	Plus	7.00	Plus	.87
S	Minus	7.59	Minus	11.51	Minus	5.25
O	Minus	6.66	Minus	5.01	Minus	2.53
N	Plus	9.98	Plus	2.24	Plus	.57
D	Plus	.53	Plus	2.24	Minus	.56

Closing High DJI:	108.67	(7/18)
Closing Low DJI:	50.16	(2/27)
Closing High DJR:	56.53	(7/7)
Closing Low DJR:	23.43	(2/25)
Closing High DJU:	37.73	(7/13)
Closing Low DJU:	19.33	(3/31)

Change from 1932

Dow Industrials:	Plus	38.74
Dow Rails:	Plus	14.52
Dow Utilities:	Minus	4.21

February 15: Anton Cermak, mayor of Chicago, slain by assassin. President-elect Roosevelt escaped.

February 27: Dow Industrials closed at 50.16, low for year, which held above the 1932 low of 41.22 and indicated an end to bear market.

March 4: FDR inaugurated. Governor of New York declared state banking holiday, following similar action by other states. NYSE closed until March 14 for banking holiday.

March 5: Roosevelt declared national banking holiday. In rapid succession Congress adopted following measures: Agricultural Adjustment Act, Banking Act, Economy Bill, Farm Mortgage Act, Home Owners' Loan Act, Securities Act.

March 9: FDR called Congress into special session ("Congress of 100 Days") to propound New Deal. Emergency Banking Act passed.

March 12: FDR's first "fireside chat."

March 31: Civilian Conservation Corps established.

April 4: U.S. off gold standard.

May 18: Tennessee Valley Authority came into being to improve navigation, flood control, and development and sale of power.

June 16: National Industrial Recovery Act established to encourage industrial recovery.

July 19–22: Market dropped on heavier volume, as top-heavy speculative structure broke. Commodities and alcohol stocks especially weak. NYSE trading hours shortened to rest tired clerks.

August 4: Gas bombs exploded near NYSE trading floor.

September 8: Second Day Delivery Plan effective, under which Exchange contracts settled on second following full business day. Previously, contracts had been settled on next following full business day.

October 14: Germany withdrew from League of Nations.

December 5: Prohibition ended.

Also: Liquor stocks strong early in year in anticipation of repeal, but boom ended in July.

U.S. had 34 security exchanges, including NYSE.

NYSE began compiling first hour-volume figures.

Congress passed Railroad Emergency Act of 1933 to help to keep railroads in business.

New era in securities and security-exchange regulation began.

1934

Trading Sessions:	301

Advances	DJI:	147
Declines	DJI:	154
Unchanged	DJI:	0
Advances	DJR:	148
Declines	DJR:	152
Unchanged	DJR:	1
Advances	DJU:	120
Declines	DJU:	176
Unchanged	DJU:	5

Closing High DJI:	110.74	(2/5)
Closing Low DJI:	85.51	(7/26)
Closing High DJR:	52.97	(2/5)
Closing Low DJR:	33.19	(9/17)
Closing High DJU:	31.03	(2/6)
Closing Low DJU:	16.83	(12/26)

Monthly Record

	Inds.		Rails		Utils.	
J	Plus	7.32	Plus	8.97	Plus	3.76
F	Minus	3.76	Minus	1.97	Minus	.60
M	Minus	1.61	Plus	.12	Minus	.43
A	Minus	1.36	Minus	.53	Minus	.97
M	Minus	6.49	Minus	4.69	Minus	2.19
J	Plus	1.72	Plus	1.28	Plus	.90
J	Minus	7.67	Minus	9.30	Minus	3.86
A	Plus	4.81	Plus	1.49	Plus	.56
S	Minus	.23	Plus	.16	Minus	.06
O	Plus	.73	Minus	1.55	Minus	1.23
N	Plus	9.58	Plus	1.91	Minus	.17
D	Plus	1.10	Minus	.25	Minus	1.20

Change from 1933

Dow Industrials:	Plus	5.37
Dow Rails:	Minus	3.98
Dow Utilities:	Minus	5.49

January 21: Gold Reserve Act of 1934 established new dollar at 59.06% of old weight. Gold price was fixed at $35 an ounce, versus $20.67.

June 1: Congress passed Securities Exchange Act of 1934.

June 6: FDR signed Securities Exchange Act.

July 2: Securities & Exchange Commission organized under Securities Exchange Act.

September 26: NYCE Governing Committee invited "Advisory Group" of 10 nonmembers to attend meeting of Governing Committee and to serve upon special standing committees.

October 1: NYCE registered as National Securities Exchange.

October 15: Initial margin requirement of 45% became effective.

Also: Teleregister service introduced by NYCE with 6 boards.

Federal Deposit Insurance Corp. created to insure bank depositors.

Federal Communications Act of 1934 gave 7 members of Federal Communications Commission power to control wire and radio communications; it later included television.

Directors, officers, and owners of 10% of a corporation's stock were barred from taking short-term profits.

1935

Trading Sessions:	301
Advances DJI:	176
Declines DJI:	125
Unchanged DJI:	0
Advances DJR:	151
Declines DJR:	149
Unchanged DJR:	1
Advances DJU:	155
Declines DJU:	133
Unchanged DJU:	13
Closing High DJI:	148.44 (11/19)
Closing Low DJI:	96.71 (3/14)
Closing High DJR:	41.84 (12/9)
Closing Low DJR:	27.31 (3/12)
Closing High DJU:	29.78 (12/7)
Closing Low DJU:	14.46 (3/14)

Monthly Record

	Inds.		Rails		Utils.	
J	Minus	2.35	Minus	2.69	Minus	.55
F	Plus	.69	Minus	3.38	Minus	1.37
M	Minus	1.57	Minus	2.40	Plus	.72
A	Plus	8.64	Plus	2.26	Plus	1.57
M	Plus	1.19	Plus	.45	Plus	2.07
J	Plus	7.57	Plus	2.19	Plus	1.65
J	Plus	8.02	Plus	2.38	Plus	1.96
A	Plus	1.66	Minus	.05	Plus	1.85
S	Plus	4.03	Minus	.27	Minus	.49
O	Plus	7.82	Minus	.32	Plus	2.50
N	Plus	2.61	Plus	4.59	Plus	.91
D	Plus	1.78	Plus	1.28	Plus	.93

Change from 1934

Dow Industrials:	Plus	40.09
Dow Rails:	Plus	4.04
Dow Utilities:	Plus	11.75

March 10: Hitler rejected Versailles Treaty.

March 16: Hitler revived German military training.

May 13: Eight Governing Members (office partners of member firms) elected to NYSE Governing Committee, increasing number of committee members from 42 to 50.

May 27: U.S. Supreme Court ruled NRA unconstitutional.

August 9: FDR signed Motor Carrier Act, giving ICC some control over buses and trucks similar to that over railroads.

August 14: Social Security Act signed.

October 3: Italy invaded Ethiopia.

November 9: Committee for Industrial Organization (later, Congress of Industrial Organization) formed by several AFL international unions and officials to foster industrial unionism.

Also: Public Utility Holding Company Act passed. Required that gas and electric holding companies register with SEC and ordered their corporate structures to be simplified.

National Labor Relations (Wagner) Act established first national labor policy of protecting rights of workers to organize and to elect their representatives for collective bargaining.

Works Progress Administration (WPA) established.

1936

Trading Sessions:		301	

			Monthly Record					
Advances	DJI:	167		*Inds.*		*Rails*		*Utils.*
Declines	DJI:	133						
Unchanged	DJI:	1	J	Plus	5.36	Plus	5.72	Plus	2.69
			F	Plus	2.66	Plus	2.38	Minus	.13
Advances	DJR:	158	M	Plus	4.19	Minus	1.65	Minus	.18
Declines	DJR:	139	A	Minus	10.67	Minus	3.65	Minus	2.74
Unchanged	DJR:	4	M	Plus	6.97	Plus	3.00	Plus	2.21
			J	Plus	5.05	Plus	1.56	Plus	1.08
Advances	DJU:	152	J	Plus	7.17	Plus	5.66	Plus	2.41
Declines	DJU:	147	A	Plus	1.43	Plus	1.28	Minus	.12
Unchanged	DJU:	2	S	Plus	1.53	Plus	1.10	Minus	.68
Closing High	DJI:	184.90 (11/17)	O	Plus	9.37	Plus	2.78	Plus	1.99
Closing Low	DJI:	143.11 (1/6)	N	Plus	6.03	Plus	3.26	Minus	.33
			D	Minus	3.32	Minus	1.77	Minus	.92
Closing High	DJR:	59.89 (10/14)						
Closing Low	DJR:	40.66 (1/2)			*Change from 1935*				
Closing High	DJU:	36.08 (10/31)		Dow Industrials:		Plus	35.77		
Closing Low	DJU:	28.63 (4/29)		Dow Rails:		Plus	13.15		
				Dow Utilities:		Plus	5.28		

February 1: Federal Reserve raised margin to 55%.

March 7: Hitler reoccupied Rhineland.

June 29: Merchant Marine Act gave control of oceanic shipping to U.S. Maritime Commission.

July 17: Spanish Civil War began.

August: AFL suspended Committee for Industrial Organization (later, Congress of Industrial Organization) for failure to comply with AFL's order in January to disband.

October 27: Rome-Berlin Axis established.

Also: In first large sit-down strike United Rubber Workers (CIO) won recognition at Goodyear Tire & Rubber Co.

Antistrikebreaker (Byrnes) Act declared it unlawful "to transport or aid in transporting strikebreakers in interstate or foreign commerce."

1937

Trading Sessions:	299
Advances DJI:	149
Declines DJI:	149
Unchanged DJI:	1
Advances DJR:	147
Declines DJR:	149
Unchanged DJR:	3
Advances DJU:	131
Declines DJU:	164
Unchanged DJU:	4

Closing High DJI:	194.40	(3/10)
Closing Low DJI:	113.64	(11/24)
Closing High DJR:	64.46	(3/17)
Closing Low DJR:	28.91	(12/28)
Closing High DJU:	37.54	(1/13)
Closing Low DJU:	19.65	(10/19)

Monthly Record

	Inds.		Rails		Utils.	
J	Plus	5.84	Plus	1.37	Plus	1.00
F	Plus	1.56	Plus	3.01	Minus	1.75
M	Minus	.89	Plus	3.72	Minus	2.00
A	Minus	12.14	Minus	3.10	Minus	3.07
M	Plus	.44	Minus	1.81	Minus	1.06
J	Minus	5.39	Minus	5.47	Minus	1.64
J	Plus	16.29	Plus	1.60	Plus	3.78
A	Minus	8.20	Minus	3.35	Minus	2.71
S	Minus	22.84	Minus	8.35	Minus	3.23
O	Minus	16.40	Minus	6.62	Minus	1.32
N	Minus	14.69	Minus	2.38	Minus	.23
D	Minus	2.63	Minus	2.79	Minus	2.25

Change from 1936

Dow Industrials:	Minus 59.05
Dow Rails:	Minus 24.17
Dow Utilities:	Minus 14.48

January 30: Federal Reserve increased reserve requirements against demand and time deposits of member banks.

March 10: Dow Industrials reached postdepression peak at 194.40 under Roosevelt bull market.

March 17–22: Government warnings against inflation and disappointment over auto-labor negotiations sparked 10-point drop to 179.82 by DJI.

April 26: Commodities plunged to new lows.

May 30: Police and members of Steel Workers Organizing Committee clashed at Republic Steel plant in Chicago.

July 1: "Little Steel" strike of five weeks broken when Inland Steel workers returned to jobs without union recognition or other gains.

September 7: DJI closed 8.16 lower on bearish developments in Europe.

October 5: International stocks hit hard in London.

October 18: U.S. Steel lost 7 points, Chrysler 11, Westinghouse 9½, American Smelting 7½, as DJI plummeted 10.57 to 125.73.

October 19: Market declined further to 115.83 intraday on DJI and 27.76 on DJR before rallying. Volume climbed to 7.3 million shares.

November 1: Margin lowered to 40%.

December 10: Charles R. Gay, president of NYSE, appointed special committee to consider all aspects of further developments of organization and administration of Exchange.

December 11: Italy quit League of Nations.

December 12: Japanese plane sank U.S. gunboat "Panay."

December 29: Minimum nonmember commissions raised by approximately 11%, effective January 3, 1938.

Also: General Motors recognized United Auto Workers (CIO) as bargaining agent for its members, to drop injunction proceedings against strikers, not to discriminate against union members and to establish grievance procedures.

U.S. Steel recognized Steel Workers Organizing Committee as bargaining agent for its members. A 10% wage increase, 8-hour day, and 40-hour week were negotiated.

1937–1938 recession caused principally by collapse of production.

1938

January 27: Conway Committee, special committee for study of the organization and administration of NYSE, recommended a simplified management structure to include salaried presidency; a chairman of the board to be chosen from members; reduction in size of the Governing Board, on which partners of member firms, out-of-town houses, and the public would receive increased representation; reduction of standing committees from 17 to 7; and increased responsibility for executive staff of the Exchange.

Trading Sessions: 301

Advances DJI: 153
Declines DJI: 147
Unchanged DJI: 1

Advances DJR: 142
Declines DJR: 152
Unchanged DJR: 7

Advances DJU: 139
Declines DJU: 162
Unchanged DJU: 0

Closing High DJI: 158.41 (11/12)
Closing Low DJI: 98.95 (3/31)

Closing High DJR: 33.98 (12/31)
Closing Low DJR: 19.00 (3/31)

Closing High DJU: 25.19 (10/27)
Closing Low DJU: 15.14 (3/31)

Monthly Record

	Inds.		Rails		Utils.	
J	Plus	1.02	Minus	1.50	Minus	1.14
F	Plus	7.77	Plus	1.94	Plus	.61
M	Minus	30.69	Minus	10.90	Minus	4.68
A	Plus	12.33	Plus	2.26	Plus	2.76
M	Minus	3.54	Minus	.95	Minus	.02
J	Plus	26.14	Plus	5.71	Plus	3.18
J	Plus	7.37	Plus	2.43	Minus	.43
A	Minus	2.04	Minus	1.04	Minus	1.35
S	Plus	2.18	Minus	.80	Plus	.16
O	Plus	10.28	Plus	4.88	Plus	4.91
N	Minus	1.91	Minus	1.73	Minus	2.20
D	Plus	4.94	Plus	4.22	Plus	.87

Change from 1937

Dow Industrials: Plus 33.91
Dow Rails: Plus 4.52
Dow Utilities: Plus 2.67

February: Ruling that short sales in round-lots may be made only at a price above last sale ("⅛ Rule") became effective.

February 10: NYSE voting procedure amended to provide for adoption of constitutional amendment by an affirmative majority of the membership voting, provided 688 ballots are cast. Previous voting procedure provided for adoption of amendments if not disapproved by membership.

March 11: NYSE member firms required to make available to any customer, upon request, a statement of financial condition based upon their reply to most recent NYSE questionnaire.

March 12: Germany annexed Austria.

March 17: Richard Whitney expelled from NYSE for embezzlement. On same day NYSE governors approved Conway Committee's plans for reorganization and administration of Exchange.

May 2: San Francisco Stock Exchange and San Francisco Curb Exchange (founded January 2, 1928) were consolidated.

May 16: NYSE's new constitution became effective.

May 27: Capital gains tax revised; undistributed profits tax was virtually eliminated.

June 30: Board of Governors of NYSE unanimously elected William McC. Martin, Jr., first salaried president.

September 28: NYSE Board of Governors elected 3 governors of Exchange as representatives of the public, bringing board to full quota of 32.

September 29–30: Munich Pact signed by France, England, Italy, Germany.

October 26: NYSE Constitution amended to require that all non-member general partners in member firms become allied members of Exchange, directly subject to Exchange control and discipline by January 1, 1939.

October 31: NYSE announced 15-point program designed to provide additional protection to public in dealings with member firms and to enlarge usefulness and serviceability of Exchange.

November 22: Exchange's Board of Governors adopted report of Committee on Stock List recommending new and flexible listing policies designed to attract additional seasoned issues, with quality rather than size as test of acceptability. Report also recommended substantially reduced initial listing fee, coupled with continuing annual fee instead of once-and-for-all fee, and enactment of federal legislation to eliminate inconsistencies between status of listed, registered securities and other similar classes of securities traded as unlisted, or OTC issues.

December 1: Second-day settlement of stock transactions re-established. Semiweekly settlements had been introduced, as experiment on September 1. Decision to return to second-day system followed returns to questionnaire, which showed that 80% of firms answering favored returning to second-day system.

Also: Maloney Act passed by Congress for purpose of regulating OTC market. From this evolved the National Association of Securities Dealers.

NYSE first opened to public view.

1939

January: Reports that Germany would make new demands on England and France, plus persistent selling from London, sparked 11-point decline by DJI to 143.76 during month.

March 15–18: Germans annexed Czechoslovakia. British ambassador recalled from Berlin for consultation.

March 31: Britain and France decided to defend Poland.

Trading Sessions:		300	
Advances	DJI:	149	
Declines	DJI:	150	
Unchanged	DJI:	1	
Advances	DJR:	143	
Declines	DJR:	157	
Unchanged	DJR:	0	
Advances	DJU:	154	
Declines	DJU:	137	
Unchanged	DJU:	9	
Closing High	DJI:	155.92	(9/12)
Closing Low	DJI:	121.44	(4/8)
Closing High	DJR:	35.90	(9/27)
Closing Low	DJR:	24.14	(4/8)
Closing High	DJU:	27.10	(8/2)
Closing Low	DJU:	20.71	(4/8)

Monthly Record

	Inds.		*Rails*		*Utils.*	
J	Minus	11.00	Minus	4.24	Plus	.38
F	Plus	3.54	Plus	2.74	Plus	2.45
M	Minus	15.46	Minus	6.10	Minus	4.15
A	Minus	3.39	Minus	.52	Plus	.36
M	Plus	9.73	Plus	2.59	Plus	1.61
J	Minus	7.55	Minus	2.60	Minus	.70
J	Plus	12.63	Plus	3.36	Plus	2.98
A	Minus	8.85	Minus	3.11	Minus	1.41
S	Plus	18.13	Plus	9.51	Plus	.59
O	Minus	.66	Minus	1.70	Plus	.67
N	Minus	6.19	Minus	2.21	Minus	.88
D	Plus	4.55	Plus	.13	Plus	.66

Change from 1938

Dow Industrials:	Minus	4.52
Dow Rails:	Minus	2.15
Dow Utilities:	Plus	2.56

April 1: Capital requirements of member firms doing general business with public were increased about 25%.

May 22: Germany and Italy signed 10-year military alliance.

June 1: Registered employees classified into two general groups (Registered Representatives and Branch Office Managers), in place of two previous classifications to facilitate more intensive supervision. Examination requirements also extended to include all registered employees.

June 26: Accounting firm of Haskins & Sells, which had been retained August, 1938, by special committee studying the feasibility of central depository for customers' securities, reported it would be impractical if average daily volume on Exchange was less than 2 million shares, and that annual operating costs of a central depository would be from $1,100,000 to $1,200,000.

July 14: Exchange President Martin announced appointment of special committee to serve as Public Examining Board to study the broad problem of customer protection.

July 15: General partners of member firms carrying margin accounts were prohibited by Exchange from trading on margin with own firm or with other brokers or dealers.

August 16–21: War of nerves. Favorable domestic business news, versus unfavorable international news.

August 19: Analysis of Exchange's efforts to encourage interim financial reports by companies disclosed that 73% of listed active domestic companies reported quarterly, 15% announced financial results of operations semiannually, and 12% reported only annually.

August 23: Lloyd's of London advanced war-risk rates.

NYSE Board of Governors adopted report of Subcommittee on Independent Audits and Audit Procedure, which recommended the assumption by boards of directors of direct responsibility, authority, and facilities for the comptroller or internal auditor, and adoption of a natural business year in lieu of calendar year.

August 24: Russia and Germany signed 10-year nonaggression pact.

August 31: Public Examining Board reported 14 specific recommendations to further increase protection afforded customers of member firms. Recommendations included increased capital requirements, enlarged auditing requirements, separation of underwriting from commission business, segregation of free credit balances, a reserve fund for Exchange, service charges, fidelity insurance, minimum charges for commodity accounts, and greater disclosure to member firms' customers.

Board of Governors announced September 13 that two recommendations had already been adopted: additional disclosure and distribution of member firms' financial statements, and an increase (effective March 1, 1940) of minimum capital requirements of firms carrying margin accounts from $25,000 to $50,000.

September 1: Germany attacked Poland.

September 3: England, France declared war on Germany.

September 8: FDR declared limited national emergency.

September 17: Russia invaded Poland.

November 4: Bill revising neutrality pact signed by FDR authorized the purchase of war equipment in U.S. for cash and shipment on vessels flying other than American flag.

November 30: Russia attacked Finland.

December 2: Arbitration panels of local business and professional men established in 8 principal cities for cases involving the public.

1940

January 22: First meeting of National Association of Securities Dealers.

May 10: Germany invaded Low Countries. British pound reached extreme low. Churchill displaced Chamberlain as prime minister.

Trading Sessions:	302

<table>
<tr><td>Advances</td><td>DJI:</td><td>158</td></tr>
<tr><td>Declines</td><td>DJI:</td><td>140</td></tr>
<tr><td>Unchanged DJI:</td><td></td><td>4</td></tr>
<tr><td>Advances</td><td>DJR:</td><td>155</td></tr>
<tr><td>Declines</td><td>DJR:</td><td>138</td></tr>
<tr><td>Unchanged DJR:</td><td></td><td>9</td></tr>
<tr><td>Advances</td><td>DJU:</td><td>142</td></tr>
<tr><td>Declines</td><td>DJU:</td><td>150</td></tr>
<tr><td>Unchanged DJU:</td><td></td><td>10</td></tr>
</table>

Closing High DJI:	152.80	(1/3)
Closing Low DJI:	111.84	(6/10)
Closing High DJR:	32.67	(1/4)
Closing Low DJR:	22.14	(5/21)
Closing High DJU:	26.45	(1/3)
Closing Low DJU:	18.03	(6/10)

Monthly Record

	Inds.		Rails		Utils.	
J	Minus	4.91	Minus	1.27	Minus	.88
F	Plus	1.21	Minus	.08	Minus	.06
M	Plus	1.41	Plus	.38	Plus	.58
A	Plus	.48	Minus	.17	Minus	.12
M	Minus	32.21	Minus	7.54	Minus	6.20
J	Plus	5.65	Plus	3.03	Plus	3.77
J	Plus	4.27	Plus	.74	Plus	.03
A	Plus	3.28	Plus	.98	Minus	.25
S	Plus	3.22	Plus	.62	Minus	.76
O	Plus	1.97	Plus	.78	Plus	1.31
N	Minus	3.61	Minus	1.33	Minus	3.03
D	Plus	.13	Plus	.16	Minus	.12

Change from 1939

Dow Industrials:	Minus	19.11
Dow Rails:	Minus	3.70
Dow Utilities:	Minus	5.73

May 12–14: "Sitzkrieg" ended. Germans blitzed across French border.

May 26–June 3: Evacuation at Dunkerque.

June 5: Germans moved on Paris.

June 10: Italy declared war on Allies, invaded France.

June 22: Armistice signed by France-Germany.

July 14: Estonia, Latvia, Lithuania taken over by Russia.

August 13: Battle of Britain started.

September 16: First peacetime draft law signed—Selective Training and Service Act.

October 8: Far East crisis worsened. American civilians advised to leave Japan, China, Indo-China.

November 14: Luftwaffe bombed Coventry.

Also: Investment Company Act of 1940 and Investment Advisors Act of 1940 initiated and designed by Federal Government to protect investors against fraud.

Merrill Lynch, Pierce, Fenner & Smith published first annual report by a brokerage firm.

1941

January 9: FDR proposed all-out aid to free nations.

January 20: FDR inaugurated for third term.

Trading Sessions: 301

Advances   DJI: 138
Declines   DJI: 162
Unchanged DJI: 1

Advances   DJR: 146
Declines   DJR: 145
Unchanged DJR: 10

Advances   DJU: 145
Declines   DJU: 148
Unchanged DJU: 8

Closing High DJI: 133.59 (1/10)
Closing Low DJI: 106.34 (12/23)

Closing High DJR: 30.88   (8/1)
Closing Low DJR: 24.25   (12/10)

Closing High DJU: 20.65   (1/13)
Closing Low DJU: 13.51   (12/19)

Monthly Record

	Inds.		Rails		Utils.	
J	Minus	7.00	Plus	.12	Minus	.30
F	Minus	2.16	Minus	.82	Plus	.07
M	Plus	.75	Plus	1.24	Plus	.07
A	Minus	7.18	Minus	.27	Minus	1.79
M	Plus	.22	Minus	.97	Minus	1.00
J	Plus	7.38	Plus	.98	Plus	.90
J	Plus	5.65	Plus	2.20	Plus	.80
A	Minus	1.09	Minus	.42	Plus	.13
S	Minus	.88	Minus	1.29	Minus	.43
O	Minus	9.00	Minus	.57	Minus	1.66
N	Minus	3.59	Minus	1.37	Minus	1.01
D	Minus	3.27	Minus	1.54	Minus	1.61

Change from 1940

Dow Industrials: Minus 20.17
Dow Rails: Minus 2.71
Dow Utilities: Minus 5.83

January 30: Hitler said ships aiding Britain would be sunk. French reported that German attack on Britain might begin in February, because of favorable Channel tides.

March 11: Lend-lease bill signed by FDR.

March 13: New long-range heavy bombers used for first time against Berlin, Hamburg, Bremen.

April 7: Yugoslavia surrendered to the Axis.

April 11: FDR created Office of Price Administration and Civilian Supply to cope with big inflationary pressures.

April 27: German tanks rolled into Athens. British evacuated Greece.

May 9: Emil Schram, chairman of RFC, elected NYSE president.

May 10: Rudolf Hess parachuted into Scotland to see Duke of Hamilton in attempt to arrange peace with England.

May 27: FDR declared unlimited national emergency.

June 22: Germany attacked Russia.

July 28: From a high of 130.06 on this date, the Dow Industrials eroded steadily to an April 28, 1942, low of 92.92.

August 28: Office of Price Administration established to control war inflation. Rent controls went into effect, along with gasoline rationing and other measures.

September 20: FDR signed biggest tax bill in nation's history to raise $3,553,400,000.

December 7: At 7:55 A.M., Honolulu time, Japanese planes attacked Pearl Harbor.

December 8: War formally declared on Japan.

December 10–11: Germany and Italy declared war on U.S.

December 24: AFL and CIO agreed to no-strike pledge for war's duration.

Also: As of late this year, about 15% of U.S. industrial capacity was devoted to war.

Standard Statistics merged with Poor's Corp. to become Standard & Poor's Corp.

1942

Trading Sessions:	301

Advances DJI:	168
Declines DJI:	130
Unchanged DJI:	3
Advances DJR:	139
Declines DJR:	153
Unchanged DJR:	9
Advances DJU:	147
Declines DJU:	143
Unchanged DJU:	11
Closing High DJI:	119.71 (12/26)
Closing Low DJI:	92.92 (4/28)
Closing High DJR:	29.28 (11/2)
Closing Low DJR:	23.31 (6/2)
Closing High DJU:	14.94 (1/6)
Closing Low DJU:	10.58 (4/28)

Monthly Record

	Inds.		Rails		Utils.	
J	Minus	1.85	Plus	2.82	Unchanged	
F	Minus	2.32	Minus	.72	Minus	.42
M	Minus	7.26	Minus	2.65	Minus	2.18
A	Minus	4.18	Minus	.57	Minus	.45
M	Plus	5.53	Minus	.42	Plus	.53
J	Plus	2.46	Plus	.29	Plus	.23
J	Plus	2.38	Plus	1.63	Minus	.37
A	Plus	.61	Plus	.39	Plus	.20
S	Plus	2.78	Plus	1.15	Plus	.71
O	Plus	4.96	Plus	1.51	Plus	1.89
N	Plus	.43	Minus	1.97	Minus	.16
D	Plus	4.90	Plus	.51	Plus	.54

Change from 1941

Dow Industrials:	Plus	8.44
Dow Rails:	Plus	1.97
Dow Utilities:	Plus	.52

January 7: War Production Board established.

January 12: War Labor Board established to settle labor arguments that affected waging of war and wage disputes.

January: NYSE Board of Governors adopted "special offerings" plan to handle large blocks of stock for sale on floor of Exchange.

February 10: Auto industry stopped manufacturing passenger cars.

February 15: British surrendered Singapore.

March 16: Higher NYSE commission rates became effective.

April: War Production Board put all kinds of construction under government control.

April 9: Bataan surrendered.

April 18: Lt. Col. James Doolittle led 16 B-25's from carrier "Hornet" for attack on Japan.

War Manpower Commission was established.

April 28: Dow Industrials reached rock-bottom low for war years: 92.92.

May 1: Battle of the Coral Sea.

May 2: Office of Defense Transportation took over direction of all rubber-borne transportation.

May 6: Fall of Corregidor.

May 18: NYSE celebrated 150th anniversary with huge bond sale on steps of Sub-Treasury Building. Exchange closed from noon to 1 P.M.

June 3–6: Battle of Midway.

July: War Labor Board granted 15% cost-of-living wage increases to Bethlehem Steel, Youngstown Sheet & Tube, Inland Steel, and Republic Steel employees. Called "Little Steel" formula, it set pattern for wage increases for some months ahead.

August 7: U.S. Marines landed at Guadalcanal.

August: Germans battled for Stalingrad.

November 8: Allies landed in North Africa.

Also: Stabilization Act authorized President to stabilize wages and salaries based on September 15, 1942, levels.

1943

January 14: Casablanca Conference.

January 18: Russians broke Stalingrad siege.

January 19: FDR ordered striking Pennsylvania coal miners back to work.

January 23: British captured Tripoli.

January 25: "Big Five" railroad brotherhoods renewed wage demands.

January 27: First big daylight raid on Wilhelmshaven-Emden.

January 30: OPA granted coal price rise.

February 2: Germans surrendered at Stalingrad.

Trading Sessions: 301

Advances	DJI:	166
Declines	DJI:	132
Unchanged	DJI:	3

Advances	DJR:	161
Declines	DJR:	138
Unchanged	DJR:	2

Advances	DJU:	165
Declines	DJU:	130
Unchanged	DJU:	6

| Closing High DJI: | 145.82 | (7/14) |
| Closing Low DJI: | 119.26 | (1/8) |

| Closing High DJR: | 38.30 | (7/24) |
| Closing Low DJR: | 27.59 | (1/2) |

| Closing High DJU: | 22.30 | (7/14) |
| Closing Low DJU: | 14.69 | (1/2) |

Monthly Record

	Inds.		*Rails*		*Utils.*	
J	Plus	6.18	Plus	1.82	Plus	2.06
F	Plus	4.53	Plus	2.85	Plus	.88
M	Plus	6.46	Plus	2.02	Plus	.80
A	Minus	1.09	Plus	1.48	Plus	1.33
M	Plus	6.58	Plus	1.75	Plus	.81
J	Plus	1.32	Minus	.83	Plus	.92
J	Minus	7.43	Minus	1.97	Minus	.65
A	Plus	.67	Plus	.04	Plus	.48
S	Plus	3.50	Plus	.56	Plus	.67
O	Minus	1.85	Plus	.13	Plus	.11
N	Minus	8.70	Minus	3.74	Minus	1.12
D	Plus	6.32	Plus	2.06	Plus	1.04

Change from 1942

Dow Industrials:	Plus	16.49
Dow Rails:	Plus	6.17
Dow Utilities:	Plus	7.33

February 9: Major Japanese resistance ended on Guadalcanal. FDR ordered 48-hour minimum work week.

February 12: FDR promised that Japan and Europe would be attacked.

February 15: Field Marshal Rommel broke through U.S. lines at Tunisia.

February 24: Churchill ill with pneumonia.

February 25: Boeing on strike.

March 12: Hitler reported suffering nervous breakdown.

March 15: John L. Lewis threatened UMW strike April 1, unless satisfactory work agreement was signed.

March 22: FDR ordered UMW and John Lewis to continue work after April 1 deadline.

April 8: FDR acted to curb inflation by urging check on excess purchasing power by higher taxes, more saving, and less spending.

May 1: War Manpower Commissioner Paul V. McNutt ordered 48-hour week for steel industry.

May 12: War ended in Africa.

June 9: Current Tax Payment Act enacted by Congress. Salaried workers placed on current basis, with income taxes withheld by employer.

June 30: WPA ceased to exist; turned back $130 million to U.S. Treasury. In 8 years of life WPA spent $10½ billion, employed 8.5 million.

A House vote against subsidies and good news from war front spiraled market to 3-year high.

July 10: U.S., British, Canadian troops invaded Sicily.

July 19: Rome bombed for first time by Allied planes.

July 25: Mussolini resigned as Italian premier. Market down. Rails and "War Babies" the main selling targets.

July 27: Italy reported negotiating for peace.

July 31: FDR's 1944 budget revision statement asked heavier taxes to offset war costs and curb inflation.

August 14: Premier Marshal Badoglio's government declared Rome an open city.

August 18: Sicily campaign ended.

September 3: Italian mainland invaded.

September 8: Italy surrendered.

September 10: Germans seized Rome.

September 30: Third War Loan passed quota.

October 1: Americans-British captured Naples.

October 13: Italy declared war on Germany.

November 28–December 1: Teheran Conference.

Also: National War Labor Board said that 1,363 strikes in war industries cost 2,095,294 man-days and involved 569,801 workers, versus 3,000 strikes in 1941 and 825,000 workers, costing 4,565,000 man-days.

A threatened strike over wages caused federal seizure of all railroads. Companies returned to private owners January 18, 1944.

Female pages ("Quote Girls") introduced on NYSE trading floor.

War Labor Disputes (Smith-Connally) Act, passed over President's veto. It authorized plant seizure, if needed, to avoid interference with war effort.

1944

February 3–11: Yalta Conference.

June 6: Allies landed in Normandy—D-day.

July: Representatives of 44 nations met at Bretton Woods, N.H., to discuss financial-monetary problems. (From it evolved International

Trading Sessions: 298

Advances   DJI: 171
Declines   DJI: 121
Unchanged DJI: 6

Advances   DJR: 176
Declines   DJR: 119
Unchanged DJR: 3

Advances   DJU: 166
Declines   DJU: 124
Unchanged DJU: 8

Closing High DJI: 152.53 (12/16)
Closing Low DJI: 134.22 (2/7)

Closing High DJR: 48.40 (12/30)
Closing Low DJR: 33.45 (1/3)

Closing High DJU: 26.37 (12/30)
Closing Low DJU: 21.74 (1/3)

Monthly Record

	Inds.		Rails		Utils.	
J	Plus	1.51	Plus	2.80	Plus	.70
F	Minus	1.10	Plus	1.87	Plus	.69
M	Plus	2.54	Plus	1.31	Minus	.15
A	Minus	2.61	Minus	.73	Minus	.66
M	Plus	6.01	Plus	1.72	Plus	.85
J	Plus	6.14	Plus	1.01	Plus	.80
J	Minus	2.27	Minus	.25	Minus	.10
A	Plus	.88	Minus	.40	Plus	1.39
S	Minus	.26	Plus	.04	Minus	.41
O	Minus	.20	Plus	.66	Plus	.52
N	Plus	.80	Plus	1.29	Plus	.05
D	Plus	4.99	Plus	5.52	Plus	.92

Change from 1943

Dow Industrials: Plus   16.43
Dow Rails: Plus   14.84
Dow Utilities: Plus   4.50

Bank for Reconstruction and Development, which began operations in June, 1946, and International Monetary Fund, established in 1946 with $7.9 billion of resources.)

July 20: Plot to kill Hitler failed.

August 25: Paris liberated.

September 5–9: Worry about postwar economic unsettlement temporarily put market on defensive.

October 3: Office of War Mobilization and Reconversion established to smooth change-over from war to peace.

October 20: U.S. forces landed in Philippines.

October 22–27: Battle of Leyte Gulf.

November 25: San Francisco Stock Exchange created office of non-member paid president.

December 16: Fifteen German divisions launched Battle of Ardennes Bulge.

1945

February 5: Margin raised to 50%.

February 19: Iwo Jima invaded.

April 1: Okinawa invaded.

April 12: FDR died. Truman became President.

Trading Sessions: 286

Advances   DJI: 163
Declines   DJI: 122
Unchanged DJI: 1

Advances   DJR: 161
Declines   DJR: 122
Unchanged DJR: 3

Advances   DJU: 177
Declines   DJU: 103
Unchanged DJU: 6

Closing High DJI: 195.82   (12/11)
Closing Low DJI: 151.35   (1/24)

Closing High DJR: 64.89   (12/8)
Closing Low DJR: 47.03   (1/31)

Closing High DJU: 39.15   (12/10)
Closing Low DJU: 26.15   (1/23)

Monthly Record

	Inds.		*Rails*		*Utils.*	
J	Plus	1.35	Minus	1.37	Plus	.54
F	Plus	6.73	Plus	4.53	Plus	1.56
M	Minus	5.99	Minus	.85	Minus	.83
A	Plus	11.03	Plus	6.37	Plus	2.82
M	Plus	2.86	Plus	.82	Plus	.54
J	Minus	3.01	Plus	2.72	Plus	2.13
J	Minus	2.41	Minus	3.50	Minus	.47
A	Plus	11.41	Minus	1.84	Plus	.35
S	Plus	7.42	Plus	3.78	Plus	1.89
O	Plus	4.89	Plus	1.06	Plus	2.06
N	Plus	4.86	Plus	3.78	Plus	1.81
D	Plus	1.45	Minus	1.10	Minus	.64

Change from 1944

Dow Industrials:	Plus	40.59
Dow Rails:	Plus	14.40
Dow Utilities:	Plus	11.76

May 2: Fall of Berlin.

May 6: Germany signed unconditional surrender.

May 7: V-E Day.

July 5: Margin raised to 75%.

July 16: First atom bomb exploded in New Mexico—so-called "Manhattan Project."

July 17–August 2: Potsdam Conference.

July: First advertising by NYSE appeared during this month.

August 6: Atom bomb on Hiroshima.

August 9: Atom bomb on Nagasaki.

August 14: Japan surrendered unconditionally.

September 2: Formal surrender of Japan—V-J Day.

October 24: United Nations established.

November 21: General Motors struck by United Auto Workers union (CIO).

Also: Government spending to prosecute war totaled $281 billion during 1941–1945. Of this amount taxation contributed about 43%; balance was obtained through borrowing. There were seven War Loans and a Victory Loan during the war. Bond sales equaled $156.9 billion; corporations subscribed $102.2 billion; individuals, $43.2 billion. Remainder of about $12 billion was subscribed by commercial banks and U.S. Treasury.

1946

Trading Sessions:		281	
Advances	DJI:	136	
Declines	DJI:	145	
Unchanged	DJI:	0	
Advances	DJR:	131	
Declines	DJR:	146	
Unchanged	DJR:	4	
Advances	DJU:	152	
Declines	DJU:	125	
Unchanged	DJU:	4	
Closing High	DJI:	212.50	(5/29)
Closing Low	DJI:	163.12	(10/9)
Closing High	DJR:	68.31	(6/13)
Closing Low	DJR:	44.69	(10/9)
Closing High	DJU:	43.74	(5/29)
Closing Low	DJU:	33.20	(10/9)

Monthly Record

	Inds.		*Rails*		*Utils.*	
J	Plus	11.76	Plus	4.82	Plus	3.12
F	Minus	14.58	Minus	5.39	Minus	2.32
M	Plus	9.66	Plus	2.03	Plus	2.88
A	Plus	7.02	Minus	.09	Plus	1.53
M	Plus	5.51	Plus	3.70	Plus	.21
J	Minus	6.66	Minus	2.06	Minus	1.45
J	Minus	4.06	Minus	3.95	Minus	.78
A	Minus	12.37	Minus	4.57	Minus	2.28
S	Minus	16.77	Minus	9.57	Minus	4.59
O	Minus	3.27	Plus	1.34	Plus	.75
N	Plus	.74	Plus	.52	Plus	.15
D	Plus	7.31	Plus	1.55	Plus	1.92

Change from 1945

Dow Industrials:	Minus	15.71
Dow Rails:	Minus	11.67
Dow Utilities:	Minus	.86

January: Steel strike in force.

January 10: League of Nations dissolved after 26 years.

January 15: 100,000 General Electric workers on strike.

January 21: Margin raised to 100%.

February 17: Steel strike settled.

March 13: General Electric and General Motors strikes ended.

April: 450,000 soft coal miners struck.

May 26: Railroad brotherhood called strike.

May 28: Railmen returned to work.

May 29: Market reached postwar top of 212.50 DJI—new high since 1930.

May 30: Coal strike settled.

September: Stocks on downgrade, but decline was brief; the public was not heavily in market.

December 31: World War II excess-profits tax, enacted in 1940, was repealed.

Also: Truman ended all wartime wage and salary controls.
Work stoppages at new high—4,985 strikes, or 116 man-days idle.

1947

Trading Sessions:	283

Monthly Record

	Inds.		Rails		Utils.	
J	Plus	3.24	Minus	.25	Minus	.35
F	Minus	1.54	Minus	.49	Minus	.11
M	Minus	1.70	Minus	1.75	Minus	.93
A	Minus	6.56	Minus	3.42	Minus	1.90
M	Minus	1.39	Minus	.98	Minus	.61
J	Plus	8.05	Plus	1.64	Plus	1.36
J	Plus	5.88	Plus	4.08	Plus	.92
A	Minus	4.33	Minus	1.19	Minus	.07
S	Minus	1.36	Minus	.34	Minus	.32
O	Plus	4.32	Plus	.31	Minus	.38
N	Minus	2.41	Minus	1.62	Minus	1.94
D	Plus	1.76	Plus	5.36	Plus	.46

Advances DJI:	147	
Declines DJI:	136	
Unchanged DJI:	0	
Advances DJR:	133	
Declines DJR:	143	
Unchanged DJR:	7	
Advances DJU:	133	
Declines DJU:	142	
Unchanged DJU:	8	
Closing High DJI:	186.85	(7/24)
Closing Low DJI:	163.21	(5/17)
Closing High DJR:	53.42	(2/8)
Closing Low DJR:	41.16	(5/19)
Closing High DJU:	37.55	(2/8)
Closing Low DJU:	32.28	(5/20)

Change from 1946

Dow Industrials:	Plus	3.96
Dow Rails:	Plus	1.35
Dow Utilities:	Minus	3.87

February 1: Margin lowered to 75%.

March: United Auto Workers ended 329-day strike against Allis-Chalmers.

June 23: Taft-Hartley law (Labor-Management Act of 1947) passed by Congress, vetoed by Truman. But it became law, nevertheless, over his veto.

July: Military mission sent to Greece.

November 1: Regulation "W" expired—the brake on consumer credit that was applied September 1, 1941.

Also: National Federation of Telephone Workers struck AT&T.
The only war control remaining this year applied to rent.

1948

January: Truman warned of inflation.

January 30: Mahatma Gandhi assassinated.

February 24: Communists took over Czechoslovakia.

Trading Sessions: 283

Advances DJI: 153
Declines DJI: 127
Unchanged DJI: 3

Advances DJR: 150
Declines DJR: 132
Unchanged DJR: 1

Advances DJU: 153
Declines DJU: 121
Unchanged DJU: 9

Closing High DJI: 193.16 (6/15)
Closing Low DJI: 165.39 (3/16)

Closing High DJR: 64.95 (7/14)
Closing Low DJR: 48.13 (2/10)

Closing High DJU: 36.04 (6/14)
Closing Low DJU: 31.65 (2/27)

Monthly Record

	Inds.		Rails		Utils.	
J	Minus	6.11	Minus	.82	Minus	.71
F	Minus	7.75	Minus	2.39	Minus	.99
M	Plus	9.90	Plus	4.46	Plus	.57
A	Plus	3.31	Plus	4.42	Plus	.81
M	Plus	10.23	Plus	2.66	Plus	1.75
J	Minus	1.28	Plus	1.95	Minus	.13
J	Minus	8.13	Minus	2.61	Minus	1.00
A	Plus	.38	Plus	1.38	Plus	.15
S	Minus	3.41	Minus	3.20	Minus	.37
O	Plus	10.32	Plus	3.01	Plus	.92
N	Minus	7.42	Minus	9.43	Minus	2.80
D	Plus	6.10	Plus	.95	Plus	.95

Change from 1947

Dow Industrials: Minus 3.86
Dow Rails: Plus   .38
Dow Utilities: Plus   .15

March 16: Bituminous coal miners began negotiations for wage hikes. General Motors negotiated contract with CIO for further wage increases.

April: United Auto Workers President Walter Reuther wounded by gunman who escaped.

May 10: Army took over railroads on Truman's order, because of wage disputes.

June 21: Berlin airlift started.

July 8: Railroads returned to private owners, after having been under control since May 10.

September 20: Federal controls reinstated on consumer credit.

November: Truman won over Dewey at the polls.

Also: Truman's pledge that he would try to get Taft-Hartley Act repealed won support from labor and was big factor in the election race.

Maritime and longshoremen struck on both coasts.

Reduction in individual income taxes gave inflation another boost.

1949

March 7: Philadelphia Stock Exchange merged with Baltimore Stock Exchange and changed name to Philadelphia-Baltimore Stock Exchange —the first regional exchange to cross state boundaries.

Trading Sessions: 282

Advances	DJI:	148
Declines	DJI:	132
Unchanged	DJI:	2
Advances	DJR:	145
Declines	DJR:	134
Unchanged	DJR:	3
Advances	DJU:	151
Declines	DJU:	115
Unchanged	DJU:	16

Closing High	DJI:	200.52 (12/30)
Closing Low	DJI:	161.60 (6/13)
Closing High	DJR:	54.29 (1/7)
Closing Low	DJR:	41.03 (6/13)
Closing High	DJU:	41.31 (12/30)
Closing Low	DJU:	33.36 (1/3)

Monthly Record

	Inds.		Rails		Utils.	
J	Plus	1.82	Minus	.29	Plus	1.13
F	Minus	6.06	Minus	4.86	Minus	.12
M	Plus	4.04	Plus	1.31	Plus	.96
A	Minus	2.94	Minus	1.75	Minus	.11
M	Minus	5.80	Minus	2.78	Minus	.36
J	Minus	.94	Minus	1.92	Minus	.64
J	Plus	8.50	Plus	2.20	Plus	1.31
A	Plus	2.74	Plus	.32	Plus	.97
S	Plus	3.85	Plus	2.78	Plus	1.17
O	Plus	7.03	Minus	.01	Plus	.67
N	Plus	2.01	Plus	.25	Plus	.73
D	Plus	8.58	Plus	4.65	Plus	2.03

Change from 1948

Dow Industrials:	Plus	22.83
Dow Rails:	Minus	.10
Dow Utilities:	Plus	7.74

March 30: Margin lowered to 50%.

April 4: Atlantic Pact signed by 12 nations (NATO).

April 12: Marshall Plan passed by House of Representatives.

April–June: Regulation "W" relaxed, then canceled entirely by Federal Reserve to spur consumer buying.

May: Short strike at Ford.

May 12: 328-day Berlin airlift ended.

June 30: State and local governments had $20.9 billion of outstanding debt.

July: Unemployment at 4.1 million on account of recession.

CIO President Philip Murray demanded various wage increases and other benefits for steelworkers.

September 14: Chicago newspapers in circulation after 22 months' idleness.

September 18: Britain devalued the pound.

September 21: Republic of West Germany established.

September 19: Coal miners on strike.

September 23: Truman announced that Russia had exploded an atomic device.

October: Steel industry virtually shut down by strikes.

Hourly minimum wage raised from 40 to 75 cents by Congress, revising Fair Labor Standards Act of 1938.

November 9: Coal miners returned to work after September 19 strike.

December 7: Chinese Nationalists fled to Formosa.

1950

Trading Sessions:	281
Advances DJI:	164
Declines DJI:	114
Unchanged DJI:	3
Advances DJR:	152
Declines DJR:	126
Unchanged DJR:	3
Advances DJU:	152
Declines DJU:	121
Unchanged DJU:	8

Closing High DJI:	235.47	(11/24)
Closing Low DJI:	196.81	(1/13)
Closing High DJR:	77.89	(12/28)
Closing Low DJR:	51.24	(6/29)
Closing High DJU:	44.26	(5/20)
Closing Low DJU:	37.40	(7/26)

Monthly Record

	Inds.		Rails		Utils.	
J	Plus	1.66	Plus	2.33	Plus	.93
F	Plus	1.65	Plus	.25	Plus	.59
M	Plus	2.61	Minus	.51	Minus	.14
A	Plus	8.28	Plus	1.24	Plus	.11
M	Plus	9.09	Plus	.21	Plus	1.02
J	Minus	14.31	Minus	4.04	Minus	3.16
J	Plus	.29	Plus	8.62	Minus	2.86
A	Plus	7.47	Plus	2.04	Plus	1.01
S	Plus	9.49	Plus	4.74	Plus	1.67
O	Minus	1.35	Minus	1.36	Minus	.44
N	Plus	2.59	Plus	2.25	Minus	.22
D	Plus	7.81	Plus	9.11	Plus	1.18

Change from 1949

Dow Industrials:	Plus	35.28
Dow Rails:	Plus	24.88
Dow Utilities:	Minus	.31

June 25: Korean War started.

June 27: U.S. sent help to South Korea.

June 30: U.S. ground forces in action in Korea.

August 27: Federal troops took over railroads to prevent general strike.

September 8: National Defense Production Act, designed to remobilize the U.S., became law.

Chrysler employees struck for 100 days.

September 15: U.S. amphibious forces made Inchon landing.

November 1: Truman escaped assassination attempt.

November 20: U.S. forces reached Manchurian border.

November 26: Communist volunteers crossed Yalu River.

Also: Five-year contract with no reopening provisions negotiated by UAW and General Motors.

1951

Trading Sessions:		283	
Advances	DJI:	145	
Declines	DJI:	134	
Unchanged	DJI:	4	
Advances	DJR:	138	
Declines	DJR:	139	
Unchanged	DJR:	6	
Advances	DJU:	152	
Declines	DJU:	125	
Unchanged	DJU:	6	
Closing High	DJI:	276.37	(9/13)
Closing Low	DJI:	238.99	(1/3)
Closing High	DJR:	90.08	(2/5)
Closing Low	DJR:	72.39	(6/29)
Closing High	DJU:	47.22	(12/31)
Closing Low	DJU:	41.47	(1/2)

Monthly Record

	Inds.		Rails		Utils.	
J	Plus	13.42	Plus	8.94	Plus	1.25
F	Plus	3.22	Minus	1.48	Plus	1.39
M	Minus	4.11	Minus	4.52	Minus	1.37
A	Plus	11.19	Plus	2.34	Plus	.11
M	Minus	9.48	Minus	3.28	Minus	.15
J	Minus	7.01	Minus	7.25	Minus	.13
J	Plus	15.22	Plus	8.15	Plus	2.78
A	Plus	12.39	Minus	.21	Plus	.14
S	Plus	.91	Plus	4.43	Plus	.67
O	Minus	8.81	Minus	4.50	Plus	.08
N	Minus	1.08	Plus	1.17	Plus	.29
D	Plus	7.96	Plus	.27	Plus	.18

Change from 1950

Dow Industrials:	Plus	33.82
Dow Rails:	Plus	4.06
Dow Utilities:	Plus	6.24

January 17: Margin raised to 75%.

January 24: Truman formed Office of Price Stabilization.

May 27: Red Chinese absorbed Tibet.

July 10: Korean truce talks began.

October 1: Branches of the Philadelphia-Baltimore Stock Exchange and the Stock Clearing Corp. of Philadelphia established in Washington.

October: First amendment to Taft-Hartley Act, permitting negotiations of union-shop agreements with previous polls of employees, became law.

1952

April 8: U.S. seized steel mills to avert strike.

May 23: Railroads returned to owners after being under federal control since August 27, 1950.

June 2: Supreme Court declared steel seizure illegal.

July 24: Steel strike of nearly 8 weeks settled.

September 29: Half-day Saturday trading discontinued. Weekday closings extended from 3 to 3:30 P.M.

October: Britain completed first atomic test.

Trading Sessions: 271

Advances DJI: 147
Declines   DJI: 122
Unchanged DJI: 2

Advances DJR: 146
Declines   DJR: 124
Unchanged DJR: 1

Advances DJU: 146
Declines   DJU: 115
Unchanged DJU: 10

Closing High DJI: 292.00 (12/30)
Closing Low DJI: 256.35 (5/1)

Closing High DJR: 112.53 (12/22)
Closing Low DJR: 82.03 (1/9)

Closing High DJU: 52.64 (12/30)
Closing Low DJU: 47.53 (1/2)

Monthly Record

	Inds.		Rails		Utils.	
J	Plus	1.46	Plus	4.09	Plus	1.41
F	Minus	10.61	Minus	.92	Minus	.20
M	Plus	9.38	Plus	9.49	Plus	1.78
A	Minus	11.83	Minus	1.55	Minus	1.78
M	Plus	5.31	Plus	4.48	Plus	1.51
J	Plus	11.32	Plus	5.44	Minus	.28
J	Plus	5.30	Plus	1.09	Plus	.89
A	Minus	4.52	Minus	.51	Plus	.24
S	Minus	4.43	Minus	2.96	Minus	.62
O	Minus	1.38	Plus	.42	Minus	.23
N	Plus	14.43	Plus	7.39	Plus	1.66
D	Plus	8.24	Plus	3.11	Plus	1.00

Change from 1951

Dow Industrials: Plus   22.67
Dow Rails: Plus   29.57
Dow Utilities: Plus   5.38

November 1: U.S. exploded first H-bomb.

November 4: Dwight D. Eisenhower elected President.

Also: Wage and price controls extended to April 30, 1953, by a revised Defense Production Act.

1953

January 5: New York Curb Exchange changed name to American Stock Exchange.

January: Bonds reacted sharply on rumors of boost in discount rate.

February 6: Eisenhower ordered end to wage and salary controls; also decontrolled various consumer product prices.

February 20: Margin lowered to 50%.

March 14: Stalin died.

March 17: All remaining price controls terminated.

June 4: NYSE amended rules to allow members to incorporate. First member corporation: Woodcock, Hess & Co.

June 17: Communists routed East Berliners with tanks.

July 27: Korean armistice signed.

August 12: AEC announced that Russia had exploded an H-bomb.

October 15: Philadelphia-Baltimore Stock Exchange merged with Washington Stock Exchange, became third largest in U.S.

Also: NYSE retired 9 of its 1,375 seats, reducing membership to the present 1,366.

Trading Sessions:		251	
Advances	DJI:	128	
Declines	DJI:	123	
Unchanged	DJI:	0	
Advances	DJR:	115	
Declines	DJR:	136	
Unchanged	DJR:	0	
Advances	DJU:	137	
Declines	DJU:	110	
Unchanged	DJU:	4	
Closing High	DJI:	293.79	(1/5)
Closing Low	DJI:	255.49	(9/14)
Closing High	DJR:	112.21	(1/30)
Closing Low	DJR:	90.56	(9/14)
Closing High	DJU:	53.88	(3/13)
Closing Low	DJU:	47.87	(6/22)

Monthly Record

	Inds.		Rails		Utils.	
J	Minus	2.13	Plus	.94	Plus	.08
F	Minus	5.50	Minus	2.16	Minus	.18
M	Minus	4.40	Minus	3.03	Minus	.25
A	Minus	5.12	Minus	3.95	Minus	1.18
M	Minus	2.47	Plus	2.35	Minus	.24
J	Minus	4.02	Minus	.65	Minus	2.29
J	Plus	7.12	Plus	1.09	Plus	.91
A	Minus	14.16	Minus	10.23	Plus	.15
S	Plus	2.82	Minus	1.73	Minus	.12
O	Plus	11.77	Plus	3.36	Plus	1.66
N	Plus	5.56	Plus	1.60	Plus	1.19
D	Minus	.47	Minus	4.83	Minus	.29

Change from 1952

Dow Industrials:	Minus	11.00
Dow Rails:	Minus	17.24
Dow Utilities:	Minus	.56

1954

Trading Sessions:		252	
Advances	DJI:	159	
Declines	DJI:	91	
Unchanged	DJI:	2	
Advances	DJR:	141	
Declines	DJR:	110	
Unchanged	DJR:	1	
Advances	DJU:	150	
Declines	DJU:	96	
Unchanged	DJU:	6	
Closing High	DJI:	404.39	(12/31)
Closing Low	DJI:	279.87	(1/11)
Closing High	DJR:	146.23	(12/29)
Closing Low	DJR:	94.84	(1/11)
Closing High	DJU:	62.47	(12/31)
Closing Low	DJU:	52.22	(1/4)

Monthly Record

	Inds.		Rails		Utils.	
J	Plus	11.49	Plus	7.81	Plus	2.05
F	Plus	2.15	Plus	.36	Plus	.58
M	Plus	8.97	Minus	.78	Plus	1.32
A	Plus	15.82	Plus	2.89	Plus	.50
M	Plus	8.16	Plus	6.29	Plus	1.58
J	Plus	6.04	Plus	2.10	Plus	.13
J	Plus	14.39	Plus	6.86	Plus	1.90
A	Minus	12.12	Minus	7.11	Plus	.01
S	Plus	24.66	Plus	2.73	Plus	.93
O	Minus	8.32	Plus	2.51	Minus	3.23
N	Plus	34.63	Plus	13.78	Plus	2.94
D	Plus	17.62	Plus	14.39	Plus	1.72

Change from 1953

Dow Industrials:	Plus	123.49
Dow Rails:	Plus	51.83
Dow Utilities:	Plus	10.43

January 21: First atomic-powered submarine ("Nautilus") launched.

March 1: Five Congressmen wounded by gunfire from gallery of House of Representatives.

May 7: Fall of Dien Bien Phu.

July 21: Communists got half of Vietnam as result of truce signed in Geneva.

September 8: SEATO agreement signed by 8 nations in Manila.

Also: NYSE member firms introduced MIP (Monthly Investment Plan) to the public.

1955

Trading Sessions: 252

Advances	DJI:	156
Declines	DJI:	96
Unchanged	DJI:	0
Advances	DJR.	137
Declines	DJR:	112
Unchanged	DJR:	3
Advances	DJU:	147
Declines	DJU:	102
Unchanged	DJU:	3

Closing High	DJI:	487.45	(9/23)
Closing Low	DJI:	388.20	(1/17)
Closing High	DJR:	167.83	(11/25)
Closing Low	DJR:	137.84	(1/17)
Closing High	DJU:	66.68	(7/26)
Closing Low	DJU:	61.39	(10/11)

Monthly Record

	Inds.		Rails		Utils.	
J	Plus	4.44	Minus	1.52	Minus	.45
F	Plus	3.04	Plus	5.13	Plus	2.03
M	Minus	2.17	Plus	.85	Minus	.48
A	Plus	15.95	Plus	10.20	Plus	1.22
M	Minus	.79	Minus	.65	Minus	1.16
J	Plus	26.52	Plus	1.08	Plus	.71
J	Plus	14.47	Minus	2.76	Plus	2.25
A	Plus	2.33	Minus	1.05	Minus	.49
S	Minus	1.56	Minus	2.09	Minus	2.96
O	Minus	11.75	Minus	5.52	Plus	.23
N	Plus	28.39	Plus	17.12	Plus	2.55
D	Plus	5.14	Minus	3.36	Minus	1.76

Change from 1954

Dow Industrials:	Plus	84.01
Dow Rails:	Plus	17.43
Dow Utilities:	Plus	1.69

January 1: Philadelphia-Baltimore-Washington Stock Exchange and Pittsburgh Stock Exchange agreed to interchange associated memberships.

January 4: Margin raised to 60%.

January 28: Congress granted Eisenhower's request for emergency powers to protect Formosa and the Pescadores.

April 23: Margin raised to 70%.

June: Ford and the UAW negotiated new 3-year contract. By end of year similar plans were negotiated for more than one million workers, including rest of auto industry.

September 24: Eisenhower had heart attack.

September 26: Dow Industrials dropped 31.89, following weekend news of heart attack.

December 5: American Federation of Labor and Congress of Industrial Organization merged.

1956

Trading Sessions:	251

Monthly Record

Advances DJI:	126
Declines DJI:	124
Unchanged DJI:	1

Advances DJR:	114
Declines DJR:	137
Unchanged DJR:	0

Advances DJU:	131
Declines DJU:	117
Unchanged DJU:	3

Closing High DJI:	521.05	(4/6)
Closing Low DJI:	462.35	(1/23)

Closing High DJR:	181.23	(5/9)
Closing Low DJR:	150.44	(11/29)

Closing High DJU:	71.17	(8/7)
Closing Low DJU:	63.03	(1/23)

	Inds.		*Rails*		*Utils.*	
J	Minus	17.66	Minus	4.93	Minus	.28
F	Plus	12.91	Plus	1.26	Plus	1.21
M	Plus	28.14	Plus	12.20	Plus	2.30
A	Plus	4.33	Plus	4.81	Minus	2.15
M	Minus	38.07	Minus	11.53	Unchanged	
J	Plus	14.73	Plus	1.59	Plus	2.14
J	Plus	25.03	Plus	3.96	Plus	3.77
A	Minus	15.77	Minus	10.00	Minus	2.52
S	Minus	26.79	Minus	6.64	Plus	.60
O	Plus	4.60	Plus	1.92	Plus	.63
N	Minus	7.07	Minus	4.24	Plus	.22
D	Plus	26.69	Plus	1.54	Plus	2.12

Change from 1955

Dow Industrials:	Plus	11.07
Dow Rails:	Minus	10.06
Dow Utilities:	Plus	4.38

January 18: Ford "went public": 10,200,000 shares ($657.9 million) offered at 64½.

June 9: Eisenhower operated upon for ileitis.

July 26: Egypt seized Suez Canal.

October 23–24: Russian tanks quelled Hungarian revolt.

October 29: Israelis crossed Egyptian border in drive toward Suez Canal.

October 31: France-Britain air-bombed Egyptian installations.

November 5–6: France-Britain landed troops in Egypt.

November 7: Cease-fire in Egypt.

1957

Trading Sessions:	252

Advances	DJI:	123
Declines	DJI:	126
Unchanged	DJI:	3
Advances	DJR:	106
Declines	DJR:	144
Unchanged	DJR:	2
Advances	DJU:	130
Declines	DJU:	121
Unchanged	DJU:	1

Closing High DJI:	520.77	(7/12)
Closing Low DJI:	419.79	(10/22)
Closing High DJR:	157.67	(1/10)
Closing Low DJR:	95.67	(12/24)
Closing High DJU:	74.61	(5/21)
Closing Low DJU:	62.10	(10/22)

Monthly Record

	Inds.		Rails		Utils.	
J	Minus	20.31	Minus	4.44	Plus	2.39
F	Minus	14.54	Minus	7.75	Minus	.53
M	Plus	10.19	Plus	3.01	Plus	1.07
A	Plus	19.55	Plus	1.79	Plus	1.54
M	Plus	10.57	Minus	.29	Plus	1.02
J	Minus	1.64	Plus	.91	Minus	4.19
J	Plus	5.23	Plus	3.33	Plus	.04
A	Minus	24.17	Minus	12.30	Minus	2.04
S	Minus	28.05	Minus	13.79	Minus	1.17
O	Minus	15.26	Minus	12.76	Minus	.92
N	Plus	8.83	Minus	6.97	Plus	1.98
D	Minus	14.18	Minus	7.01	Plus	.85

Change from 1956

Dow Industrials:	Minus	63.78
Dow Rails:	Minus	61.42
Dow Utilities:	Plus	.04

January 2: San Francisco and Los Angeles Stock Exchanges consolidated to form Pacific Coast Exchange.

March 25: Common Market, or European Economic Community, came into being in Rome.

October 4: Russia launched Sputnik I.

October 23: Market staged one of strongest rebounds ever on 4.6 million share volume, as DJI soared 17.34, Rails 5.91, Utilities 1.45—market's biggest daily gain since 1929.

December: Teamsters, bakery, and laundry workers expelled at biennial convention of AFL-CIO on charges of domination by corrupt influences.

December 17: First U.S. ICBM successfully test-fired.

Also: Philadelphia-Baltimore-Washington Stock Exchange set up an associate membership agreement with Boston Stock Exchange, similar to that arranged with Pittsburgh Stock Exchange in 1955.

NYSE tightened rules on participation of members, allied members, member firms, or corporations and their employees in proxy fights.

1958

Trading Sessions:		252
Advances	DJI:	145
Declines	DJI:	106
Unchanged	DJI:	1
Advances	DJR:	132
Declines	DJR:	120
Unchanged	DJR:	0
Advances	DJU:	161
Declines	DJU:	85
Unchanged	DJU:	6
Closing High	DJI:	583.65 (12/31)
Closing Low	DJI:	436.89 (2/25)
Closing High	DJR:	157.91 (11/19)
Closing Low	DJR:	99.89 (1/2)
Closing High	DJU:	91.00 (12/31)
Closing Low	DJU:	68.94 (1/2)

Monthly Record

	Inds.		Rails		Utils.	
J	Plus	14.53	Plus	12.08	Plus	3.69
F	Minus	10.10	Minus	6.09	Plus	.22
M	Plus	6.84	Plus	.33	Plus	1.51
A	Plus	9.10	Plus	8.59	Plus	3.37
M	Plus	6.84	Plus	4.13	Plus	.82
J	Plus	15.48	Plus	2.75	Plus	.92
J	Plus	24.81	Plus	12.92	Plus	.66
A	Plus	5.64	Plus	.85	Minus	1.61
S	Plus	23.46	Plus	12.09	Plus	2.74
O	Plus	11.13	Plus	3.95	Plus	2.51
N	Plus	14.24	Plus	7.12	Plus	2.03
D	Plus	26.19	Plus	1.97	Plus	5.75

Change from 1957

Dow Industrials:	Plus	147.96
Dow Rails:	Plus	60.69
Dow Utilities:	Plus	22.42

January 16: Margin lowered to 50%.

January 31: Explorer I, first U.S. satellite, went into orbit.

March 27: Khrushchev became Russian premier.

May 1: Higher brokerage commission rates became effective.

July 15: U.S. marines landed in Lebanon.

August 5: Margin raised to 70%.

October 16: Margin raised to 90%.

October 28: Mary G. Roebling became first woman governor of American Stock Exchange.

Also: Congress authorized SBIC's (Small Business Investment Companies).

1959

January 1: Batista fled Cuba; Castro took over.

January 4: Soviets launched Lunik I, first man-made satellite.

July 15: Steel strike began.

November 7: Longest-ever steel strike ended by Taft-Hartley injunction.

Trading Sessions: 253

Advances	DJI:	144
Declines	DJI:	107
Unchanged	DJI:	2

Advances	DJR:	116
Declines	DJR:	135
Unchanged	DJR:	2

Advances	DJU:	123
Declines	DJU:	122
Unchanged	DJU:	8

Closing High	DJI:	679.36 (12/31)
Closing Low	DJI:	574.46 (2/9)

Closing High	DJR:	173.56 (7/8)
Closing Low	DJR:	146.65 (11/17)

Closing High	DJU:	94.70 (3/18)
Closing Low	DJU:	85.05 (9/21)

Monthly Record

	Inds.		Rails		Utils.	
J	Plus	10.31	Plus	4.26	Minus	.12
F	Plus	9.54	Plus	.29	Plus	1.17
M	Minus	1.79	Minus	3.55	Plus	1.38
A	Plus	22.04	Plus	8.17	Minus	2.10
M	Plus	20.04	Plus	.52	Minus	1.53
J	Minus	.19	Plus	.39	Minus	2.50
J	Plus	31.28	Plus	.08	Plus	2.69
A	Minus	10.47	Minus	4.35	Plus	1.12
S	Minus	32.73	Minus	6.05	Minus	3.20
O	Plus	14.92	Minus	2.90	Minus	.44
N	Plus	12.58	Minus	4.39	Minus	.91
D	Plus	20.18	Plus	3.94	Plus	1.27

Change from 1958

Dow Industrials:	Plus	95.71
Dow Rails:	Minus	3.60
Dow Utilities:	Minus	3.17

December 30: "USS George Washington" commissioned—first Polaris submarine.

1960

Trading Sessions: 252

Advances	DJI:	119
Declines	DJI:	132
Unchanged	DJI:	1

Advances	DJR:	109
Declines	DJR:	138
Unchanged	DJR:	5

Advances	DJU:	145
Declines	DJU:	104
Unchanged	DJU:	3

Closing High	DJI:	685.47 (1/5)
Closing Low	DJI:	566.05 (10/25)

Closing High	DJR:	160.43 (1/5)
Closing Low	DJR:	123.37 (9/29)

Closing High	DJU:	100.07 (12/29)
Closing Low	DJU:	85.02 (2/16)

Monthly Record

	Inds.		Rails		Utils.	
J	Minus	56.74	Minus	2.45	Minus	2.27
F	Plus	7.50	Minus	1.65	Plus	1.20
M	Minus	13.53	Minus	6.21	Plus	1.54
A	Minus	14.89	Minus	3.91	Plus	.41
M	Plus	23.80	Minus	.17	Minus	.71
J	Plus	15.12	Plus	3.53	Plus	5.39
J	Minus	23.89	Minus	7.93	Minus	.56
A	Plus	9.26	Plus	1.46	Plus	2.87
S	Minus	45.85	Minus	11.30	Minus	4.41
O	Plus	.22	Plus	.35	Plus	1.25
N	Plus	16.86	Plus	4.27	Plus	2.65
D	Plus	18.67	Plus	1.51	Plus	4.83

Change since 1959

Dow Industrials:	Minus	63.47
Dow Rails:	Minus	23.20
Dow Utilities:	Plus	12.19

January 4: Ticker tape transmission increased to 500 characters per minute on ASE. Threatened resumption of steel strike averted.

January 7: Eisenhower State of Union message: 1960 "promises to be the most prosperous year in our history."

January 10: U.S. pledged to defend Quemoy and Matsu Islands.

February: Titan ICBM successfully completed first full-range test.

February 13: France exploded an atomic device.

May 1: U-2 plane shot down over Russia.

May 17: Khrushchev exploded Paris Summit Conference over U-2 incident.

June 29–July 1: Castro seized U.S. oil refineries.

July 7: U.S. virtually sealed off Cuban sugar imports.

July 28: Margin lowered to 70%.

August 7: Castro started seizure of other U.S. Cuban properties.

September 1–2: Strike against Pennsylvania Railroad — first complete shutdown in its 114-year history.

September 24: World's biggest ship and first nuclear-powered carrier, "Enterprise," launched.

September 28: Treasury Secretary Robert B. Anderson: "The outlook for economic activity in the country is favorable, both for the near future and many years ahead."

November 1: Eisenhower pledged to defend Guantánamo.

November 16: Attempting to halt gold drain, Eisenhower ordered federal agencies to cut foreign spending.

1961

January 3: U.S.-Cuba broke diplomatic relations.

January 20: John F. Kennedy inaugurated.

January 16: Fidelity insurance became compulsory for Exchange member firms.

April: Stock market credit topped $5 billion for first time in 20 years.

April 12: Russia sent first man into earth orbit.

April 17: Attempted invasion of Cuba at Bay of Pigs failed.

May 5: Alan B. Shepard, Jr., in space.

May 30: Trujillo assassinated in Dominican Republic.

June 27: Secondary distribution of 2¾ million shares of Ford by Ford Foundation at 80½.

August 6: Soviet spaceman, Titov, orbited earth 17½ times.

Trading Sessions:		250
Advances	DJI:	135
Declines	DJI:	115
Unchanged	DJI:	0
Advances	DJR:	119
Declines	DJR:	130
Unchanged	DJR:	1
Advances	DJU:	152
Declines	DJU:	95
Unchanged	DJU:	3

Closing High DJI:	734.91	(12/13)
Closing Low DJI:	610.25	(1/3)
Closing High DJR:	152.92	(10/11)
Closing Low DJR:	131.06	(1/3)
Closing High DJU:	135.90	(11/20)
Closing Low DJU:	99.75	(1/3)

Monthly Record

	Inds.		Rails		Utils.	
J	Plus	32.31	Plus	10.86	Plus	6.48
F	Plus	13.88	Plus	4.30	Plus	1.99
M	Plus	14.55	Plus	.19	Plus	3.42
A	Plus	2.08	Minus	5.13	Minus	.19
M	Plus	18.01	Plus	3.84	Plus	1.05
J	Minus	12.76	Minus	5.44	Minus	1.03
J	Plus	21.41	Minus	1.58	Plus	4.11
A	Plus	14.57	Plus	6.42	Plus	4.97
S	Minus	18.73	Minus	.35	Plus	1.62
O	Plus	2.71	Plus	4.16	Plus	7.63
N	Plus	17.68	Minus	2.32	Plus	4.15
D	Plus	9.54	Minus	1.96	Minus	5.06

Change from 1960

Dow Industrials:	Plus	115.25
Dow Rails:	Plus	12.99
Dow Utilities:	Plus	29.14

August 13: Communist East Germans built wall dividing East and West Germany.

September 1: Russia broke ban on atomic testing.

October 29: Russia exploded biggest bomb in history.

Also: Philadelphia-Baltimore-Washington Stock Exchange set up an associate membership agreement with Montreal Stock Exchange, rather similar to those arranged with Pittsburgh Stock Exchange (1955) and Boston Stock Exchange (1957).

U.S. railroads recorded smallest net income since 1946, earning only 1.97% on average net property investment — their sixth straight drop in rate of return.

1962

January 16: Dominican Government overthrown.

January 17: DJI fell 7.98, largest drop since September 25, 1961.

January 18: U.S. considered applying pressure on new Dominican military government.

January 19: Another government upheaval in Dominican Republic.

January 25: Geneva Conference to end nuclear testing failed.

February 7: Almost 60% of ground lost by market between December 13 and January 29 recovered by this date.

Trading Sessions: 252

Advances DJI: 118
Declines DJI: 132
Unchanged DJI: 2

Advances DJR: 120
Declines DJR: 130
Unchanged DJR: 2

Advances DJU: 136
Declines DJU: 112
Unchanged DJU: 4

Closing High DJI: 726.01 (1/3)
Closing Low DJI: 535.76 (6/26)

Closing High DJR: 149.83 (2/2)
Closing Low DJR: 114.86 (10/1)

Closing High DJU: 130.85 (3/19)
Closing Low DJU: 103.11 (6/25)

Monthly Record

	Inds.		Rails		Utils.	
J	Minus	31.14	Plus	3.93	Minus	5.08
F	Plus	8.05	Minus	1.47	Plus	4.24
M	Minus	1.10	Minus	2.02	Plus	1.69
A	Minus	41.62	Minus	5.80	Minus	3.05
M	Minus	51.97	Minus	9.29	Minus	13.42
J	Minus	52.08	Minus	10.56	Minus	5.26
J	Plus	36.65	Plus	3.49	Plus	9.04
A	Plus	11.25	Plus	1.63	Plus	3.51
S	Minus	30.20	Minus	8.07	Minus	3.22
O	Plus	10.79	Plus	5.03	Minus	.72
N	Plus	59.53	Plus	18.26	Plus	8.38
D	Plus	2.80	Plus	2.07	Plus	3.96

Change from 1961

Dow Industrials: Minus 79.04
Dow Rails: Minus 2.80
Dow Utilities: Plus .07

February 12: Smallest volume in 6½ months: 2,620,000 shares.

February 20: John H. Glenn, Jr., orbited earth 3 times.

March 7: National Stock Exchange opened for business in New York with 8 listings.

April 12: DJI dropped 9.23, breaking January 29 low of 689.92, on Kennedy's remarks about steel industry.

April 13: New individual lows totaled 124, largest for a day since October 24, 1960.

April 16: Heavy selling of steels, although previous price boosts were rescinded.

April 23: According to "The Trader," writing in *Barrons* ". . . there is no fundamental warrant for general selling of stocks after a precipitate four-month decline."

April 24: Secondary distribution of 2¼ million shares of Ford by Ford Foundation at 97.

April: Strikes this month involved 40% more workers than in 1961.

May 1: Individual new stock lows totaled 364, largest since October 22, 1957.

May 8: Secondary distribution of 430,000 shares of General Motors from heirs of Fisher Body at 53⅛.

May 23: NYSE ticker lagged 143 minutes behind floor transactions

—the greatest ever except for 160-minute lag by slower-speed tickers in 1929.

June 5: Odd-lot short sales were 8.2% of all odd-lot sales, largest proportion in about 20 years.

June 15: Ewan Clague, head of Bureau of Labor Statistics, said a 1963 recession was probable.

June 25: DJI selling around 539 and yielding 4.32%, versus 4.26% for high-grade bonds, most favorable ratio since September 5, 1958. ASE membership approved major reorganization and revision of constitution.

June 30: Volume of market credit totaled $2,325 million in June, lowest since March 29, 1961.

July 10: Margin lowered to 50%.

July 11: New Telstar satellite successfully transmitted messages and pictures overseas. AT&T advanced $3\frac{1}{2}$ points.

July 25: Secondary distribution of 1,590,000 shares General Motors at $49\frac{5}{8}$.

July: Auto sales this month largest since 1955.

August: Cuban missile crisis started to warm up.

August 5: Russia began second series of nuclear tests.

August 10: Silver stocks strong. Silver reached $1.08 per ounce, highest since 1920.

August 13: JFK promised an "across-the-board, top to bottom" reduction in corporate and personal taxes, with a retroactively effective tax date of January 1, 1963. DJI closed up 6.61 next day.

August 17: DJI closed 17.70 higher on week, largest weekly gain since recovery got under way from June panic bottom.

September 29: JFK sent troops to Mississippi in racial crisis.

September: Sales of open-end fund shares declined for fourth straight month, the smallest in more than 4 years. Redemptions increased to 61% of new sales, loftiest since 1954, when records were first kept.

October 19: Chinese-Indian troops clashed in Himalayas.

October 22: JFK announced presence of Soviet missile bases in Cuba; ordered sea blockade.

October 29: Khrushchev to remove missile bases. Market rallied sharply.

November 15: Treasury Secretary Dillon promised "sizable [tax] rate cuts across-the-board."

November 21: Blockade of Cuba lifted.

December 5: Ninety-six point recovery by DJI since October 23 was largest ever for 6-week period.

Also: Exchange distributions exceeded 2 million shares for first time. NYSE's initiation fee for seats increased from $4,000 to $7,500, first change since 1920.

1963

Trading Sessions:	251

Advances	DJI:	142
Declines	DJI:	108
Unchanged	DJI:	1
Advances	DJR:	138
Declines	DJR:	111
Unchanged	DJR:	2
Advances	DJU:	137
Declines	DJU:	110
Unchanged	DJU:	4

Closing High DJI:	767.21	(12/18)
Closing Low DJI:	646.79	(1/2)
Closing High DJR:	179.46	(12/18)
Closing Low DJR:	142.03	(1/2)
Closing High DJU:	144.37	(8/23)
Closing Low DJU:	129.19	(1/2)

Monthly Record

	Inds.		*Rails*		*Utils.*	
J	Plus	30.75	Plus	9.03	Plus	6.44
F	Minus	19.91	Plus	.30	Minus	2.67
M	Plus	19.58	Plus	2.55	Plus	3.19
A	Plus	35.18	Plus	10.86	Plus	2.75
M	Plus	9.26	Plus	9.60	Plus	1.39
J	Minus	20.08	Plus	.28	Minus	1.25
J	Minus	11.45	Minus	6.70	Plus	.92
A	Plus	33.89	Plus	9.90	Plus	3.96
S	Plus	3.47	Minus	6.33	Minus	4.01
O	Plus	22.44	Minus	1.07	Minus	.89
N	Minus	4.71	Plus	2.39	Minus	2.62
D	Plus	12.43	Plus	6.69	Plus	2.55

Change from 1962

Dow Industrials:	Plus	110.85
Dow Rails:	Plus	37.50
Dow Utilities:	Plus	9.76

January 25: Longshoremen's strike ended.

March 31: New York newspaper strike ended.

April 5: Cleveland newspaper strike ended.

June: A $75 million offering by Firestone Tire & Rubber; first major corporate debt issue in form of registered bonds.

August 20: First "F" transaction made under proposed Interest Equalization Tax. Sale followed by "F," meaning an American bought stock from foreigner and would pay U.S. taxes of 15%.

November 2: South Vietnam Government overthrown.

November 6: Margin raised to 70%.

November 22: President Kennedy assassinated. Lyndon B. Johnson became President.

November 25: U.S. securities exchanges closed for JFK funeral.

December: Economy rounded out 3 years of business expansion; 14 years of rising stock prices.

Also: Federal tax collections topped $100 billion for first time.

Ira Haupt & Co. collapsed, a victim of Great Salad Oil scandal.

1964

Trading Sessions:	249

Advances	DJI:	146
Declines	DJI:	103
Unchanged	DJI:	0
Advances	DJR:	141
Declines	DJR:	105
Unchanged	DJR:	3
Advances	DJU:	134
Declines	DJU:	106
Unchanged	DJU:	9

Closing High	DJI:	891.71	(11/18)
Closing Low	DJI:	766.08	(1/2)
Closing High	DJR:	224.91	(10/26)
Closing Low	DJR:	178.81	(1/3)
Closing High	DJU:	155.71	(11/20)
Closing Low	DJU:	137.30	(3/31)

Monthly Record

	Inds.		Rails		Utils.	
J	Plus	22.39	Plus	2.85	Plus	.50
F	Plus	14.80	Plus	9.35	Plus	1.01
M	Plus	13.15	Plus	1.14	Minus	2.74
A	Minus	2.52	Plus	3.25	Plus	1.93
M	Plus	9.79	Plus	10.82	Plus	.83
J	Plus	10.94	Plus	7.61	Plus	3.34
J	Plus	9.60	Plus	4.24	Plus	6.49
A	Minus	2.62	Minus	11.55	Minus	.17
S	Plus	36.89	Plus	11.92	Plus	3.44
O	Minus	2.29	Plus	5.37	Minus	.20
N	Plus	2.35	Minus	11.27	Plus	1.03
D	Minus	1.30	Minus	6.93	Plus	1.18

Change from 1963

Dow Industrials:	Plus	111.18
Dow Rails:	Plus	26.80
Dow Utilities:	Plus	16.18

January 4: Big Board's 33 registered traders obliged to meet new capital requirement of $250,000. Stricter specialists' rules also became effective on NYSE and ASE.

January 8: LBJ's State of Union message asked for reduction in federal budget to $97.9 billion; also, programs to combat poverty and discrimination.

January 9: Anti-U.S. riots in Panama Canal Zone.

January 10: Panama suspended U.S. relations, demanded treaty revision.

January 17: Volume for week ended this day was largest (30.5 million shares) since week of May 31, 1962, when panic was underway and 40.6 million shares traded. Latter, in turn, was greatest since July 22, 1933 week (based on 6 trading sessions).

January 20: LBJ's economic report projected 1964 rise in GNP to $623 billion from $585 billion in 1963.

January 21: Geneva disarmament talks resumed.

Congress received President's $97.9 billion budget.

January 27: France recognized Red China.

February 13: Dow Rails topped previous all-time high of 189.11 set September 3, 1929.

February 26: Johnson signed $11½ billion tax-cut bill.

February: AT&T raised annual dividend from $3.90 to $4 and announced a 12,250,000 new share offering.

First ticker service to Puerto Rico, Hawaii, Switzerland.

March 13: Market closed higher for week, thus extending string of consecutive weekly gains to 13—longest on record.

March 16: LBJ's $962.5 million antipoverty program reached Congress.

March 27: Alaska earthquake.

April 3: Diplomatic relations restored with Panama.

April 7: Federal grand jury indicted 8 large steel companies.

April 12: Texas Gulf Sulphur issued press release playing down reported mineral strike.

April 16: News of big copper strike by Texas Gulf Sulphur in Timmins, Ontario, sharply boosted stock price.

April 22: Nationwide rail strike averted by settlement of 5-year dispute.

May 11: Amex inaugurated an automated telephone quotation service: "Am-Quote."

May 18: Johnson asked Congress for $125 million additional aid for South Vietnam.

June 1: Important trade agreement between U.S.-Rumania.

June 2: Five million shares of Comsat, widely heralded as romance-glamor company of the century, offered initially at $20 a share.

July 2: Johnson signed Civil Rights bill.

August 3: New NYSE member classification—Registered Trader.

October 15: Khrushchev out; replaced by Brezhnev and Kosygin. Labor won British election.

October 16: Red China exploded nuclear bomb.

December 1: New 900-character-per-minute tickers put in service.

1965

Trading Sessions: 252

Advances   DJI: 140
Declines   DJI: 110
Unchanged DJI: 2

Advances   DJR: 137
Declines   DJR: 115
Unchanged DJR: 0

Advances   DJU: 124
Declines   DJU: 124
Unchanged DJU: 4

Closing High DJI: 969.26 (12/31)
Closing Low DJI: 840.59   (6/28)

Closing High DJR: 249.55 (12/17)
Closing Low DJR: 187.29   (6/28)

Closing High DJU: 163.32   (4/20)
Closing Low DJU: 149.84 (12/20)

Monthly Record

	Inds.		Rails		Utils.	
J	Plus	28.73	Plus	7.44	Plus	5.51
F	Plus	.62	Minus	1.40	Plus	.54
M	Minus	14.43	Minus	.61	Plus	1.14
A	Plus	33.26	Plus	1.86	Minus	.60
M	Minus	4.27	Minus	7.59	Minus	1.59
J	Minus	50.01	Minus	11.35	Minus	6.02
J	Plus	13.71	Plus	14.04	Plus	1.21
A	Plus	11.36	Plus	10.94	Minus	.12
S	Plus	37.48	Plus	4.24	Plus	2.36
O	Plus	30.24	Plus	12.95	Plus	.36
N	Minus	14.11	Plus	6.67	Minus	4.06
D	Plus	22.55	Plus	4.95	Minus	1.27

Change from 1964

Dow Industrials:	Plus	93.15
Dow Rails:	Plus	42.14
Dow Utilities:	Minus	2.54

January 8: Treasury warned that speculators' attempts to inflate gold above $35 would fail.

January 11: Record "Exchange Distribution" in terms of dollar value handled by one firm—270,000 shares of RCA.

January 12: Federal Reserve concerned about rising consumer-wholesale prices.

January 19: Global money jitters.

January 25: Johnson's budget indicated record spending close to $100 billion in fiscal year starting July 1.

January 27: Defense stocks strong on possibility U.S. may explore moon, photograph it.

January 28: DJI closed above 900 for first time.

February 8: Possibility of stepped-up Southeast Asia War sparked sell off.

February 10: U.S. gold stocks reached lowest level since March 8, 1939.

February 11: Dow dropped 11 points on worry over Vietnam.

February 12: NYSE firms dealing with public asked to outline costs and profits of business in 1964.

February 15: New quotation system started for OTC stocks.

February 17: Johnson announced easier depreciation deduction rules.

February 26: Martin of Federal Reserve said he didn't expect "much in the way of long term interest rates," but balance-of-payments position might cause tighter money.

March 1: 9,336.0 million shares listed on NYSE versus about 5 million in 1958 and 2 million in 1948.

March 3: Increased public participation indicated by heavier speculation.

March 4: International oil companies worried that Indonesia might nationalize foreign holdings.

March 8: Fully automated quote service introduced.

March 11: FRB's Martin warned economy close to overheating.

March 17: Secondary offering of 2.8 million General Motors, last of four large offerings from court-ordered divestiture of Du Pont's GM holdings.

March 23: Gemini III launched and landed successfully—first multimanned spaceship.

March 24: Pacific Coast Exchange stalled membership try by Investors Diversified Services.

March 26: Justice Department started investigation of NYSE and other securities markets.

April 1: AT&T profit for year ended February 28 largest of any company for 12-month period.

April 7: Soviet jets harassed West Berlin.

April 8: Drug stocks strong on Medicare passage by House.

April 13: NYSE ruled that member firms be allowed for first time to raise capital by selling own debentures, but not stocks, to public.

April 19: Federal mediators sought to reach interim settlement, postponing May 1 steel strike deadline.

April 20: Various officers and directors of Texas Gulf Sulphur named defendants in SEC suit, charging that inside information was used to trade in stock before public was told of ore find.

April 23: NYSE upgraded listing requirements for common stocks. In 1964 new listings totaled 64, highest since 1934 when records first started.

April 27: Steel strike deadline postponed four months.

April 28: LBJ ordered marines to Dominican Republic.

April 30: Forty-eight-year-old Wheeling Stock Exchange dissolved because of declining business. First time in 25 years an exchange had dissolved.

May 3: Paratroop brigade sent to Vietnam; more troops to Dominican Republic.

May 4: LBJ requested $700 million to support Dominican and Vietnam operations.

May 6: Top businessmen expressed optimism for balance of 1965.

May 18: House Ways and Means Committee approved excise tax repeal on wide variety of items.

May 24: Unconfirmed reports that Red China had moved military equipment toward North Vietnam border.

May 25: Treasury asked Congress to raise legal national debt limit to $329 billion from $324 billion.

May 26: U.S. gold stocks at lowest since November 23, 1938.

June 1: FRB Chairman Martin's warning about "disquieting similarities" with 1929 sparked 9½ point break by DJI.

June 9: Market sold off on rumor about LBJ stroke or heart attack.

June 14: 1,036 NYSE stocks declined—largest ever in single session.

June 17: House approved $4.7 million excise tax cut.

June 22: Ford Foundation's secondary offering of 6 million Ford shares sold out.

June 23: American stockholders topped 20 million, more than triple 1952.

June 28: Many stock offerings postponed due to "market conditions."

June 29: Climactic decline on 10½ million shares—largest since May 31, 1962—preceded abrupt recovery.

July 6: Market cautious on news that two North Vietnam missile bases nearly completed.

July 9: Red China claimed four U.S. planes violated air space.

July 13: LBJ: "New and serious decisions" lie ahead in Vietnam.

July 14: House approved new content for coins, eliminating silver from dimes and quarters.

July 26: Commodities and defense stocks advanced sharply.

July 27: Jets hit Red missile sites.

July 28: Draft calls to be doubled.

August 2: DJI formed triple top around 885–890.

August 5: London gold price reached highest level since November, 1961.

August 18: Marines won first big Vietnam victory.

August 19: Steel-labor talks at crucial point.

August 20: NYSE reserved right to ban stop orders in volatile issues. First stock: Fairchild Camera.

August 25: Johnson ordered a $1.5 billion military space venture.

August 31: Steel strike deadline extended 8 days.

September 1: India-Pakistan in undeclared war.

September 2: LBJ increased efforts to settle steel dispute.

September 3: Indians attacked Pakistanis aiming at Lahore.

September 7: Weekend settlement of steel-labor difficulties.

September 10: Ten nations (including U.S., but not France) agreed to help Britain in times of financial stress.

September 15: Pakistani president urged LBJ to mediate end to undeclared war.

September 16: Red China gave India 3 days to dismantle border bases.

September 22: India-Pakistan ordered cease-fire.

October 6: News of LBJ's scheduled operation touched off selling.

October 11: British-Rhodesian talks collapsed.

October 15: Electronic Systems Center created.

October 25: Santo Domingo occupied by inter-American force at government request.

October 28: AT&T weakened after FCC said company's rates would be "thoroughly investigated."

November 1: NYSE announced tighter credit rules for stocks showing unusual activity.

November 3: FCC called off AT&T investigation.

November 10: Massive power failure delayed NYSE and ASE openings. Big Board volume dropped to 4.9 million shares, lowest since August 30.

November 12: Britain imposed stiff economic sanctions on Rhodesia after nation declared independence.

November 18: Mrs. Phyllis S. Peterson and Mrs. Julia Montgomery, first women elected to ASE membership.

November 21: Treasury Secretary Fowler warned that wage-price hikes deemed inflationary would be opposed by Government.

November 26: Dow Rails continued moving into new high ground.

November 30: Possibly higher interest rates and McNamara's remarks that Vietnam War would be long caused price unsettlement.

December 2: Moderately tight rein on credit by Federal Reserve.

December 6: Discount rate increased.

December 13: NYSE member firms instructed to send at least one member to trading floor every day by 9 A.M. to clear up any questions about previous trades.

December 15: Dow Rails at record high.

December 22: Dow Industrials at new peak closing, confirming prior Rail action.

December 31: Federal taxes no longer levied on security transactions.

1966

Trading Sessions:	252

Monthly Record

	Inds.		Rails		Utils.	
J	Plus	14.25	Plus	14.21	Minus	3.88
F	Minus	31.62	Plus	5.07	Minus	7.00
M	Minus	27.12	Minus	17.59	Minus	.51
A	Plus	8.91	Plus	4.51	Minus	1.03
M	Minus	49.61	Minus	26.40	Minus	4.61
J	Minus	13.97	Minus	1.22	Minus	4.00
J	Minus	22.72	Minus	5.87	Plus	.82
A	Minus	58.97	Minus	24.43	Minus	11.09
S	Minus	14.19	Minus	2.27	Plus	3.39
O	Plus	32.85	Plus	7.39	Plus	12.00
N	Minus	15.48	Plus	1.39	Minus	2.54
D	Minus	5.90	Plus	.70	Plus	2.00

Advances DJI:	114	
Declines DJI:	137	
Unchanged DJI:	1	
Advances DJR:	123	
Declines DJR:	129	
Unchanged DJR:	0	
Advances DJU:	100	
Declines DJU:	145	
Unchanged DJU:	7	
Closing High DJI:	995.15	(2/9)
Closing Low DJI:	744.32	(10/7)
Closing High DJR:	271.72	(2/15)
Closing Low DJR:	184.34	(10/7)
Closing High DJU:	152.39	(1/12)
Closing Low DJU:	118.96	(8/29)

Change from 1965

Dow Industrials:	Minus 183.57
Dow Rails:	Minus 44.51
Dow Utilities:	Minus 16.45

January 3: N.Y. transit strike began.

January 5: U.S. Steel and Government reached compromise in price battle.

January 6: Both New York exchanges closed at 2 P.M. on account transit tie-up.

January 13: Transit strike ended.

January 18: DJI crossed 1,000 intraday for first time.

January 19: Short interest recorded largest monthly drop—1,616,818 shares.

January 21: NYSE tightened credit restrictions.

January 26: Dow Rails at record high; Utilities at new low for 1965–1966.

January 31: Johnson ordered renewed bombing North Vietnam bases after 30-day moratorium. Mutual-fund sales crossed half-billion-dollar mark for first time in January.

February 16: Dow Utilities at 1966 low.

February 21: Dow Industrials dropped 8.74, biggest loss since July 20, 1965.

February 24: Worry over tightening credit and tax boosts sparked further declines.

March 3: NYSE threatened to move when Mayor Lindsay proposed 50% rise in stock transfer taxes of New York State.

March 7: Dow down 14.58, sharpest drop since JFK assassination.

March 10: Commercial banks raised prime rate on building loans.

March 17: NYSE abandoned plans for $50 million building.

March 30: DJI fell 9.63 on idea of tax rise.

April 1: Rail firemen agreed to end short strike against 8 railroads.

April 4: March new car sales at peak level.

April 6: Amex seat sold for $100,000, highest since April 27, 1931.

April 7: Howard Hughes to sell 75.18% of TWA.

April 14: Federal Reserve stepped harder on credit brakes.

April 19: Big Board drafted plan to move.

April 21: NYSE and ASE raised from $1,000 to $2,000 the minimum equity required to open brokerage account. Both exchanges announced plans for computing and publishing their own stock indices.

April 24: NYSE and ASE moved to curb speculation by stiffening Day Trader rules.

April 25: Detroit agreed that Government should have "ultimate authority" to set safety standards.

April 29: ASE installed new electronic equipment on trading floor, to speed transmission of market data to ticker network.

May 1: Philadelphia-Baltimore-Washington Stock Exchange opened new trading quarters.

May 4: Martin of FRB said tax hikes were needed to curb inflation.

May 5: Dow Theory signaled bear market.

June 2: FRB bank borrowings at 6-year high.

June 3: National Association of Purchasing Agents said economic boom cooled perceptibly in May.

June 6: Stock market watchers began getting information more quickly on ticker tape, as Big Board linked its ticker system directly to 2 of 18 trading posts, using a computerized setup that reduced the interval between execution of a trade and its appearance on ticker tape.

June 9: Short-term interest rates at all-time peak.

June 15: AT&T demonstrated world-wide direct telephone dialing from Philadelphia to Geneva, Switzerland. ASE introduced own market averages.

June 17: NYSE toned down warnings it would move.

June 24: Market worried by rumors of heavier North Vietnam bombing. Douglas Aircraft dropped abruptly on lower-than-expected earnings. Resulting lawsuits charged that this nonpublic information was leaked to preferred individuals, enabling them to sell, or sell short, prior to public disclosure.

June 30: Prime rate boosted by many banks.

July 1: Higher New York State transfer tax became effective. NYSE reduced fee charged for buying and selling listed stocks in odd-lots. New fee, or odd-lot differential: 12½ cents on each share of stock selling below $55 and 25 cents on each share selling at $55 or above.

July 7: Warsaw Pact nations offered volunteers to Vietnam.

July 11: U.S. government bonds dropped sharply.

July 14: NYSE introduced own market averages.

July 25: Dow Industrials had biggest decline in 32 months—16.32.

July 29: DJI closed at new low for year.

August 5: LBJ virtually conceded defeat over steel price hikes.

August 16: First National City Bank raised prime rate.

August 26: Dow Industrials fell to 776.22 intraday, canceling 50% of rise from October missile-crisis low in 1962 to February 1966 closing high.

September 6: Prime Minister Verwoerd of East Africa assassinated.

September 12: Funston announced resignation from NYSE presidency.

September 14: Senate adopted minimum-wage legislation.

September 15: Big Board agreed to let members engage in stock transactions with nonmember firms in listed stocks.

September 22: Ambassador Goldberg's speech about Vietnam peace sparked rally.

September 23: Gromyko rejected Goldberg's peace proposals.

September 28: Market tested 760–770 DJ support zone for third time.

September 30: Goldberg said truce door in South Vietnam still open.

October 6: Johnson said business indications never better and 1967 would be as good as 1966.

October 18: Blue chips strong. General Electric settled contract dispute.

October 21: Bonds strongest in eight weeks.

October 31: Treasury official said 1967 tax rise might be necessary.

November 4: Market accepted LBJ surgery in stride.

November 7: Rule 394 (b) went into effect, enabling Big Board firms to go "off floor" under certain conditions if it produced better order executions for customers. Ralph S. Saul began first day as ASE president.

November 15: Rails reversed pattern of declining tops and bottoms by rising decisively above September high of 203–204 DJ.

November 21: Blue Monday caused by auto cutbacks.

December 7: DJI soared $10\frac{1}{2}$ points on 9 million shares.

December 13: Triple top indicated at 825–830 (Sept. 16, Nov. 16, Dec. 13).

December 20: Transmission of trade and quote data from NYSE trading floor fully automated.

December 27: Commerce Secretary Connor: "Worst of the credit stringency is over."

December 28: Red China exploded fifth nuclear device.

December 30: Associated Press computer failure caused more than 400 errors in NYSE closing prices. Ticker ran late 124 days in 1966; the greatest on May 6—23 minutes.

During this month ASE installed a computer complex, as an electronic basis for ticker, surveillance, and compared-clearance operations.

1967

January 1: M. H. Myerson & Co. moved to New Jersey to avoid increased N.Y. State stock transfer tax—first firm to do so.

Trading Sessions: 251

	Advances DJI:	131
	Declines DJI:	118
	Unchanged DJI:	2

	Advances DJR:	130
	Declines DJR:	117
	Unchanged DJR:	4

	Advances DJU:	115
	Declines DJU:	133
	Unchanged DJU:	3

Closing High DJI: 943.08   (9/25)
Closing Low DJI: 786.41   (1/3)

Closing High DJR: 274.49   (8/4)
Closing Low DJR: 205.16   (1/3)

Closing High DJU: 140.43   (4/20)
Closing Low DJU: 120.97   (11/8)

Monthly Record

	Inds.		*Rails*		*Utils.*	
J	Plus	64.20	Plus	25.04	Plus	3.01
F	Minus	10.52	Minus	1.37	Minus	3.20
M	Plus	26.61	Plus	3.95	Plus	2.56
A	Plus	31.07	Plus	1.32	Plus	.80
M	Minus	44.49	Plus	11.70	Minus	6.36
J	Plus	7.70	Plus	11.23	Minus	1.60
J	Plus	43.98	Plus	17.10	Plus	1.95
A	Minus	2.95	Minus	10.00	Minus	3.42
S	Plus	25.37	Minus	.11	Plus	.42
O	Minus	46.92	Minus	24.38	Minus	7.23
N	Minus	3.93	Minus	3.59	Plus	1.41
D	Plus	29.30	Minus	.62	Plus	3.39

Change from 1966

Dow Industrials:	Plus	119.42
Dow Rails:	Plus	30.27
Dow Utilities:	Minus	8.27

January 3: Commerce Secretary Connor said industrial growth would slacken this year.

January 11: Johnson's State of Union message proposed 6% surcharge on corporate and most individual income tax bills to help finance Vietnam War. First hour volume at record high of 4.2 million, vs. previous peak of 3.9 million on December 6, 1965.

January 13: NYSE pushed back its May deadline for finding new president.

January 18: Fowler told Congress the $330 billion debt ceiling would have to be raised.

January 20: Interest rates continued to ease.

January 24: LBJ budget proposed another speed-up in corporate tax payments.

January 26: Chase Bank cut prime rate; first reduction in over 6 years.

January 30: Administration requested $7 billion boost in public debt limit.

February 2: Johnson said he was not aware of serious Hanoi effort to halt war.

February 7: Blizzard caused NYSE to open 15 minutes late, close 90 minutes early.

February 8: ASE seat price equaled 1931 high—$120,000.

February 9: Martin of Federal Reserve said economy may resume rate of rapid growth shortly.

February 13. North Vietnam bombing resumed after 4-day truce.

February 16: NYSE opposed stiffer tax deterrents on foreign securities purchased by Americans. Computer failure caused 92 previously unreported stock sales to be carried on Big Board ticker after market closed.

February 20: Edward M. Gilbert, former president of E. L. Bruce Co., pleaded guilty to stealing $1.1 million from company.

February 23: U.S. launched biggest offensive of Vietnam War.

February 28: LBJ acted to increase credit supplies.

March 3: U Thant said Vietnam fighting "is going to be long and bloody."

March 6: Treasury bill yields dropped to lowest level since 1965 as result of FRB's credit-easing moves.

March 9: LBJ said he would ask Congress to restore 7% tax credit on new investment in equipment. Stocks soared on West Coast.

March 10: NYSE had busiest opening hour on record—5.1 million shares.

March 13: To curb tape lateness, volume to be deleted from all transactions when ticker becomes two minutes late.

March 15: House Ways and Means Committee voted that the tax incentive be restored.

March 17: Johnson and Ky started talks at Guam.

March 21: NYSE seat sold at $305,000—highest since 1931.

March 22: Morgan Guaranty cut prime rate.

March 27: N.Y. Central and Pennsylvania Railroads denied authority by Supreme Court to proceed immediately with merger.

March 28: U Thant offered peace proposal.

April 5: U.S. mediators moved to avert rail and trucking strikes.

April 6: Discount rate chopped. Stocks boomed on West Coast.

April 10: Rail strike, set for April 13, headed for another 20-day truce until May 3.

April 20: Haiphong bombed for first time.

April 21: Russia launched Soyuz I over weekend.

April 24: North Vietnam MIG fighter bases bombed for first time.

May 1: SEC sent mutual fund reform legislation to Capitol Hill.

May 2: Ackley warned that price inflation likely to intensify again.

May 3: Johnson reaffirmed that 6% income tax surcharge would be sought later in year.

May 4: Bank of England cut discount rate for third time in 1967. DJI closed above 900 for first time since June 22, 1966.

May 11: U Thant worried that Washington-Peking confrontation over Vietnam was inevitable.

May 16: Martin of Federal Reserve said short-term speculation reminiscent of "pool operations in the 1920's."

May 18: Egypt-Israel at loggerheads. U.N. removed supervisory force. U.S. Treasury halted silver sales for export. Silver strong.

May 19: U.S. forces invaded DMZ in Vietnam.

May 22: Egypt closed Gulf of Aqaba to Israeli shipping.

June 5: Outbreak of Middle East War over weekend. Volume 11.1 million shares, largest since May 4.

June 6: Hopes rose for transfer of war from battlefield to conference table.

June 7: Israel claimed victory. Gulf of Aqaba blockade broken.

June 13: Sixth straight market session on upside.

June 22: LBJ and Kosygin agreed to Summit Conference.

June 26: Martin of FRB called for tax increase exceeding 6%.

June 27: Ackley backed Administration's proposal for tax hike.

July 6: AT&T hit new low; result of FCC announcement that fair rate of return for Bell System interstate services should be set at 7%–7½%.

July 10: ASE imposed 100% margin on additional stocks in effort to curb speculation. Total at record of 26.

July 14: Treasury made wide changes in mechanics of interest-equalization tax, in attempt to halt large-scale tax evasion on foreign securities purchases.

July 17: Nationwide rail strike averted.

July 19: Short interest at record high—15,879,852 shares. Rails closed at all-time top; previous peak was 271.72 on February 15, 1966.

July 24: Federal troops curbed Detroit race riots. Ticker to report volume of 5,000 shares or more, even during heavy trading periods when volume of other transactions is deleted.

August 4: DJR posted high for month—274.49.

August 9: DJI posted high for month—926.72. NYSE closed at 2

P.M. nine days in August to enable back offices to catch up on clerical work.

September 11: Robert W. Haack became NYSE president.

September 14: FTC modified ruling on AT&T rates.

September 18: Further depreciation of dollar's value expected.

September 26: Hanoi rejected appeal for negotiated settlement in Vietnam.

October 3: Tax question still stalemated.

October 4: New York banks reported record profits.

October 18: Short interest at new record—17.8 million shares.

October 20: Federal Reserve moved to apply current 70% stock margin to unregulated lenders: banks, corporations, and partnerships that make loans on stocks.

October 23: Egypt sank Israeli destroyer.

October 24: Israelis shelled Egyptian oil installations.

October 30: Two Russian satellites docked in space. High interest rates continued worrisome.

October 31: A record 1,153,700 shares Alcan Aluminum traded at $23.

November 3: Spread on yields between high-grade bonds and common stocks reached 2.7% in bond's favor—highest in modern history.

November 13: Supreme Court held NYSE immune from antitrust challenge in fixing uniform commission rates that Exchange members charge investors.

November 14: U.S. Steel postponed $225 million debenture offering due to "unsettled market conditions."

November 17: Short interest at new high—18,331,711 shares.

November 20: Market dropped on weekend news of British pound devaluation and hike in U.S. discount rate. London Stock Exchange closed. ASE tightened listing rules.

November 21: LSE reopened. DJI surged 13.17 on news that Congress would restudy Administration's proposed income tax increase. Rise in prime rate spread nationwide.

November 22: Bulletproof glass installed at NYSE Visitors' Gallery.

November 27: Justice Department said N.Y. Central and Pennsylvania Railroads should be allowed to complete merger without delay.

November 28: Louis Wolfson sentenced to prison and payment of $100,000 for violations of securities laws.

December 6: Capital spending of U.S. corporations continued to rise.

December 7: U.S. gold stocks fell to lowest level in 30 years.

December 11: NYSE imposed 100% initial margin on 19 stocks of 13 companies—largest number to be subjected to rule in single step.

December 13: King Constantine led revolt against ruling junta in Athens.

December 18: Supreme Court adjourned again without ruling on Pennsy-Central merger plan.

December 20: Short position at record 20,961,965 shares.

December 21: Big Board opened membership door to qualified Canadian brokerage firms. FRB headed toward tighter credit.

December 27: FRB announced it would increase the amount of reserves member banks must maintain against demand deposits in excess of $5 million.

December 28: First woman member admitted to NYSE—Muriel F. Siebert.

December 29: Market closed 1967 on strong note.

During the year ASE undertook major capital improvement program to increase trading floor capacity.

1968

Trading Sessions: 226

Advances   DJI: 117
Declines   DJI: 108
Unchanged DJI: 1

Advances   DJR: 111
Declines   DJR: 112
Unchanged DJR: 3

Advances   DJU: 101
Declines   DJU: 122
Unchanged DJU: 3

Closing High DJI: 985.21   (12/3)
Closing Low DJI: 825.13   (3/21)

Closing High DJR: 279.48   (12/2)
Closing Low DJR: 214.58   (3/5)

Closing High DJU: 141.30   (11/19)
Closing Low DJU: 119.79   (3/25)

Monthly Record

	Inds.		Rails		Utils.	
J	Minus	49.64	Minus	4.22	Plus	1.15
F	Minus	14.97	Minus	10.33	Minus	1.22
M	Plus	.17	Plus	.30	Minus	6.26
A	Plus	71.55	Plus	18.01	Plus	.38
M	Minus	13.22	Plus	18.66	Plus	1.06
J	Minus	1.20	Plus	6.11	Plus	9.58
J	Minus	14.80	Minus	10.66	Minus	1.31
A	Plus	13.01	Unchanged		Minus	.76
S	Plus	39.78	Plus	16.58	Minus	.16
O	Plus	16.60	Minus	1.29	Plus	.89
N	Plus	32.69	Plus	12.88	Plus	9.08
D	Minus	41.33	Minus	7.68	Minus	3.17

Change from 1967

Dow Industrials: Plus   38.64
Dow Rails: Plus   38.36
Dow Utilities: Plus   9.26

January 2: SEC received Big Board's proposal for revising volume discount rates and give-up practices. Resort stocks weakened after Johnson suggested restricting U.S. citizens' foreign travel. ASE increased maximum ticker speed to 900 characters per minute.

January 5: Vietnam peace prospects boosted utilities.

January 9: ASE seat sold at highest since 1929—$240,000.

January 15: Supreme Court ruled that N.Y. Central and Pennsylvania Railroads could merge.

January 16: Britain's Prime Minister Wilson announced austerity program.

January 22: U.S. admitted forces crossed into Cambodia. Ackley urged tax hike. Markets closed 2 P.M. first time, to ease paper logjam.

January 23: House Ways and Means Committee ruled out income tax rise.

January 24: Market dropped on "Pueblo" seizure.

January 25: LBJ called up reservists.

January 30: Viet Cong shelled Saigon; attacked U.S. embassy.

February 1: Penn Central began trading.

February 8: South Korea president reported saying war could erupt any time. Federal Reserve continued moderately restrictive credit policy.

February 9: U.S. jets bombed communications center 10 miles from Hanoi. Securities settlement time extended from 4 days to 5 days.

February 13: Market in tailspin on news of more men sent to Vietnam. DJI dropped 8.27; about 30 points in 4 days.

February 14: Martin of Federal Reserve warned: "We're in a wartime economy." Red China shot down U.S. plane in its air space.

February 21: Russian embassy in Washington bombed.

March 4: Securities markets resumed 3:30 P.M. closings.

March 7: U.S.-Russia agreed to protect nonnuclear nations from attack. Lack of confidence in paper money caused heavy gold buying in London.

March 11: U.S. and various nations pledged to keep $35 gold price at Switzerland weekend meeting.

March 12: Treasury gold supply dropped another $450 million.

March 14: Discount rate rise imminent.

March 18: Weekend gold agreement—which freed the hitherto sacred $35 price—met enthusiastically, but selling on strength limited market gain.

March 22: LBJ called for austerity, promised spending cuts.

March 27: Living costs rose in February for thirteenth straight month. Last sale data of ASE stocks made available abroad, with first transmissions to 6 European countries.

April 1: Weekend news that LBJ would not run again, plus announced curtailment of North Vietnam bombing and outcome of Stockholm monetary negotiations, sparked explosive rally. DJI soared 20.58—biggest daily gain since JFK assassination. Ten percent income tax surcharge became effective.

April 4: Martin Luther King assassinated.

April 8: North Vietnam agreed to open peace talks.

April 9: Markets closed for King funeral.

April 10: First 20-million-share day—20,410,000 shares.

April 15: U.S. and Hanoi dickered over peace talk site.

April 18: Discount rate boosted.

April 19: Martin of Federal Reserve: The U.S. is in "the worst financial crisis since 1931."

April 29: Hanoi rejected all 15 U.S.-proposed peace talk sites. Monthly fail figures first compiled in this month. NYSE tightened listing standards.

May 3: Paris chosen for peace talks.

May 7: Tax proposal progress carried DJI and DJR to new highs for year.

May 9: Reports that Russian troops moved toward Czechoslovakia triggered sharpest drop in 3 weeks.

May 13: British pound fell. Bank of England director resigned.

May 20: Gold at new high in Europe. Strikes enveloped France.

May 22: Heavy speculation in low-priced stocks.

May 24: Interest rates continued to climb. France in turmoil.

May 31: Better prospects for tax bill passage sparked market rise.

June 5: Robert F. Kennedy shot.

June 6: RFK died.

June 10: Margin raised to 80%.

June 12: Major exchanges began operating on 4-day week on account of "back office" problems.

June 13: 730,312 shares American Standard Pfd. traded at 104¼; record block in terms of dollars—$76.1 million.

June 14: Heavy speculation. Some ASE stocks traded over 300% of their floating supply in one month.

June 17: East Germans squeezed Berlin travel.

June 18: U Thant: Paris peace talks "will be deadlocked for a long time."

July 9: DJI at new high closing for 1968.

July 15: FTC announced plans to probe conglomerates.

July 18: Russia demanded that Czechoslovakia modify its program of democratic reform.

July 22: Czech-Russian tension and indications that tax increase might slow or halt economic boom caused deepest setback since June 5, 1967.

July 30: Steel-union pact announced after close; strike averted.

August 8: LBJ illness caused precautionary selling.

August 20: LBJ said no further de-escalation unless Reds reciprocate.

August 29: Federal Reserve continued to ease credit reins. Exchanges scheduled 4-day trading weeks for September.

August 30: Discount rate cut.

September 3: Prospects for Soviet invasion of Rumania diminished.

September 11: Exchanges resumed Wednesday closings.

September 17: LBJ condemned Chrysler for raising car prices.

September 24: New high for DJI sparked by cut in prime rate.

October 1: DJI and DJR "in gear" on upside.

October 3: Nixon said securities industry regulations would be relaxed if he was elected.

October 8: Rumors in Paris of peace talk break before November elections.

October 17: Peace outlook pushed DJI to 2½-year high. First hour volume heaviest in history—7,660,000 shares.

October 23: ASE seat sold for record price—$277,000.

October 29: NYSE seat sold for $500,000, equaling 1929 high.

October 31: After markets closed LBJ announced suspension of North Vietnam bombing.

November 6: Nixon won Presidency in down-to-wire finish, but Humphrey gained popular vote.

November 12: The N.Y. Times: "NYSE should shut down between Christmas and New Year's to clear brokerage paper logjam."

November 14: Europe bothered by money jitters.

November 19: France ordered all markets closed on account of money crisis.

November 22: De Gaulle resisted pressure to devalue franc.

November 29: Europeans heavy buyers of U.S. stocks.

December 2: Prime rate raised.

December 17: Discount rate increased. Price rate up again.

December 23: Money/credit noose tightened. DJI dropped 13¼ points.

December 28: Apollo VIII splashed down after moon flight.

December 31: DJI closed at December low. No year-end rally. Eleventh time in 75 years that prices were not higher by New Year than they were Christmas Eve.

Customer-directed give-ups banned by nation's stock markets.

1969

Trading Sessions:	250		*Monthly Record*			

			Inds.	*Rails*	*Utils.*
Advances	DJI:	120			
Declines	DJI:	129			
Unchanged DJI:		1	J Plus 2.30	Plus 3.28	Plus 2.78
			F Minus 40.84	Minus 21.20	Minus 7.38
Advances	DJR:	95	M Plus 30.27	Minus 9.99	Minus 2.90
Declines	DJR:	150	A Plus 14.70	Minus 5.35	Plus .38
Unchanged DJR:		5	M Minus 12.62	Minus 4.94	Minus .90
			J Minus 64.37	Minus 21.41	Minus 7.06
Advances	DJU:	110	J Minus 57.72	Minus 16.11	Minus 5.05
Declines	DJU:	142	A Plus 21.25	Plus 5.30	Minus .73
Unchanged DJU:		3	S Minus 23.63	Minus 4.58	Minus 5.15
Closing High DJI:	968.85	(5/14)	O Plus 42.90	Plus 3.60	Plus 7.86
Closing Low DJI:	769.93	(12/17)	N Minus 43.69	Minus 13.56	Minus 7.63
			D Minus 11.94	Minus 10.30	Minus 1.31
Closing High DJR:	279.88	(2/7)			
Closing Low DJR:	169.03	(12/17)	*Change from 1968*		
Closing High DJU:	139.95	(1/31)	Dow Industrials:	Minus 143.39	
Closing Low DJU:	106.31	(12/9)	Dow Rails:	Minus 95.26	
			Dow Utilities:	Minus 27.09	

January 2: Exchange initiated 4-hour trading sessions (10 A.M.– 2 P.M.), cut out Wednesday closings in force since June 12, 1968.

January 7: First National City Bank of N.Y. lifted prime rate—third rise since early December.

January 20: Nixon inaugurated.

February 4: ASE banned off-floor trading by members for their own account in 103 volatile stocks.

February 10: Heavy snow forced closings of NYSE and ASE, the first such weekday closing by Big Board in this century. Only other all-day closing was Saturday in January, 1948, due also to snow.

February 11: Market battled between forces of inflation and deflation.

February 12: Pittsburgh Stock Exchange members voted merger with Philadelphia-Baltimore-Washington Stock Exchange.

February 17: Trading stalemate broken on downside.

February 24: Cede & Co. began operations—the nominee for all shares held in the NYSE's Central Certificate Service, an automated method of transferring stock ownership.

February 26: Federal Reserve restated determination to tighten credit to cool economy.

March 3: Russians and Chinese clashed.

March 6: Gold at new high under two-tiered system.

March 12: Antitrust broadsides from Washington caused selling in conglomerates.

March 17: Prime rate raised to record level.

March 18: Dow Industrials showed double bottom at 895–905.

March 24: Antitrust action against LTV sparked selling in other conglomerates.

March 25: Rails-Utilities at 1969 lows. Martin of Federal Reserve said he hoped prime rate would not be hiked again.

March 28: Eisenhower died. Market closed the following Monday.

April 2: Gold strong.

April 4: Discount rate raised.

April 7: Stocks dived on discount rate boost.

April 8: Peace hopes, good first-quarter earnings helped support market.

April 11: Tension in Mid-East. Rail strike averted at last minute. DJR at new low. U.S. Vietnam deaths topped Korean total.

April 14: Utilities at new low. Conglomerates weak.

April 15: North Korea shot down U.S. plane.

April 16: Market weakened on Korean news.

April 18: Worry that FRB credit squeeze would cause recession.

April 21: Nixon requested repeal of investment tax credit.

April 22: U Thant said near state of war existed along Suez.

April 25: ASE to investigate trading in Parvin Dohrmann.

April 28: De Gaulle beaten at polls.

April 29: Market scored biggest rise in almost 2 months.

May 2: Funds invested "impatient money." Near panic buying in some blue chips.

May 5: Money/credit pinch started taking bite out of economy. Westec Corp. plunged $36.50 on ASE as trading resumed after 2 years, 8 months, 11 days.

May 8: Viet Cong offered peace plan.

May 26: Apollo X landed safely.

June 6: Morgan Guaranty boosted broker loan rate.

June 11: Administration ruled out wage-price controls.

June 12: Credit clamps tightened. All three Dow Averages hit new lows for year.

June 19: NYSE appropriated $7.5 million for future automation projects; computerized routing of odd-lot orders from brokerage houses to trading floor and expansion of Exchange's market-data system, which drives stock ticker.

July 1: DJI posted first back-to-back plus days since May highs were reached.

July 7: Exchanges returned to longer sessions (closings extended to 2:30 P.M.).

July 8: Threat of price controls caused big drop.

July 10: Chrysler's 5-point fall sparked 13.83 decline by DJI.

July 16: Apollo XI moon launch succeeded.

July 17: Peace hopes dashed.

July 21: Markets closed to celebrate moon landing.

July 31: Sharp rally caused by clearing in Senate of bill to extend 10% income tax surcharge.

August 8: France devalued franc by 11.1%.

August 11: Volume smallest since August 27, 1967, despite franc devaluation.

August 12: Heavy pressure on British pound.

August 14: Martin of Federal Reserve: ". . . less inflationary momentum in the economy than there was three months ago."

August 19: Industrials-Rails showed strong pattern of ascending tops-bottoms.

August 20: Short interest increased first time in 5 months.

September 2: AFL-CIO President George Meany said only wage-price controls can halt inflationary spiral.

September 3: Ho Chi Minh died. Power failure halted trading temporarily on Exchange.

September 4: Concern about Ho's death caused heavy selling.

September 9: Israel launched large raid across Suez Canal.

September 15: Possibility of more troop removals from Vietnam helped market rally.

September 17: AT&T and Du Pont at new lows.

September 29: Civilian government in Bolivia overthrown by military. Exchanges extended trading to 3:00 P.M.

October 14: Peace hopes bolstered market. Volume highest in nearly a year.

October 17: Arthur Burns succeeded Martin as FRB chairman.

October 20: Sugar strong on government ban of cyclamates.

October 27: German mark revalued over weekend. Profit taking hit market.

November 4: Market reacted bearishly to Nixon's speech.

November 10: DJI at new high since July.

November 12: Penn Central at new low.

November 17: Economy showed signs of slipping.

November 19: Second moon landing successful.

November 21: Bond yields competed strongly with stocks.

November 25: Losses outnumbered gains for twelfth straight day.

November 28: "Eyes of Wall Street are on FRB"—*Wall Street Journal.*

December 2: Dow Industrials "in gear" with Rails-Utilities on downside.

December 5: Volume discounts initiated, giving large investors a commission price break on most trades exceeding 1,000 shares.

December 8: All Dow Averages closed at new lows for past 3 years or more.

December 11: Market down almost 100 points from November high.

December 15: U.S. Steel at 14-year bottom.

December 18: Stocks rallied after Burns said he hoped FRB would reconsider tight money policy.

December 31: 10% income tax surcharge, in effect since April 1, 1968, reduced to 5%.

1970

Trading Sessions:		254
Advances	DJI:	126
Declines	DJI:	126
Unchanged	DJI:	2
Advances	DJT:	125
Declines	DJT:	128
Unchanged	DJT:	1
Advances	DJU:	125
Declines	DJU:	124
Unchanged	DJU:	5

Closing High DJI:	842.00	(12/29)
Closing Low DJI:	631.16	(5/26)
Closing High DJT:	183.31	(1/5)
Closing Low DJT:	116.69	(7/7)
Closing High DJU:	121.84	(12/31)
Closing Low DJU:	95.86	(6/30)

Monthly Record

	Inds.		Trans.		Utils.	
J	Minus	56.30	Minus	12.62	Minus	4.89
F	Plus	33.53	Plus	13.86	Plus	10.06
M	Plus	7.98	Minus	4.52	Plus	2.50
A	Minus	49.50	Minus	16.69	Minus	9.08
M	Minus	35.63	Minus	11.91	Minus	6.42
J	Minus	16.91	Minus	23.89	Minus	6.39
J	Plus	50.59	Plus	10.16	Plus	9.07
A	Plus	30.46	Plus	7.08	Plus	5.10
S	Minus	3.90	Plus	15.64	Minus	1.84
O	Minus	5.07	Minus	7.73	Minus	1.82
N	Plus	38.48	Plus	7.64	Plus	9.40
D	Plus	44.83	Plus	18.16	Plus	6.07

Change from 1969

Dow Industrials:	Plus	38.56
Dow Trans.:	Minus	4.82
Dow Utilities:	Plus	11.76

January 2: DJ Rail Average became Transportation Average. Some rails were deleted; certain airline, freight carrier issues added.

January 16: IBM hit by poor earnings; weakness spread to other glamors.

January 19: DJI fell for seventh straight day.

January 22: Street disappointed by lack of anything definite in Nixon's State of Union message.

January 26: DJI at new low for 1969–1970.

January 28: Indications of rising wholesale prices, plus auto production cutbacks, caused another bad slide.

February 3: Market climbed on 16-million-share volume after Treasury Secretary Kennedy suggested that easier interest rates may be nearer than expected.

February 9: Stocks strong on hopes for easier credit.

February 11: Chrysler cut dividend to 15 cents from 50 cents.

February 12: Middle East situation worsened.

February 16: Record balance-of-payments deficit reported for 1969.

February 17: Du Pont, Procter & Gamble weakness paced 6½ point drop by DJI.

February 20: Street consensus believed that market had reached or was near bottom, that money/credit would soon be eased.

February 24: Arab-Israeli conflict heated up.

February 25: DJI soared 14 points on news of prime rate cut by Philadelphia bank.

March 4: Market worried about possible rail strike.

March 13: McDonnell & Co. announced closing.

March 17: Mail strike started in New York City.

March 18: Post Office tie-up in full swing.

March 23: Nixon called in troops for P.O. strike—first time ever against a civil service.

March 24: Brighter P.O. outlook and easier short-term interest rates helped market.

March 25: DJI soared 16.32 on sudden cut in prime rate by leading bank.

April 2: Institutions dumped glamor stocks. Market concerned about spreading strikes by Teamsters, Mid-East turmoil, enemy action in Vietnam, Cambodia, first quarter earnings.

April 6: Ninety-day test of $15 service charge on orders of 1,000 shares or less became effective.

April 13: AT&T's huge rights offering began. Company's warrants became listed, after NYSE lifted a 51-year ban on such listings.

April 24: Dow Industrials had biggest drop in 9 months. During this month Donaldson, Lufkin & Jenrette blazed trail to public ownership with first offering of a NYSE member firm.

May 1: Cambodia a major market depressant.

May 4: Exchanges resumed 3:30 P.M. closings. DJI plunged 19.07— biggest loss since November 22, 1963.

May 6: Margin lowered to 65%.

May 7: Colleges closed; peace rallies held.

May 12: Israel raided Lebanon. Laird said all U.S. troops out of Vietnam by June, 1971.

May 15: ASE began implementing a computer system to route odd-lot orders directly from member-firm order rooms to posts on trading floor.

May 26: All Dow Averages reached new lows. Government National Mortgage Association ("Ginnie Mae") made first public offering of mortgage-backed bonds this month.

May 27: Market staged very strong rally.

June 4: Market worried by Nixon's statement that Middle East "is bubbling up and about to explode."

June 8: North Korea reported sinking of U.S. gunboat; proven false over weekend.

June 10: AT&T dropped to 10-year low.

June 16: Market strengthened in anticipation of Nixon's speech on the economy.

June 19: DJI began to show bullish pattern of higher highs.

June 22: Bankruptcy involving Penn Central cast pall over whole market. Stock dropped 4⅝ to 6½.

June 23: Market worried about liquidity crisis. Chrysler especially weak.

June 27: Odd-lot short sales soared to 42,815 shares.

June 29: Transportation Average hit 12-year low on weakness among rails.

June 30: U.S. troops withdrawn from Cambodia. NYSE presented its brokerage commission proposal to SEC. Income tax surcharge, in effect since April 1, 1968, ended.

July 2: Nixon appointed David Bruce to head Paris Vietnam talks.

July 7: Rail strike averted by Nixon's calling 90-day moratorium.

July 13: SEC began hearings on extension of brokerage surcharge.

July 15: DJI at new recovery high. Volume up. Du Pont strong.

July 22: False rumors about softer Viet Cong stand in Paris.

July 23: Nasser reported more amenable to peace talks.

July 27: Small pipe bomb exploded at entrance to Bank of America's Wall Street office.

August 4: Peace hopes brightened for Middle East.

August 7: Ninety-day Mid-East cease-fire arranged.

August 10: U.S. Steel hit new low.

August 13: IBM slid 7 points to new low.

August 18: Biggest trading day in 122-year history of Chicago Board of Trade. Record 309 million bushels of grain changed hands, 13% above previous record on June 16, 1966.

August 19: Oils paced upside action. Cities Service, Mobil, Jersey Standard at new highs.

August 20: Government officials made bullish comments on business.

August 24: FRB's move to ease monetary pressures in area of bank reserve requirements helped spark rally.

August 25: Short-term interest rates declined.

August 31: Concern over Arab-Israeli charges, countercharges.

September 1: Auto industry's proposals received coolly by union.

September 8: Israel said it would pull out of peace talks.

September 9: Airliners hijacked.

September 11: Unions chose General Motors for strike target.

September 14: Big Philadelphia bank cut prime rate.

September 15: Possibility of long GM strike stalled market.

September 17: Viet Cong offered new peace proposals.

September 21: Prime rate reduced. NYSE short interest at highest in over 4 years. Jordan and guerrillas battled in Syrian War.

September 23: Rail strike postponed two weeks.

September 24: Market advanced on second highest volume.

September 28: Nasser died.

October 8: Communists' negative response to Nixon's Vietnam speech caused sell off.

October 14: Investors concerned by forecasts of record federal deficit for fiscal 1971.

October 19: Turmoil in Canada a market depressant.

October 21: Rumors of Vietnam cease-fire fueled recovery.

October 28: Goodbody & Co.'s difficulties began to surface.

October 29: Merrill Lynch to acquire Goodbody.

November 9: General Motors strike ended.

November 10: Discount rate cut.

November 19: Interest rates continued to drop.

November 20: Chase Bank chopped prime rate.

November 23: Market unsettled by U.S. commandolike raid near Hanoi, renewed bombing of North Vietnam.

November 30: DJI advanced 12.74 to highest level since January.

December 1: Discount rate lowered.

December 2: DJI closed above 800 for first time since January.

December 3: Chase Bank reduced consumer loan rate.

December 7: DJI extended daily gains to 12 straight.

December 8: Rail strike threatened for midnight December 9 put damper on market.

December 10: Indicated end to abortive rail strike enabled resumption of uptrend, with DJI at new high closing for year.

December 14: Comsat paid initial quarterly dividend—12½ cents.

December 22: Preopening news of lowered prime rate by Chase Bank construed bullishly.

December 24: DJI reached 13-month high.

December 30: Nixon signed Securities Investor Protection Act of 1970 into law.

December 31: Year's volume at record high of 2,937,400,000 shares, versus previous record of 2,931 million in 1968 and 2,850 million in 1969.

1971

Trading Sessions:	253

				Monthly Record					
Advances	DJI:	132			*Inds.*		*Trans.*		*Utils.*
Declines	DJI:	120							
Unchanged	DJI:	1		J	Plus 29.58	Plus	20.54	Plus	2.46
				F	Plus 10.33	Plus	4.34	Minus	2.88
Advances	DJT:	142		M	Plus 25.54	Plus	3.60	Plus	1.41
Declines	DJT:	110		A	Plus 37.38	Plus	25.89	Minus	3.04
Unchanged	DJT:	1		M	Minus 33.94	Minus	8.49	Minus	5.37
				J	Minus 16.67	Minus	1.80	Plus	4.03
Advances	DJU:	113		J	Minus 32.71	Minus	9.21	Minus	3.36
Declines	DJU:	134		A	Plus 39.64	Plus	33.12	Minus	3.41
Unchanged	DJU:	6		S	Minus 10.88	Minus	2.36	Minus	2.37
				O	Minus 48.19	Minus	7.97	Plus	2.59
Closing High DJI:	950.82	(4/28)		N	Minus 7.66	Minus	6.89	Minus	1.53
Closing Low DJI:	797.97	(11/23)		D	Plus 58.86	Plus	21.40	Plus	7.38

Closing High DJT:	248.33	(9/7)
Closing Low DJT:	169.70	(1/4)

Change from 1970

Closing High DJU:	128.39	(1/19)		Dow Industrials:	Plus	51.28
Closing Low DJU:	108.03	(11/24)		Dow Trans.:	Plus	72.20
				Dow Utilities:	Minus	4.09

January 4: First Penn Banking & Trust Co. cut prime rate.

January 7: Other banks accepted prime rate cut. Federal Reserve lowered discount rate. Big Board governors approved increase in Exchange's Special Trust Fund to $75 million from $55 million.

January 13: Conflict between U.S. oil companies and Libya-Algeria sparked selling in oils. Steels weak too after Nixon blasted industry on Bethlehem Steel price boost.

January 15: Evidence that Government would shore up economy, plus prime rate cut, pushed Dow Averages to new highs.

January 18: Prime rate reduced again; discount rate lowered.

January 21: Short interest reported down. General Electric an upside leader on good earnings.

January 22: Big Board volume at record peak—21.7 million shares. Institutions active on buying side.

January 27: Bethlehem Steel lowered quarterly dividend.

January 29: NYSE weekly volume topped 100 million shares for first time.

February 2: New high volume—22 million shares. Mystery surrounding Laos invasion and U.S. role there used as excuse for selling.

February 3: Generally bad fourth-quarter earnings failed to hinder further advance on heavier volume.

February 4: Egypt said it would observe month-long extension of Mid-East cease-fire.

February 5: National Quotation Bureau Index of OTC issues discontinued. New indexes compiled by NASD, through its automated system for quoting OTC securities (called NASDAQ), became effective.

February 8: DJI closed at highest level since July 7, 1969, despite news of drive into Laos. Volume: 25.6 million shares. 3,248,000 shares Allis-Chalmers traded at 18; largest block in history and second largest in total dollar volume.

February 9: Volume at new peak: $28\frac{1}{4}$ million shares.

February 12: Some FRB banks cut discount rate after market closed.

February 16: Prime rate lowered.

February 18: NYSE added "Incorporated" after its name. Higher short interest on both N.Y. exchanges.

February 22: South Vietnamese drive into Laos stalled. Market enthusiasm slowed by FRB Chairman Burns' remark that he was not optimistic as Administration on economy.

February 25: Improved business spurred market strength, despite new worries over Southeast Asia.

March 2: Corporate bonds weakened.

March 3: Uncertainty over extension Mid-East cease-fire.

March 5: Rail-union negotiations still stalled.

March 8: Market concerned that South Vietnam might invade North, bring China into war.

March 11: Chase Bank cut prime rate.

March 15: DJI closed above 900 for first time in 21 months.

April 1: NYSE listing fees increased; first major overhaul in 20 years. Rebels seized East Pakistan city. U.S. ordered official personnel to leave area.

April 5: NYSE first permitted negotiated brokerage rates on portions of orders over $500,000. Quotes for 32 OTC issues added to new NASDAQ facility, which began operating in February.

April 13: Administration released first "inflation alert" about future, rather than past, price-wage actions.

April 14: Some restrictions relaxed on trade-travel between U.S. and Red China.

April 15: DJI crossed 940 intraday; Transportation Index topped 200.

April 19: Paul McCracken termed economic indicators "very encouraging." Russia orbited satellite (said to be step toward manned space station).

April 20: China accepted invitation to send ping-pong team to U.S.

April 21: NYSE short interest down from previous month.

April 22: Chase Bank boosted prime rate.

April 28: Market at 23-month high.

May 4: Disturbing European monetary news.

May 5: Swiss, German, other banks withdrew support of dollar.

May 6: Street worried that monetary crisis might cause U.S. to tighten credit, slow domestic economic growth, take stronger stand against inflation.

May 10: West Germany decided to let mark float to higher level in relation to dollar.

May 14: Prime rate under heavier pressure for increase.

May 17: Biggest market setback in 11 months. Nationwide rail strike began, caused other work stoppages.

May 18: Rail strike ended.

May 20: Short interest dropped half a million shares from April 15.

May 21: NYSE further tightened capital rules proposals.

June 14: Market dived on anticipated prime-discount rate hikes.

June 18: News that mutual-fund redemptions topped sales for first time ever prompted heavy selling.

June 23: Merrill Lynch, Pierce, Fenner & Smith went public.

June 24: Daniels & Bell, Inc. became first black-owned Big Board member.

July 6: Prime rate increased.

July 13: Telephone strike began. IBM dropped 13 points on bad earnings.

July 15: Discount rate increased. NYSE tightened standards for original-continued listings. Nixon announced plan to visit Red China before May 1, 1972.

July 20: Telephone tie-up settled.

July 22: Gold at 2-year high.

July 27: U.S. Steel cut quarterly dividend.

August 2: Steel strike averted; rail walkout ended.

August 6: U.S. dollar faced growing crisis.

August 13: NYSE and Amex reported short interests at lowest in over a year.

August 16: Market soared on peak volume (31.7 million) after Nixon announced freeze on wages, prices, rents until November 13.

August 20: DJT at new 1971 high.

August 26: FNMA publicly offered $1 billion of debentures, largest in its history. Three maturities included in one sale for first time. Major foreign holding in a member firm became effective with Big Board approval.

September 9: Market officials indorsed concept of a central securities market.

September 14: Eastern dock strike threatened for October 1.

September 22: Bond interest rates at highest level since Nixon's new economic policy unveiled. September mutual-fund redemptions at record peak.

October 1: Coal-shipping industries began strike.

October 4: Nixon invoked Taft-Hartley on shipping strike.

October 6: Congress passed bill to reinstate 7% investment tax credit and cut individual income taxes.

October 12: Nixon to visit Moscow in May for summit meeting. Labor said it would cooperate with Phase Two.

October 20: Prime rate cut.

November 1: NASDAQ published OTC volume statistics for first time.

November 4: Prime rate cut—second time in 2½ weeks.

November 10: Discount rate lowered.

November 13: Ninety-day wage-price freeze ended.

November 16: Chesapeake & Ohio dived 11¾ points on dividend omission.

November 18: NYSE approved in principle member firms' selling life insurance.

November 22: Big Board amended rules to let independent bank or trust company act both as transfer agent and registrar for any listed security other than its own.

November 23: DJI at year's low.

November 30: Wall Street awaited outcome of Rome monetary conference.

December 1: NYSE said that, starting January 3, it would print on ticker hourly volume totals of Exchange-traded warrants.

December 2: Dollar dropped on devaluation possibilities.

December 6: Margin lowered to 55% from 65%. India-Pakistan War. South Korea proclaimed state of emergency.

December 9: Pakistan accepted UN cease-fire proposal.

December 10: Nixon signed into law tax cuts to give economy a shot in the arm. Discount rate reduced.

December 13: Public became more active in market.

December 14: Nixon-Pompidou conferred in Azores. Agreed on prompt realignment of exchange rates through "a devaluation of the dollar and a revaluation of some other currencies."

December 15: Pakistan commander requested cease-fire.

December 16: East Pakistan army surrendered. India set West Pakistan cease-fire.

December 20: Dollar devalued officially over weekend. Gold raised to $38 per ounce from $35. Ten percent import surcharge removed. Federal Reserve pressed monetary expansion. More banks lowered prime rate.

December 22: Short interest increased 790,331 shares. November mutual-fund sales topped redemptions.

December 27: Heavy bombing North Vietnam resumed over weekend.

December 28: SEC requested greater power over exchanges. Short-term interest rates dropped. FCC called off investigation of telephone rates.

December 30: North Vietnam bombing halted after 5 days.

SECTION 2

The Exchanges

PART 1

Founding and Subsequent Fathers

A. THE "BUTTONWOOD TWENTY-FOUR" OF MAY 17, 1792

Leonard Bleecker	16 Wall Street
Hugh Smith	Tontine Coffee House
Armstrong & Barnewell	58 Broad Street
Samuel March	243 Queen Street
Bernard Hart	55 Broad Street
Sutton & Hardy	20 Wall Street
Benjamin Seixas	8 Hanover Square
John Henry	13 Duke Street
John A. Hardenbrook	24 Nassau Street
Samuel Beebe	21 Nassau Street
Alexander Zuntz	97 Broad Street
Andrew D. Barclay	136 Pearl Street
Ephraim Hart	74 Broadway
Julian McEvers	140 Greenwich Street
G. N. Bleecker	21 Broad Street
Peter Anspach	3 Great Dock Street
Benjamin Winthrop	2 Great Dock Street
John Ferrers	205 Water Street
Isaac M. Gomez	32 Maiden Lane
Augustine H. Lawrence	132 Water Street
John Bush	195 Water Street
Charles McIvers, Jr.	194 Water Street
Robinson & Hartshorne	198 Queen Street
David Reedy	58 Wall Street

145

B. PRESIDENTS OF THE NEW YORK STOCK EXCHANGE

Anthony Stockholm	1817	Salem T. Russell	1876–77
G. S. Mumford	1818–23	Henry Meigs	1877–78
Edward Lyde	1824–26	Brayton Ives	1878–80
James W. Bleecker	1827–29	Donald Mackay	1880–82
Russell H. Nevins	1830	Frederick N. Lawrence	1882–83
John Ward	1831–33	Alfrederick S. Hatch	1883–84
R. D. Weeks	1834	J. Edward Simmons	1884–86
Edward Prime	1835	James D. Smith	1886–88
R. D. Weeks	1836	William L. Bull	1888–90
David Clarkson	1837–51	Watson B. Dickerman	1890–92
Henry G. Stebbins	1851–52	Frank K. Sturgis	1892–94
Charles R. Marvin	1852–55	Francis L. Eames	1894–98
Charles R. Marvin	1855–57	Rudolph Keppler	1898–00
John H. Gourlie	1857–58	Rudolph Keppler	1900–03
Henry G. Stebbins	1858–59	Ransom H. Thomas	1903–04
William H. Neilson	1859–61	Henry K. Pomroy	1904–05
W. R. Vermilye	1861–62	Henry K. Pomroy	1905–07
Abraham B. Baylis	1862–63	Ransom H. Thomas	1907–12
Henry G. Stebbins	1863–64	James B. Mabon	1912–14
William Seymour, Jr.	1864–65	Henry G. S. Noble	1914–19
R. L. Cutting	1865–66	William R. Remick	1919–21
Wm. Alexander Smith	1866–67	Seymour L. Cromwell	1921–24
John Warren	1867–68	Edward H. H. Simmons	1924–28
William Searls	1868–69	Edward H. H. Simmons	1928–30
William H. Neilson	1869–70	Richard Whitney	1930–35
William Seymour, Jr.	1870–71	Charles R. Gay	1935–36
William B. Clerke	1871–72	Charles R. Gay	1936–38
Edward King	1872–73	William McC. Martin, Jr.*	1938–41
Henry G. Chapman	1873–74	Emil Schram	1941–51
George H. Brodhead	1874–75	G. Keith Funston **	1951–67
George W. McLean	1875–76	Robert W. Haack ***	1967–72

* Under the amended constitution of the Exchange, effective May 16, 1938, the presidency became a salaried office.
** May 24, 1951, appointment date. Assumed office September 10, 1951. Richard M. Crooks, chairman of the board, acted as the president pro tem from May to September, 1951.
*** Assumed office September 10, 1967.

C. PRESIDENTS OF THE AMERICAN STOCK EXCHANGE

	Effective Date	
John L. McCormack	March	1911
Edward R. McCormick	June	1914
John W. Curtis	February	1923
David U. Page	February	1925
William S. Muller	February	1928
Howard C. Sykes	February	1932
E. Burd Grubb	February	1934
Fred C. Moffatt	February	1935
George P. Rea *	April	1939
Fred C. Moffatt (pro tem)	July	1942
Edwin Posner (pro tem)	February	1945
Edward C. Werle (pro tem)	February	1947
Francis Adams Truslow	March	1947
Edward T. McCormick	April	1951
Joseph F. Reilly (pro tem)	December	1961
Edwin Posner (pro tem)	January	1962
Edwin D. Etherington	September	1962
Ralph S. Saul	November	1966
Paul Kolton	June	1971

* First paid president.

D. CHAIRMEN OF THE ASE BOARD OF GOVERNORS

	Effective Date
Clarence A. Bettman	February 1939 *
Fred C. Moffatt	February 1941
Edwin Posner	February 1945
Edward C. Werle	February 1947
Mortimer Landsberg	February 1950
John J. Mann	February 1951
James R. Dyer	February 1956
Joseph F. Reilly	February 1960
Edwin Posner	February 1962
David S. Jackson	February 1965
Macrae Sykes	February 1968
Frank C. Graham, Jr.	February 1969

* Prior to 1939, there was no board chairman. The president was elected from among the Board of Governors.

E. HOURS OF BUSINESS

The New York and American Stock Exchanges maintain business hours of 10 A.M. to 3:30 P.M. on weekdays. Member firms must be open on every full business day during these hours. However, there have been occasions when the markets were closed, or closed early, or operated under restrictions.

September 18–30, 1873: NYSE closed on account of panic.

July 31, 1914: Outbreak of World War I prompted closing of NYSE and N.Y. Curb Market. Wall Street authorities feared the markets might be inundated by selling for the European account, estimated at $2.4 billion. The possibility of panic, or bear raiding from domestic sources, was a contributing factor.

NYSE reopened for bond trading under restrictions on *November 28.* Trading in certain stocks resumed at pegged prices on *December 12.* Dealings in all stocks resumed under restrictions on *December 15.* Normal and unrestricted trading privileges restored *April 1, 1915.* An outlaw market flourished in New Street, while the exchanges were closed.

January, 1918: Certain Monday closings initiated to conserve electricity for war effort.

September 16, 1920: NYSE closed early after explosion outside J. P. Morgan & Co. killed 30 persons.

March 4–14, 1933: Securities markets closed during banking holiday.

July 19–23, 1933: Trading hours shortened to give tired clerks a rest.

August 15–16, 1945: Exchanges closed two days to celebrate end of World War II.

September 29, 1952: Half-day Saturday trading discontinued. Weekday closings extended from 3 to 3:30 P.M.

November 22, 1963: Securities markets closed immediately when John F. Kennedy's assassination became known. All trading banned also on day of the funeral, November 25.

August, 1967: Exchanges closed at 2 P.M. for 9 days to enable back-office employees to catch up on clerical work.

June 12, 1968: Major markets began operating on 4-day week, generally closing on Wednesdays, as result of delivery, processing, bookkeeping problems arising from high trading volume of 1967–1968.

January 2, 1969: Exchanges returned to 5-day week, but operated on truncated (10 A.M.–2 P.M., Eastern Time) schedule. Additions of 30 minutes a day were made July 7, September 29, and on May 4, 1970, when 3:30 P.M. closings resumed.

There have also been such "special closings" as March 31, 1969—observance of former President Eisenhower's death; July 21, 1969—celebration of lunar landing; et cetera.

NYSE has been closed on every Good Friday since 1900, excepting 1906 and 1907. Subject to an affirmative vote, it is closed on following legal holidays in New York State: New Year's Day, Washington's Birthday, Memorial Day, Independence Day, Labor Day, Thanksgiving Day, Christmas Day.

PART 2

Historical Records

A. SEAT (MEMBERSHIP) PRICES

1. New York Stock Exchange

Year		High		Low	Year		High		Low
1869 *	....	$ 7,500	$	3,000	1885	....	$ 34,000	$	20,000
1870	....	4,500		4,000	1886	....	33,000		23,000
1871	....	4,500		2,750	1887	....	30,000		19,000
1872	....	6,000		4,300	1888	....	24,000		17,000
1873	....	7,700		5,000	1889	....	23,000		19,000
1874	....	5,000		4,250	1890	....	22,500		17,000
1875	....	6,750		4,250	1891	....	24,000		16,000
1876	....	5,600		4,000	1892	....	22,000		17,000
1877	....	5,750		4,500	1893	....	20,000		15,250
1878	....	9,500		4,000	1894	....	21,250		18,000
1879	....	16,000		5,100	1895	....	20,000		17,000
1880	....	26,000		14,000	1896	....	20,000		14,000
1881	....	30,000		22,000	1897	....	22,000		15,500
1882	....	32,500		20,000	1898	....	29,750		19,000
1883	....	30,000		23,000	1899	....	40,000		29,500
1884	....	27,000		20,000	1900	....	47,500		37,500

* Seats first made salable October 23, 1868.

Year		High	Low	Year		High	Low
1901	....	$ 80,000	$ 48,500	1936	....	$174,000	$ 89,000
1902	....	81,000	65,000	1937	....	134,000	61,000
1903	....	82,000	51,000	1938	....	85,000	51,000
1904	....	81,000	57,000	1939	....	70,000	51,000
1905	....	85,000	72,000	1940	....	60,000	33,000
1906	....	95,000	78,000	1941	....	35,000	19,000
1907	....	88,000	51,000	1942	....	30,000	17,000
1908	....	80,000	51,000	1943	....	48,000	27,000
1909	....	94,000	73,000	1944	....	75,000	40,000
1910	....	94,000	65,000	1945	....	95,000	49,000
1911	....	73,000	65,000	1946	....	97,000	61,000
1912	....	74,000	55,000	1947	....	70,000	50,000
1913	....	53,000	37,000	1948	....	68,000	46,000
1914	....	55,000	34,000	1949	....	49,000	35,000
1915	....	74,000	38,000	1950	....	54,000	46,000
1916	....	76,000	60,000	1951	....	68,000	52,000
1917	....	77,000	45,000	1952	....	55,000	39,000
1918	....	60,000	45,000	1953	....	60,000	38,000
1919	....	110,000	60,000	1954	....	88,000	45,000
1920	....	115,000	85,000	1955	....	90,000	80,000
1921	....	100,000	77,500	1956	....	113,000	75,000
1922	....	100,000	86,000	1957	....	89,000	65,000
1923	....	100,000	76,000	1958	....	127,000	69,000
1924	....	101,000	76,000	1959	....	157,000	110,000
1925	....	150,000	99,000	1960	....	162,000	135,000
1926	....	175,000	133,000	1961	....	225,000	147,000
1927	....	305,000	170,000	1962	....	210,000	115,000
1928	....	595,000	290,000	1963	....	217,000	160,000
1929 **	......	625,000	550,000	1964	....	230,000	190,000
1929 ***	.....	495,000	350,000	1965	....	250,000	190,000
1930	....	480,000	205,000	1966	....	270,000	197,000
1931	....	322,000	125,000	1967	....	450,000	220,000
1932	....	185,000	68,000	1968	....	515,000	385,000
1933	....	259,000	90,000	1969	....	515,000	260,000
1934	....	190,000	70,000	1970	....	320,000	130,000
1935	....	140,000	65,000	1971	....	300,000	145,000

** To February 18, 1929.
*** Ex-rights. New York Stock Exchange members voted 25% in the form of rights on the 1,100 seats existing on February 18, 1929. The rights created 275 new memberships and brought the total to 1,375. Nine of these were retired by the Exchange in 1953, which reduced the number to the present 1,366.

Source: Fact Book, New York Stock Exchange, Inc.

2. American Stock Exchange

Year	High	Low	Year	High	Low
1921 *	$ 6,800	$ 3,750	1947	$ 25,000	$ 13,500
1922	10,000	4,200	1948	23,000	12,500
1923	9,500	3,600	1949	10,000	5,500
1924	9,000	4,000	1950	11,000	6,500
1925	37,500	8,500	1951	15,500	9,500
1926	35,000	17,500	1952	14,000	12,000
1927	67,000	22,000	1953	15,000	10,100
1928	170,000	56,000	1954	19,000	10,000
1929	254,000	150,000	1955	22,000	17,500
1930	225,000	70,000	1956	31,500	21,500
1931	137,500	38,000	1957	26,000	21,500
1932	55,000	16,500	1958	42,000	18,000
1933	50,000	25,000	1959	65,000	44,000
1934	40,000	17,000	1960	60,000	51,000
1935	33,000	12,000	1961	80,000	52,000
1936	48,000	26,000	1962	65,000	40,000
1937	35,000	17,500	1963	66,000	52,500
1938	17,500	8,000	1964	63,000	52,000
1939	12,000	7,000	1965	80,000	55,000
1940	7,250	6,900	1966	120,000	70,000
1941	2,600	1,000	1967	230,000	100,000
1942	1,700	650	1968	315,000	220,000
1943	8,500	1,600	1969	350,000	150,000
1944	16,000	7,500	1970	185,000	70,000
1945	32,000	12,000	1971	150,000	65,000
1946	37,500	19,000			

* From June 27, 1921.

Source: Amex Databook 1971 (American Stock Exchange, Inc.)

B. MINIMUM LISTING REQUIREMENTS

1. New York Stock Exchange (1958–1971)

Effective Date	Net Income Latest Year	Net Income Preceding Year	Pre-Tax Income Latest Year	Pre-Tax Income Preceding 2 Years	Net Tangible Assets	Aggregate Market Value Shares Outstanding	Aggregate Market Value Publicly Held Shares	Shares Outstanding	Shares not Concentrated (Publicly Held)	No. of Stockholders of Record	No. of Holders of Round Lots (100 Shs. or More)
Apr. 23, 1958	$1,000,000	.....	.....	.....	$ 8,000,000	$ 8,000,000	.....	.....	400,000	.....	1,500**
Apr. 20, 1961	1,000,000	.....	.....	.....	10,000,000	10,000,000	.....	.....	500,000	.....	1,500**
Mar. 19, 1964	1,200,000	$1,200,000 *	$2,000,000	$2,000,000 *	10,000,000	.....	$10,000,000	.....	600,000	.....	1,500
Apr. 15, 1965	1,200,000	1,200,000 *	2,000,000	2,000,000 *	10,000,000	.....	12,000,000	1,000,000	700,000	2,000	1,700
May 23, 1968	.....	.....	2,500,000	2,000,000	14,000,000	.....	14,000,000	1,000,000	800,000	2,000	1,800
July 15, 1971	.....	.....	2,500,000	2,000,000	16,000,000	.....	16,000,000	.....	1,000,000	.....	2,000

* Normally earning's yardsticks should have been exceeded for 3 years.
** Some credit given for odd-lot holdings. None in later years.

Source: Fact Book, New York Stock Exchange, Inc.

2. American Stock Exchange (1962–1971)

Effective Date	Shares Publicly Held (a)	Market Value Publicly Held Shares	Market Value Shares Outstanding	No. of Stockholders (Round-Lot Holders)	Net Income Last Fiscal Year (Pre-Tax)	Net Income Last Fiscal Year (After All Charges)	Net Income 3-Year Average (After All Charges)	Net Tangible Assets
Apr. 5, 1962	200,000	$1,000,000 (b)	$2,000,000	750 (500)	.....	$150,000	$100,000	$1,000,000
Feb. 1, 1964	250,000	1,000,000 (c)	.....	750 (500)	.....	150,000	100,000	1,000,000
Nov. 21, 1967	300,000	2,000,000 (d)	.....	900 (600)	$500,000	300,000	.....	3,000,000

(a) Exclusive of the holdings of officers and directors and other concentrated or family holdings.
(b) Amended November 13, 1963, for issues selling below $5 per share to substantially in excess of $1,000,000.
(c) Plus 10,000 more shares publicly held for each 50 cents below $5.
(d) Price per share: $5 for a reasonable period of time prior to the filing of a listing application.

Source: Amex Databook 1971 (American Stock Exchange, Inc.)

C. NUMBER ISSUES — ANNUAL VOLUME

1. New York Stock Exchange

| Year | Number Issues | | Reported Volume | |
	Stocks	Bonds	Stocks (Shs.)	Bonds (Par Val.)
1900	376	827	138,981,000	$ 579,293,000
1901	379	855	264,935,000	994,554,000
1902	384	891	186,715,000	893,049,000
1903	383	903	158,497,000	686,435,000
1904	374	907	186,921,000	1,032,655,000
1905	381	929	260,569,000	1,026,254,000
1906	393	937	282,206,000	677,184,000
1907	389	929	194,635,000	529,843,000
1908	402	984	194,545,000	1,081,175,000
1909	426	1,013	212,421,000	1,314,425,000
1910 *	454	1,053	163,705,000	634,863,000
1911	480	1,069	125,835,000	889,076,000
1912	521	1,083	131,488,000	675,429,000
1913	511	1,082	82,849,000	501,532,000
1914	511	1,096	47,431,000	461,652,000
1915	540	1,149	172,497,000	961,700,000
1916	613	1,171	232,633,000	1,148,161,000
1917	627	1,102	184,623,000	1,034,663,000
1918	612	1,131	143,280,000	2,092,751,000
1919	691	1,114	318,273,000	3,676,101,000
1920	756	1,115	227,636,000	3,868,422,000
1921	792	1,156	172,778,535	3,386,159,000
1922	778	1,234	260,890,802	4,132,731,558
1923	889	1,262	236,482,731	2,744,966,900
1924	927	1,332	284,044,082	3,810,471,000
1925	1,043	1,367	459,717,623	3,427,042,210
1926	1,081	1,420	451,868,353	3,015,344,915
1927	1,097	1,491	581,702,342	3,308,002,382
1928	1,176	1,534	930,893,276	2,906,611,160
1929	1,293	1,543	1,124,800,410	2,996,398,000
1930	1,308	1,607	810,632,546	2,720,301,800
1931	1,278	1,601	576,765,412	2,969,848,000
1932	1,237	1,549	425,234,294	2,991,244,000
1933	1,209	1,568	654,816,452	3,355,646,000
1934	1,187	1,540	323,845,634	3,702,820,000
1935	1,185	1,463	381,635,752	3,339,458,000

* Figures up to and including March 10, 1910, include unlisted trading.

	Number Issues		Reported Volume	
Year	Stocks	Bonds	Stocks (Shs.)	Bonds (Par Val.)
1936	1,212	1,409	496,046,869	$3,576,878,000
1937	1,259	1,376	409,464,570	2,792,531,000
1938	1,237	1,393	297,466,722	1,859,865,000
1939	1,233	1,395	262,029,599	2,046,083,000
1940	1,230	1,295	207,599,749	1,669,438,000
1941	1,232	1,173	170,603,671	2,111,805,000
1942	1,238	1,136	125,685,298	2,311,479,250
1943	1,237	1,096	278,741,765	3,254,717,725
1944	1,259	1,063	263,074,018	2,694,704,000
1945	1,269	982	377,563,575	2,261,985,110
1946	1,334	925	363,709,312	1,364,174,150
1947	1,379	900	253,623,894	1,075,541,420
1948	1,419	911	302,218,965	1,013,829,210
1949	1,457	915	272,203,402	817,949,070
1950	1,472	926	524,799,621	1,112,425,170
1951	1,495	918	443,504,076	824,002,920
1952	1,522	958	337,805,179	772,875,640
1953	1,530	984	354,851,325	775,940,140
1954	1,532	1,014	573,374,622	979,500,000
1955	1,508	1,024	649,602,291	1,045,900,000
1956	1,502	1,043	556,284,172	1,068,900,000
1957	1,522	1,106	559,946,890	1,081,600,000
1958	1,507	1,149	747,058,306	1,382,200,000
1959	1,507	1,180	820,296,279	1,585,700,000
1960	1,528	1,191	766,693,818	1,346,400,000
1961	1,541	1,186	1,021,264,589	1,636,000,000
1962	1,559	1,202	962,200,000	1,454,600,000
1963	1,572	1,185	1,146,300,000	1,483,300,000
1964	1,606	1,186	1,236,600,000	2,524,500,000
1965	1,627	1,210	1,556,300,000	2,975,200,000
1966	1,665	1,272	1,899,500,000	3,092,800,000
1967	1,700	1,388	2,530,000,000	3,955,500,000
1968	1,767	1,455	2,931,600,000	3,814,200,000
1969	1,789	1,574	2,850,800,000	3,646,200,000
1970	1,840	1,729	2,937,400,000	4,494,900,000
1971	1,927	1,988	3,891,300,000	6,563,800,000

Source: Fact Book, New York Stock Exchange, Inc.

2. American Stock Exchange

	Listed Issues		Unlisted Issues		Volume	
Year	Stocks	Bonds	Stocks	Bonds	Stocks (Shs.)	Bonds (Par Val.)
1938	501	71	605	313	49,640,238	$366,974,000
1939	499	63	578	270	45,729,888	444,497,000
1940	493	33	566	247	42,928,377	303,902,000
1941	472	33	546	212	34,656,354	249,705,000
1942	459	29	516	185	22,301,852	176,704,500
1943	439	28	496	173	71,374,283	231,109,000
1944	422	23	461	140	71,061,713	181,073,500
1945	421	22	438	116	143,309,292	167,333,000
1946	437	18	402	89	137,313,214	79,770,000
1947	441	19	374	74	72,376,027	88,638,000
1948	434	19	367	70	75,016,108	59,757,000
1949	431	18	347	65	66,201,828	49,636,000
1950	424	11	333	58	107,792,340	47,549,000
1951	443	14	320	49	111,629,218	38,832,000
1952	470	16	308	47	106,237,657	28,565,000
1953	498	17	296	47	102,378,937	32,114,800
1954	520	19	288	60 *	162,948,716	30,697,000
1955	544	19	274	50	228,956,315	35,330,000
1956	588	21	261	47	228,231,047	22,282,000
1957	609	23	246	36	214,011,566	16,538,000
1958	618	24	237	35	240,358,524	22,790,000
1959	647	29	224	33	374,058,546	32,171,000
1960	726	33	216	30	286,039,982	32,670,000
1961	797	45	204	28	488,831,037	55,184,000
1962	834	57	184	27	308,609,304	77,508,000
1963	841	60	162	23	316,735,062	77,293,000
1964	883	70	139	21	374,183,842	103,886,000
1965	910	79	118	19	534,221,999	146,927,000
1966	929	81	109	17	690,762,585	159,724,000
1967	960	124	101	13	1,145,090,300	554,824,000
1968	995	156	89	11	1,435,765,734	970,403,000
1969	1,088	164	64	11	1,240,742,012	913,940,000
1970	1,160	164	62	5	843,116,260	641,270,000
1971	1,249	178	59	4	1,070,924,002	932,000,000

* Seventeen previously suspended bond issues reinstated.

Source: Amex Databook 1971 (American Stock Exchange, Inc.)

D. MONTHLY VOLUME NEW YORK STOCK EXCHANGE

| Year | *HIGH* | | *LOW* | |
	Shs. (Thous.)	Month	Shs. (Thous.)	Month
1900	23,696	Nov.	3,928	Aug.
1901	42,138	Apr.	10,692	Aug.
1902	25,846	Apr.	7,766	June
1903	15,767	Jan.	10,612	Sept.
1904	32,853	Jan.	4,879	June
1905	29,972	Oct.	12,101	June
1906	39,205	Dec.	16,207	July
1907	32,129	Mar.	9,630	Nov.
1908	24,919	Nov.	9,351	June
1909	24,201	Aug.	12,202	Feb.
1910 *	23,821	Jan.	7,743	Sept.
1911	17,282	Sept.	5,000	Apr.
1912	15,883	Apr.	7,014	Feb.
1913	9,547	June	3,726	Nov.
1914	9,992	Jan.	3,991	June
1915	26,624	Oct.	4,343	Feb.
1916	34,472	Nov.	9,199	July
1917	19,560	May	11,698	Aug.
1918	21,111	May	6,860	Aug.
1919	37,370	Oct.	11,861	Jan.
1920	29,000	Mar.	9,333	June
1921	18,409	June	9,255	July
1922	30,675	Apr.	15,425	July
1923	25,938	Mar.	12,635	July
1924	43,876	Dec.	13,588	May
1925	54,692	Oct.	25,335	Apr.
1926	52,322	Mar.	23,452	May
1927	62,802	Dec.	34,604	Jan.
1928	116,053	Nov.	38,827	July
1929	141,668	Oct.	69,548	June
1930	111,041	Apr.	39,870	Aug.
1931	65,658	Mar.	24,829	Aug.
1932	82,626	Aug.	23,001	June
1933	125,620	June	18,718	Jan.
1934	56,830	Feb.	12,636	Sept.
1935	57,460	Nov.	14,405	Feb.
1936	67,202	Jan.	20,614	May
1937	58,671	Jan.	16,449	June
1938	41,558	Oct.	14,004	May

* Figures up to and including March 10, 1910 include unlisted trading.

	HIGH		LOW	
Year	*Shs. (Thous.)*	*Month*	*Shs. (Thous.)*	*Month*
1939	57,091	Sept.	11,964	June
1940	38,965	May	7,304	July
1941	36,390	Dec.	8,969	Feb.
1942	19,313	Dec.	7,229	May
1943	36,997	Mar.	13,923	Oct.
1944	37,713	June	13,847	Apr.
1945	41,310	June	19,977	July
i946	51,510	Jan.	20,595	July
1947	28,635	Oct.	14,153	Aug.
1948	42,769	May	15,039	Aug.
1949	39,293	Dec.	17,180	Feb.
1950	59,820	Dec.	33,406	Feb.
1951	70,181	Jan.	25,677	Nov.
1952	40,516	Dec.	20,905	Aug.
1953	42,472	Mar.	22,234	July
1954 **	92,090	Dec.	41,787	Jan.
1955	94,047	Jan.	53,335	Aug.
1956	78,219	Mar.	46,130	Sept.
1957	80,589	Oct.	45,598	Mar.
1958	118,112	Oct.	51,841	Feb.
1959	108,470	Mar.	67,534	Sept.
1960	94,756	Dec.	70,210	Oct.
1961	153,454	Mar.	71,381	July
1962	155,617	June	73,794	Sept.
1963	136,111	Oct.	90,686	Mar.
1964	155,529	Apr.	100,180	Aug.
1965	230,967	Dec.	116,462	July
1966	223,753	Mar.	141,124	July
1967	267,658	Mar.	206,197	Apr.
1968	332,512	May	205,369	Feb.
1969	319,999	Oct.	233,471	Sept.
1970	350,289	Dec.	215,947	Aug.
1971	427,779	Feb.	285,865	Sept.

** From 1954–1971, inclusive, volume includes nonreported round-lot sales and odd-lot purchases and sales.

Source: Fact Book, New York Stock Exchange, Inc.

Biggest Monthly Volume: 427,778,710 shares, February, 1971
Smallest Monthly Volume: 3,726,176 shares, November, 1913

Most Active Volume Months: March, October, December
Least Active Volume Months: June, July, August

E. DAILY VOLUME

1. New York Stock Exchange

Year	HIGH DAY Shs. (Thous.)	Date	LOW DAY Shs. (Thous.)	Date
1900	1,627	11/12	89	8/22
1901	3,337	5/9	183	7/2
1902	1;956	4/21	167	6/3
1903	1,540	1/9	147	8/27
1904	2,911	12/8	73	3/10
1905	2,042	2/27	132	6/15
1906	2,728	8/20	302	10/30
1907	2,496	3/14	139	6/24
1908	1,716	11/13	67	7/3
1909	1,650	6/4	294	3/15
1910 *	1,656	2/3	111	12/23
1911	1,704	9/27	87	7/14
1912	1,252	12/11	100	12/26
1913	864	6/10	57	11/24
1914	1,281	7/30	50	12/30
1915	1,673	9/28	114	3/17
1916	3,002	12/21	119	8/7
1917	2,048	2/1	236	10/24
1918	1,692	5/16	136	8/2
1919	2,697	11/12	299	2/7
1920	2,008	4/21	227	6/29
1921	1,290	3/23	280	8/8
1922	2,008	4/17	236	7/3
1923	1,559	11/22	283	7/16
1924	2,584	11/20	316	6/2
1925	3,391	11/10	790	4/13
1926	3,860	3/3	607	5/6
1927	3,214	10/4	1,219	1/28
1928	6,943	11/23	1,090	6/25
1929	16,410	10/29	1,996	12/24
1930	8,279	5/5	1,090	8/1
1931	5,346	2/24	536	9/1
1932	5,461	8/8	385	10/31
1933	9,572	7/21	477	1/30
1934	4,940	2/5	275	8/20
1935	3,948	11/14	345	2/4
1936	4,718	2/17	586	5/13

* Figures up to and including March 10 include unlisted trading.

Year	HIGH DAY Shs. (Thous.)	Date	LOW DAY Shs. (Thous.)	Date
1937	7,288	10/19	424	6/21
1938	3,100	11/9	278	6/8
1939	5,934	9/5	235	7/3
1940	3,940	5/21	130	8/19
1941	2,925	12/29	224	5/19
1942	1,441	12/29	207	7/1
1943	2,805	5/4	335	8/30
1944	2,517	6/16	337	5/15
1945	2,936	6/28	492	8/6
1946	3,624	9/4	487	7/5
1947	2,197	4/14	476	8/27
1948	3,837	5/14	465	8/16
1949	2,212	12/14	541	6/17
1950	4,859	6/27	1,061	3/13
1951	3,877	1/17	973	7/11
1952	2,352	11/19	780	5/19
1953	3,119	3/31	738	9/8
1954	4,433	12/29	1,215	1/11
1955	7,717	9/26	1,230	8/15
1956	3,921	2/29	1,223	10/9
1957	5,093	10/22	1,256	9/4
1958	5,368	10/17	1,566	2/24
1959	4,884	3/13	1,745	10/12
1960	5,303	12/30	1,894	10/12
1961	7,077	4/4	2,184	7/3
1962	14,746	5/29	1,946	10/8
1963	9,324	11/26	2,513	7/26
1964	6,851	4/2	3,051	8/10
1965	11,434	12/6	3,028	7/7
1966	13,121	5/6	4,268	6/6
1967	14,954	12/29	5,998	1/3
1968	21,351	6/13	6,707	3/25
1969	19,950	10/14	6,683	8/11
1970	21,345	9/24	6,660	5/11
1971	31,731	8/16	7,349	10/25

Source: Fact Book, New York Stock Exchange, Inc.

2. American Stock Exchange

Year	HIGH DAY Shs. (Thous.)	Date	LOW DAY Shs. (Thous.)	Date
1938	669	10/17	62	6/17
1939	950	9/5	40	7/3
1940	660	5/21	26	8/26
1941	636	12/29	46	5/19
1942	378	12/29	29	7/20
1943	1,259	5/10	91	1/6
1944	638	7/5	114	5/15
1945	2,354	11/13	166	4/4
1946	1,748	1/29	202	8/19
1947	872	2/7	115	8/27
1948	921	5/14	133	9/16
1949	524	12/2	123	6/17
1950	917	12/18	230	7/3
1951	953	10/8	174	7/11
1952	1,389	4/3	203	9/11
1953	983	9/15	213	6/19
1954	1,698	12/20	341	1/11
1955	1,853	9/26	459	11/1
1956	1,879	3/26	500	10/9
1957	2,023	12/31	429	11/11
1958	1,955	12/4	389	2/8
1959	3,523	3/20	640	10/12
1960	2,441	12/30	740	8/1
1961	5,431	5/12	780	7/3
1962	5,333	5/29	461	10/8
1963	2,796	12/31	637	1/2
1964	2,883	4/3	901	9/16
1965	4,963	12/8	793	7/22
1966	6,567	4/14	1,043	10/14
1967	8,292	10/26	1,740	1/3
1968	10,809	6/13	2,112	3/25
1969	11,355	12/31	2,540	8/12
1970	7,877	9/24	1,445	8/17
1971	8,615	8/16	1,897	8/6

Source: *Amex Databook 1971* (American Stock Exchange, Inc.)

F. SHORT SALES (Thousands)
NEW YORK STOCK EXCHANGE

Year	*ROUND LOTS* Total	Members	Nonmembers	Customers' Odd Lots
1939	6,649	5,114	1,534	137
1940	7,449	5,415	2,034	542
1945	11,737	8,586	3,152	338
1950	20,812	14,356	6,457	518
1951	19,241	13,704	5,537	584
1952	12,113	9,210	2,904	247
1953	14,731	9,969	4,761	357
1954	23,252	16,756	6,496	456
1955	26,033	19,651	6,382	345
1956	24,498	19,338	5,160	335
1957	31,191	22,195	8,996	684
1958	43,521	30,553	12,967	719
1959	35,092	28,817	6,275	519
1960	39,091	30,254	8,837	738
1961	44,356	36,757	7,599	595
1962	63,810	41,424	22,386	2,303
1963	58,630	44,555	14,075	960
1964	63,632	49,005	14,627	1,064
1965	94,687	75,923	18,764	972
1966	147,102	109,315	37,787	2,719
1967	182,195	148,642	33,552	1,823
1968	216,031	164,657	51,374	2,082
1969	193,438	145,151	48,287	1,341
1970	238,895	161,794	77,101	1,985
1971	288,014	230,375	57,639	973

Source: Fact Book, New York Stock Exchange, Inc.

G. SHORT SALES (Number of Shares)
AMERICAN STOCK EXCHANGE

Year	Total	By Members	By Public
1940	516,885	468,265	48,620
1941	350,570	308,855	41,715
1942	216,325	195,040	21,285
1943	479,105	393,505	85,600
1944	731,735	590,100	141,635
1945	1,695,370	1,366,465	328,905
1946	1,745,000	1,444,205	300,795
1947	1,071,165	791,260	279,905
1948	1,219,090	860,550	358,540
1949	1,450,075	955,780	494,295
1950	1,932,780	1,349,775	583,005
1951	1,536,750	1,124,025	412,725
1952	1,458,490	1,084,055	374,435
1953	1,405,230	864,290	540,940
1954	2,663,620	1,989,465	674,155
1955	3,807,905	2,225,765	1,582,140
1956	8,092,850	3,877,995	4,214,855
1957	10,419,590	4,464,330	5,955,260
1958	13,763,485	5,624,450	8,139,035
1959	18,319,415	7,946,750	10,372,665
1960	11,535,965	6,160,425	5,375,540
1961	18,514,955	13,615,095	4,899,860
1962	12,111,290	7,616,760	4,494,530
1963	13,380,935	8,482,850	4,898,085
1964	18,938,590	11,979,585	6,959,005
1965	29,035,655	20,650,230	8,385,425
1966	35,711,585	23,472,380	12,239,205
1967	58,495,240	41,131,170	17,364,070
1968	66,197,205	46,162,212	20,034,993
1969	59,517,725	39,183,062	20,334,663
1970	48,521,120	28,396,948	20,124,172
1971	49,007,743	36,881,930	12,125,813

Source: Amex Databook 1971 (American Stock Exchange, Inc.)

H. ANNUAL SHORT INTEREST *

1. New York Stock Exchange

Year	HIGH		LOW	
	Shs. (Thous.)	Date	Shs. (Thous.)	Date
1931	5,590	5/25	2,164	10/9
1932	3,965	2/11	1,657	9/16
1933	1,895	2/14	713	12/29
1934	1,030	1/31	714	12/31
1935	1,033	11/29	742	2/28
1936	1,247	2/28	974	8/31
1937	1,435	2/26	945	6/30
1938	1,384	4/29	501	12/30
1939	668	5/31	382	12/29
1940	531	4/30	428	5/31
1941	538	3/31	349	12/31
1942	558	10/30	461	1/30
1943	980	5/28	579	1/29
1944	1,436	11/30	847	1/31
1945	1,583	2/15	1,306	8/14
1946	1,270	1/15	628	9/13
1947	1,540	6/17	798	1/15
1948	1,326	5/14	932	11/15
1949	2,267	12/15	1,054	1/14
1950	2,572	3/15	1,744	8/15
1951	2,651	10/15	2,237	6/15
1952	2,478	2/15	1,571	12/15
1953	2,610	12/15	1,556	1/15
1954	3,352	9/15	2,564	1/15
1955	3,097	2/15	2,581	12/15
1956	2,530	4/13	2,165	6/15
1957	3,355	11/15	2,239	1/15
1958	6,087	7/15	2,833	1/15
1959	4,381	1/15	3,023	8/14
1960	4,400	12/15	2,736	2/15
1961	3,889	1/13	3,014	9/15

* Circulars requesting information relative to their short position were first distributed to individuals and member firms on May 25, 1931, by the NYSE. The statistics were compiled daily or weekly until June 30, 1933, when monthly reporting began. In February, 1945, the reporting date was changed from the last monthly settlement day to the fifteenth of the month, or the preceding settlement day.

Source: Fact Book, New York Stock Exchange, Inc.

	HIGH		LOW	
Year	*Shs. (Thous.)*	*Date*	*Shs. (Thous.)*	*Date*
1962	6,858	11/15	3,025	1/15
1963	7,059	12/13	5,654	7/15
1964	6,983	12/15	5,693	2/14
1965	11,724	12/15	6,038	1/15
1966	14,619	12/15	10,107	1/14
1967	20,965	12/15	12,531	1/13
1968	22,215	6/14	19,437	5/15
1969	18,639	1/15	16,394	7/15
1970	20,075	8/14	13,789	3/13
1971	20,773	3/15	15,517	10/15

2. American Stock Exchange

	HIGH		LOW	
Year	*Shs. (Thous.)*	*Month*	*Shs. (Thous.)*	*Month*
1956	477	Sept.	365	June
1957	611	Apr.	435	Oct.
1958	897	Nov.	530	Jan.
1959	1,382	Apr.	875	Jan.
1960	983	Sept.	738	Mar.
1961	1,672	May	726	Jan.
1962	1,369	Nov.	1,020	May
1963	1,831	Nov.	1,230	Jan.
1964	2,340	Nov.	1,498	Jan.
1965	4,312	Dec.	2,052	Jan.
1966	5,206	Apr.	3,267	Oct.
1967	10,300	Dec.	3,421	Jan.
1968	11,473	June	8,376	Apr.
1969	9,289	Feb.	5,796	Dec.
1970	5,663	Aug.	4,660	Mar.
1971	5,346	Mar.	4,009	Aug.

Source: Amex Databook 1971 (American Stock Exchange, Inc.)

I. FAILS TO DELIVER SECURITIES
NEW YORK STOCK EXCHANGE

A "fail" is a broker's inability to deliver, within the required 5 business days, the securities he owes another broker. One broker's failure to deliver becomes another broker's failure to receive. If the second broker also owes the securities, he, in turn, likewise has a failure to deliver on his books. An "aged fail" is one 30 days or more old.

The level of fails is a barometer of the securities industry's operational health. During the peak of the paperwork logjam in the summer of 1968, NYSE member firms had fails totaling well over $3 billion. Monthly fail figures were first compiled in April, 1968, and reached a record high of $4.1 billion in December.

	1968		1969		1970		1971	
End of Month	Total Fails (mils.)	Aged Fails (mils.)	Total Fails (mils.)	Aged Fails (mils.)	Total Fails (mils.)	Aged Fails (mils.)	Total Fails (mils.)	Aged Fails (mils.)
Jan.	n.a.*	n.a.	$3,300	$596	$1,457	$137	$1,559	$51
Feb.	n.a.	n.a.	2,969	529	1,316	111	1,801	70
Mar.	n.a.	n.a.	2,477	433	1,060	70	1,738	53
Apr.	$2,670	$478	2,319	352	968	56	1,804	74
May	3,466	535	2,551	259	830	44	1,523	61
June	3,769	715	2,183	271	790	37	1,460	66
July	3,675	837	1,668	253	780	38	1,106	52
Aug.	3,095	724	1,399	166	782	34	1,247	35
Sept.	3,082	751	1,468	123	898	34	1,138	38
Oct.	3,358	586	1,869	106	825	31	1,202	46
Nov.	3,274	556	1,691	135	1,087	39	941	41
Dec.	4,127	620	1,837	136	1,392	53	1,363	28

* n.a. — not available.

Source: Fact Book, New York Stock Exchange, Inc.

J. BLOCK TRANSACTIONS *

1. New York Stock Exchange

Year	No. of Blocks	Shs. (Thous.)	% of Sh. Vol.	Mkt. Val. (Mils.)
1965	2,171	48,262	3.1	$ 1,857.4
1966	3,642	85,298	4.5	3,303.2
1967	6,685	169,365	6.7	6,810.9
1968	11,254	292,680	10.0	12,971.6
1969	15,132	402,063	14.1	15,609.5
1970	17,217	450,908	15.4	13,354.1
1971	26,941	692,536	17.8	24,000.0

Source: Fact Book, New York Stock Exchange, Inc.

2. American Stock Exchange

Year	No. of Blocks	Shs. (Thous.)	% of Sh. Vol.	Mkt. Val. (Mils.)
1967	1,065	18,808	1.6	333.3
1968	1,682	36,064	2.5	1,108.8
1969	2,463	60,421	4.9	1,567.8
1970	2,260	57,649	6.8	989.3
1971	2,706	66,940	6.3	1,283.7

* 10,000 shares or more.

Source: Amex Databook 1971 (American Stock Exchange, Inc.)

K. ODD-LOT TRANSACTIONS NEW YORK STOCK EXCHANGE

Year	SHARES				VALUE			
	Customers' Purchases (millions)	Customers' Sales (millions)	Purchases and Sales (millions)	Purchase (+) or Sale (−) Balance (millions)	Customers' Purchases (millions)	Customers' Sales (millions)	Purchases and Sales (millions)	Purchases (+) or Sales (−) Balance (millions)
1920 *	35.2	30.0	65.2	+ 5.2				
1921 *	27.5	23.3	50.8	+ 4.3				
1922 *	38.4	36.7	75.0	+ 1.7				
1923 *	31.9	30.2	62.1	+ 1.7				
1924 *	34.3	35.0	69.3	− 0.8				
1925 *	52.2	52.9	105.1	− 0.7				
1926 *	52.3	51.5	103.7	+ 0.8	Not Available			
1927 *	67.6	65.9	133.5	+ 1.7				
1928 *	116.2	113.0	229.2	+ 3.2				
1929 *	156.1	140.7	296.8	+15.5				
1930 *	114.9	101.5	216.4	+13.4				
1931 *	95.4	79.9	175.2	+15.5				
1932 *	66.4	62.3	128.7	+ 4.1				
1933 *	93.3	93.4	186.7	− 0.1				
1934 *	46.8	47.9	94.7	− 1.1				
1935 *	49.2	53.6	102.8	− 4.4				
1936	68.8	68.4	137.2	+ 0.3				
1937	72.2	60.3	132.5	+11.8				
1938	48.4	47.0	95.3	+ 1.4				
1939	38.9	37.5	76.4	+ 1.4				
1940	29.0	27.5	56.6	+ 1.5	$1,042.3	$ 892.9	$ 1,935.2	+$ 149.4
1941	21.6	22.9	44.5	− 1.3				
1942	15.7	15.9	31.6	− 2.0				
1943	28.3	26.0	54.4	+ 2.3				
1944	28.5	26.4	54.9	+ 2.0				
1945	44.4	38.5	82.9	+ 5.9	1,770.1	1,449.9	3,220.0	+ 320.2
1946	55.7	45.0	100.7	+10.7				
1947	34.0	30.8	64.7	+ 3.2				

	SHARES				VALUE			
Year	Customers' Purchases (millions)	Customers' Sales (millions)	Purchases and Sales (millions)	Purchase (+) or Sale (−) Balance (millions)	Customers' Purchases (millions)	Customers' Sales (millions)	Purchases and Sales (millions)	Purchases (+) or Sales (−) Balance (millions)
1948	36.9	33.8	70.7	+ 3.1				
1949	29.3	28.7	58.1	+ 0.6				
1950	49.0	48.3	97.2	+ 0.7	$2,045.4	$1,818.7	$ 3,864.1	+$ 226.7
1951	48.7	41.3	90.1	+ 7.4	2,154.8	1,705.1	3,859.9	+ 449.7
1952	40.4	34.1	74.4	+ 6.3	1,853.4	1,418.3	3,271.7	+ 435.1
1953	38.1	34.7	72.8	+ 3.4	1,670.6	1,349.0	3,019.6	+ 321.6
1954	52.6	53.3	105.9	− 0.7	2,443.1	2,328.0	4,771.1	+ 115.1
1955	66.4	57.7	124.1	+ 8.7	3,484.7	2,885.4	6,370.1	+ 599.3
1956	66.0	51.7	117.6	+14.3	3,520.6	2,615.4	6,136.0	+ 905.2
1957	68.7	53.8	122.5	+14.9	3,252.1	2,508.5	5,760.6	+ 743.6
1958	69.2	65.6	134.8	+ 3.6	3,173.9	2,935.9	6,109.8	+ 238.0
1959	95.7	81.5	177.1	+14.2	5,043.0	4,155.6	9,198.6	+ 887.4
1960	86.9	77.7	164.5	+ 9.2	4,216.1	3,676.2	7,892.3	+ 539.9
1961	106.7	107.3	214.0	− 0.6	5,691.9	5,319.2	11,011.1	+ 372.7
1962	89.1	88.3	177.4	+ 0.8	4,552.7	4,436.2	8,988.9	+ 116.5
1963	80.5	95.4	175.9	−14.9	4,335.3	4,716.5	9,051.8	− 381.2
1964	99.6	101.6	201.3	− 2.0	5,415.2	5,001.4	10,416.6	+ 413.8
1965	112.3	115.2	227.5	− 2.9	5,607.2	5,659.6	11,266.8	− 52.4
1966	135.0	122.0	257.0	+13.0	7,128.3	6,439.3	13,567.6	+ 689.0
1967	143.2	158.7	301.8	−15.5	7,424.0	8,201.4	15,625.4	+ 777.4
1968	137.5	163.5	301.0	−26.0	7,230.2	8,314.1	15,544.4	− 1,083.9
1969	115.9	126.9	242.8	−11.0	5,232.8	6,006.6	11,239.4	+ 773.8
1970	86.5	99.6	186.1	−13.1	3,234.9	3,997.1	7,231.9	− 762.2
1971	71.8	132.1	203.9	−60.3	2,991.0	5,597.0	8,588.0	− 2,606.0

* Up to 1936, data are for the 3 major odd-lot firms, as reported in "Odd-Lot Trading on the New York Stock Exchange," by Charles O. Hardy. For the 2 years (1937–1938) in which data overlap, these firms did 99.5% of the odd-lot volume.

Source: Fact Book, New York Stock Exchange, Inc.

SECTION 3

The Averages

PART 1

The Dow Jones
Stock Averages

Dow Jones & Co. has been publishing the average closing prices of active representative stocks since 1884. Nine of the 11 stocks originally used in this average were rails. Indeed, rails comprised also the majority of the New York Stock Exchange trading list. Utilities were virtually unknown; scattered industrial companies were only just gaining prominence.

In 1897, to accommodate new economic and stock market factors, the Dow Average was divided into 2 groups: 12 Industrials and 20 Rails. Subsequent changes coincided with gradually altered security fashions; as certain stocks became inactive, or were no longer representative, they were weeded out. And, in September, 1916, 20 Industrials were substituted for the old list of 12.

As of October, 1928, the Industrial Index was based on 30, rather than 20, stocks and a few substitutions were made in the earlier list. These were to accommodate a greatly expanded, more active market and were intended to minimize the influence that unusual fluctuations in any one stock might have on the average as a whole. The number of stocks in the Transportation Average (prior to 1970 called the Rail Average) has always remained at 20. The Utility Average began with 20 stocks in the fall of 1929, but was since whittled to 15.

The Dow Averages today consist of 30 Industrials, 20 Transportation

173

issues, 15 Utilities. They are based on closing prices, but hourly and intraday highs and lows are recorded also. Representative stocks are top-quality common stocks, leaders in their corporate fields. If a particular issue fails to sell on any day, its previous closing price is used.

The Averages were initially calculated by dividing the total of the daily closing prices of stocks used in each average by the number of its component parts. However, to offset occasional distortions and to maintain continuity, a new system of computation was introduced in 1928. This system, still used today, is based upon an artificial divisor, which remains unchanged until a stock is split, its price is reduced substantially by a stock dividend, or another stock is substituted.

The fallacy or accuracy of the Dow Averages, or any averages, as a true yardstick of market measurement is readily debatable. Yet the Dow is certainly the oldest and probably the best-known index currently in use. Whenever any question is asked respecting the condition of the market, up or down, the answer invariably is given in terms of its prevailing status.

DOW JONES STOCK AVERAGES

Thirty Industrials

Allied Chemical	General Electric	Sears, Roebuck
Aluminum Co.	General Foods	Std. Oil of Calif.
Amer. Brands	General Motors	Std. Oil of N.J.
Amer. Can	Goodyear	Swift & Co.
Amer. Tel. & Tel.	Inter. Harvester	Texaco
Anaconda	Inter. Nickel	Union Carbide
Bethlehem Steel	Inter. Paper	United Aircraft
Chrysler	Johns-Manville	U.S. Steel
Du Pont	Owens-Illinois	Westinghouse Elec.
Eastman Kodak	Procter & Gamble	Woolworth

Twenty Transportation Cos.

American Air	Norfolk & Western	Southern Pacific
Burlington North.	Northwest Air.	Southern Railway
Canadian Pacific	Pan Am. World Air.	Trans World Air.
Ches. & Ohio	Penn Central	UAL, Inc.
Consolid. Freight	St. Louis-San Fran.	Union Pacific Corp.
Eastern Air Lines	Santa Fe Indust.	U.S. Freight Co.
McLean Trucking	Seaboard Coast.	

Fifteen Utilities

Am. Electric Power	Consol. Nat. Gas	Panhandle E.P.L.
Cleveland El. Ill.	Detroit Edison	Peoples Gas
Columbia Gas Syst.	Houston Lt. & Pwr.	Phila. Electric
Commonwealth Ed.	Niag. Mohawk Pwr.	Pub. Service El. & Gas
Consolidated Ed.	Pacific Gas & El.	So. Cal. Edison

A. PERFORMANCE OF THE DOW (1897–1971)

1. Annual Price Performance

Year	Inds.		Close 12/31	Rail-Trans.		Close 12/31	Utils.*		Close 12/31
1897	Plus	8.67	(49.41)	Plus	10.58	(62.29)			
1898	Plus	11.11	(60.52)	Plus	12.70	(74.99)			
1899	Plus	5.56	(66.08)	Plus	2.74	(77.73)			
1900	Plus	4.63	(70.71)	Plus	17.26	(94.99)			
1901	Minus	6.15	(64.56)	Plus	19.86	(114.85)			
1902	Minus	0.27	(64.29)	Plus	4.13	(118.98)			
1903	Minus	15.18	(49.11)	Minus	20.65	(98.33)			
1904	Plus	20.50	(69.61)	Plus	19.10	(117.43)			
1905	Plus	26.59	(96.20)	Plus	15.83	(133.26)			
1906	Minus	1.85	(94.35)	Minus	3.46	(129.80)			
1907	Minus	35.60	(58.75)	Minus	41.03	(88.77)			
1908	Plus	27.40	(86.15)	Plus	31.28	(120.05)			
1909	Plus	12.90	(99.05)	Plus	10.36	(130.41)			
1910	Minus	17.69	(81.36)	Minus	16.35	(114.06)			
1911	Plus	0.32	(81.68)	Plus	2.77	(116.83)			
1912	Plus	6.19	(87.87)	Plus	0.01	(116.84)			
1913	Minus	9.09	(78.78)	Minus	13.12	(103.72)			
1914	Minus	24.20	(54.58)	Minus	15.19	(88.53)			
1915	Plus	44.57	(99.15)	Plus	19.52	(108.05)			
1916	Minus	4.15	(95.00)	Minus	2.90	(105.15)			
1917	Minus	20.62	(74.38)	Minus	25.42	(79.73)			
1918	Plus	7.82	(82.20)	Plus	4.59	(84.32)			
1919	Plus	25.03	(107.23)	Minus	9.02	(75.30)			
1920	Minus	35.28	(71.95)	Plus	0.66	(75.96)			
1921	Plus	9.85	(81.10)	Minus	1.69	(74.27)			
1922	Plus	17.63	(98.73)	Plus	11.84	(86.11)			
1923	Minus	3.21	(95.52)	Minus	5.25	(80.86)			
1924	Plus	24.99	(120.51)	Plus	17.47	(98.33)			
1925	Plus	36.15	(156.66)	Plus	14.60	(112.93)			
1926	Plus	0.54	(157.20)	Plus	7.93	(120.86)			
1927	Plus	45.20	(202.40)	Plus	19.44	(140.30)			
1928	Plus	97.60	(300.00)	Plus	10.84	(151.14)			
1929	Minus	51.52	(248.48)	Minus	6.42	(144.72)	Plus	2.63	(88.27)
1930	Minus	83.90	(164.58)	Minus	48.14	(96.58)	Minus	27.47	(60.80)
1931	Minus	86.68	(77.90)	Minus	62.95	(33.63)	Minus	29.39	(31.41)
1932	Minus	17.97	(59.93)	Minus	7.73	(25.90)	Minus	3.91	(27.50)
1933	Plus	38.74	(99.90)	Plus	14.52	(40.80)	Minus	4.21	(23.29)
1934	Plus	5.37	(104.04)	Minus	3.98	(36.44)	Minus	5.49	(17.80)
1935	Plus	40.09	(144.13)	Plus	4.04	(40.48)	Plus	11.75	(29.55)
1936	Plus	35.77	(179.90)	Plus	13.15	(53.63)	Plus	5.28	(34.83)
1937	Minus	59.05	(120.85)	Minus	24.17	(29.46)	Minus	14.48	(20.35)
1938	Plus	33.91	(154.76)	Plus	4.52	(33.98)	Plus	2.67	(23.02)
1939	Minus	4.52	(150.24)	Minus	2.15	(31.63)	Plus	2.56	(25.58)
1940	Minus	19.11	(131.13)	Minus	3.70	(28.13)	Minus	5.73	(19.85)
1941	Minus	20.17	(110.96)	Minus	2.71	(25.42)	Minus	5.83	(14.02)
1942	Plus	8.44	(119.40)	Plus	1.97	(27.39)	Plus	0.52	(14.54)
1943	Plus	16.49	(135.89)	Plus	6.17	(33.56)	Plus	7.33	(21.87)
1944	Plus	16.43	(152.32)	Plus	14.84	(48.40)	Plus	4.50	(26.37)

Year	Inds.		Close 12/31	Rail-Trans.		Close 12/31	Utils.*		Close 12/31
1945	Plus	40.59	(192.91)	Plus	14.40	(62.80)	Plus	11.76	(38.13)
1946	Minus	15.71	(177.20)	Minus	11.67	(51.13)	Minus	0.86	(37.27)
1947	Plus	3.96	(181.16)	Plus	1.35	(52.48)	Minus	3.87	(33.40)
1948	Minus	3.86	(177.30)	Plus	0.38	(52.86)	Plus	0.15	(33.55)
1949	Plus	22.83	(200.13)	Minus	0.10	(52.76)	Plus	7.74	(41.29)
1950	Plus	35.28	(235.41)	Plus	24.88	(77.64)	Minus	0.31	(40.98)
1951	Plus	33.82	(269.23)	Plus	4.06	(81.70)	Plus	6.24	(47.22)
1952	Plus	22.67	(291.90)	Plus	29.57	(111.27)	Plus	5.38	(52.60)
1953	Minus	11.00	(280.90)	Minus	17.24	(94.03)	Minus	0.56	(52.04)
1954	Plus	123.49	(404.39)	Plus	51.83	(145.86)	Plus	10.43	(62.47)
1955	Plus	84.01	(488.40)	Plus	17.43	(163.29)	Plus	1.69	(64.16)
1956	Plus	11.07	(499.47)	Minus	10.06	(153.23)	Plus	4.38	(68.54)
1957	Minus	63.78	(435.69)	Minus	61.42	(96.96)	Plus	0.04	(68.58)
1958	Plus	147.96	(583.65)	Plus	60.69	(157.65)	Plus	22.42	(91.00)
1959	Plus	95.71	(679.36)	Minus	3.60	(154.05)	Minus	3.17	(87.83)
1960	Minus	63.47	(615.89)	Minus	23.20	(130.85)	Plus	12.19	(100.02)
1961	Plus	115.25	(731.14)	Plus	12.99	(143.84)	Plus	29.14	(129.16)
1962	Minus	79.04	(652.10)	Minus	2.80	(141.04)	Plus	0.07	(129.23)
1963	Plus	110.85	(762.95)	Plus	37.50	(178.54)	Plus	9.76	(138.99)
1964	Plus	111.18	(874.13)	Plus	26.80	(205.34)	Plus	16.18	(155.17)
1965	Plus	95.13	(969.26)	Plus	42.14	(247.48)	Minus	2.54	(152.63)
1966	Minus	183.57	(785.69)	Minus	44.51	(202.97)	Minus	16.45	(136.18)
1967	Plus	119.42	(905.11)	Plus	30.27	(233.24)	Minus	8.27	(127.91)
1968	Plus	38.64	(943.75)	Plus	38.36	(271.60)	Plus	9.26	(137.17)
1969	Minus	143.39	(800.36)	Minus	95.26	(176.34)	Minus	27.09	(110.08)
1970	Plus	38.56	(838.92)	Minus	4.82	(171.52)	Plus	11.76	(121.84)
1971	Plus	51.28	(890.20)	Plus	72.20	(243.72)	Minus	4.09	(117.75)

Advancing Years (Industrials): 47
Declining Years (Industrials): 28

Advancing Years (Rail-Trans.): 44
Declining Years (Rail-Trans.): 31

Advancing Years (Utilities): 25
Declining Years (Utilities): 18

"Split Close" years, when the DJ Industrial and Rail-Transportation Averages showed divergent action: 11

* Utility Average was not computed until January 1, 1929.

2. Annual Closing Highs-Lows (Prices and Dates)

	Annual Closing Highs			Annual Closing Lows		
	Ind.	Rail-Trans.	Util.*	Ind.	Rail-Trans.	Util.*
1897	55.82 (9/10)	67.23 (9/17)		38.49 (4/23)	48.12 (4/19)	
1898	60.97 (8/26)	74.99 (12/30)		42.00 (3/25)	55.89 (4/21)	
1899	77.61 (9/5)	87.04 (4/3)		58.27 (12/18)	72.48 (12/22)	
1900	71.04 (12/27)	94.99 (12/31)		52.96 (9/24)	72.99 (6/23)	
1901	78.26 (6/17)	117.86 (5/1)		61.52 (12/24)	92.66 (1/3)	
1902	68.44 (4/24)	129.36 (9/9)		59.57 (12/15)	111.73 (1/14)	
1903	67.70 (2/16)	121.28 (1/9)		42.15 (11/9)	88.80 (9/28)	
1904	73.23 (12/5)	119.46 (12/3)		46.41 (3/12)	91.31 (3/14)	
1905	96.56 (12/29)	133.54 (12/29)		68.76 (1/25)	114.52 (5/22)	
1906	103.00 (1/19)	138.36 (1/22)		85.18 (7/13)	120.30 (5/3)	
1907	96.37 (1/7)	131.95 (1/5)		53.00 (11/15)	81.41 (11/21)	
1908	88.38 (11/13)	120.05 (12/31)		58.62 (2/13)	86.04 (2/17)	
1909	100.53 (11/19)	136.46 (8/14)		79.91 (2/23)	113.90 (2/23)	
1910	98.34 (1/3)	129.90 (1/4)		73.62 (7/26)	105.59 (7/26)	
1911	87.06 (6/19)	123.86 (7/21)		72.94 (9/25)	109.80 (9/27)	
1912	94.15 (9/30)	124.35 (10/5)		80.15 (2/10)	114.92 (2/5)	
1913	88.57 (1/9)	118.10 (1/9)		72.11 (6/11)	100.50 (6/11)	
1914	83.43 (3/20)	109.43 (1/31)		53.17 (12/24)	87.40 (12/24)	
1915	99.21 (12/27)	108.28 (1/4)		54.22 (2/24)	87.85 (2/24)	
1916	110.15 (11/21)	112.28 (10/4)		84.96 (4/22)	99.11 (4/22)	
1917	99.18 (1/3)	105.76 (1/3)		65.95 (12/19)	70.75 (12/19)	
1918	89.07 (10/18)	92.91 (11/9)		73.38 (1/15)	77.21 (1/15)	
1919	119.62 (11/3)	91.13 (5/26)		79.15 (2/8)	73.63 (12/12)	
1920	109.88 (1/3)	85.37 (11/3)		66.75 (12/21)	67.83 (2/11)	
1921	81.50 (12/15)	77.56 (1/15)		63.90 (8/24)	65.52 (6/20)	
1922	103.43 (10/14)	93.99 (9/11)		78.59 (1/10)	73.43 (1/9)	

Year						
1923	105.38 (3/20)	90.63 (3/3)		85.76 (10/27)	76.78 (8/4)	
1924	120.51 (12/31)	99.50 (12/18)		88.33 (5/20)	80.23 (2/18)	
1925	159.39 (11/6)	112.93 (12/31)		115.00 (3/30)	92.98 (3/30)	
1926	166.64 (8/14)	123.33 (9/3)		135.20 (3/30)	102.41 (3/30)	
1927	202.40 (12/31)	144.82 (10/3)		152.73 (1/25)	119.29 (1/28)	
1928	300.00 (12/31)	152.70 (11/27)		191.33 (2/20)	132.60 (2/20)	
1929	381.17 (9/3)	189.11 (9/3)	144.61 (9/21)	198.69 (11/13)	128.07 (11/13)	64.72 (11/13)
1930	294.07 (4/17)	157.94 (3/29)	108.62 (4/12)	157.51 (12/16)	91.65 (12/16)	55.14 (12/16)
1931	194.36 (2/24)	111.58 (2/24)	73.40 (3/19)	73.79 (12/17)	31.42 (12/17)	30.55 (12/28)
1932	88.78 (3/8)	41.30 (1/15)	36.11 (9/7)	41.22 (7/8)	13.23 (7/8)	16.53 (7/8)
1933	108.67 (7/18)	56.53 (7/7)	37.73 (7/13)	50.16 (2/27)	23.43 (2/25)	19.33 (3/31)
1934	110.74 (2/5)	52.97 (2/5)	31.03 (2/6)	85.51 (7/26)	33.19 (9/17)	16.83 (12/26)
1935	148.44 (11/19)	41.84 (12/9)	29.78 (12/7)	96.71 (3/14)	27.31 (3/12)	14.46 (3/14)
1936	184.90 (11/17)	58.89 (10/14)	36.08 (10/31)	143.11 (1/6)	40.66 (1/2)	28.63 (4/29)
1937	194.40 (3/10)	64.46 (3/17)	37.54 (1/13)	113.64 (11/24)	28.91 (12/28)	19.65 (10/19)
1938	158.41 (11/12)	33.98 (12/31)	25.19 (10/27)	98.95 (3/31)	19.00 (3/31)	15.14 (3/31)
1939	155.92 (9/12)	35.90 (9/27)	27.10 (8/2)	121.44 (4/8)	24.14 (4/8)	20.71 (4/8)
1940	152.80 (1/3)	32.67 (1/4)	26.45 (1/3)	111.84 (6/10)	22.14 (5/21)	18.03 (6/10)
1941	133.59 (1/10)	30.88 (8/1)	20.65 (1/13)	106.34 (12/23)	24.25 (12/10)	13.51 (12/19)
1942	119.71 (12/26)	29.28 (11/2)	14.94 (1/6)	92.92 (4/28)	23.31 (6/2)	10.58 (4/28)
1943	145.82 (7/14)	38.30 (7/24)	22.30 (7/14)	119.26 (1/8)	27.59 (1/2)	14.69 (1/2)
1944	152.53 (12/16)	48.40 (12/30)	26.37 (12/30)	134.22 (2/7)	33.45 (1/3)	21.74 (1/3)
1945	195.82 (12/11)	64.89 (12/8)	39.15 (12/10)	151.35 (1/24)	47.03 (1/31)	26.15 (1/23)
1946	212.50 (5/29)	68.31 (6/13)	43.74 (5/29)	163.12 (10/9)	44.69 (10/19)	33.20 (10/9)
1947	186.85 (7/24)	53.42 (2/8)	37.55 (2/8)	163.21 (5/17)	41.16 (5/19)	32.28 (5/20)
1948	193.16 (6/15)	64.95 (7/14)	36.04 (6/14)	165.39 (3/16)	48.13 (2/10)	31.65 (2/27)
1949	200.52 (12/30)	54.29 (1/7)	41.31 (12/30)	161.60 (6/13)	41.03 (6/13)	33.36 (1/3)
1950	235.47 (11/24)	77.89 (12/28)	44.26 (5/20)	196.81 (1/13)	51.24 (6/29)	37.40 (7/26)
1951	276.37 (9/13)	90.08 (2/5)	47.22 (12/31)	238.99 (1/3)	72.39 (6/29)	41.47 (1/2)
1952	292.00 (12/30)	112.53 (12/22)	52.64 (12/30)	256.35 (5/1)	82.03 (1/9)	47.53 (1/2)
1953	293.79 (1/5)	112.21 (1/30)	53.88 (3/13)	255.49 (9/14)	90.56 (9/14)	47.87 (6/22)

* Utilities were not computed until January 1, 1929.

	Annual Closing Highs				Annual Closing Lows		
	Ind.	Rail-Trans.	Util.*		Ind.	Rail-Trans.	Util.*
1954	404.39 (12/31)	146.23 (12/29)	62.47 (12/31)	1954	279.87 (1/11)	94.84 (1/11)	52.22 (1/4)
1955	487.45 (9/23)	167.83 (11/25)	66.68 (7/26)	1955	388.20 (1/17)	137.84 (1/17)	61.39 (10/11)
1956	521.05 (4/6)	181.23 (5/9)	71.17 (8/7)	1956	462.35 (1/23)	150.44 (11/29)	63.03 (1/23)
1957	520.77 (7/12)	157.67 (1/10)	74.61 (5/21)	1957	419.79 (10/22)	95.67 (12/24)	62.10 (10/22)
1958	583.65 (12/31)	157.91 (11/19)	91.00 (12/31)	1958	436.89 (2/25)	99.89 (1/2)	68.94 (1/2)
1959	679.36 (12/31)	173.56 (7/8)	94.70 (3/18)	1959	574.46 (2/9)	146.65 (11/17)	85.05 (9/21)
1960	685.47 (1/5)	160.43 (1/5)	100.07 (12/29)	1960	566.05 (10/25)	123.37 (9/29)	85.02 (2/16)
1961	734.91 (12/13)	152.92 (10/11)	135.90 (11/20)	1961	610.25 (1/3)	131.06 (1/13)	99.75 (1/3)
1962	726.01 (1/3)	149.83 (2/2)	130.85 (3/19)	1962	535.76 (6/26)	114.86 (10/1)	103.11 (6/25)
1963	767.21 (12/18)	179.46 (12/18)	144.37 (8/23)	1963	646.79 (1/2)	142.03 (1/2)	129.19 (1/2)
1964	891.71 (11/18)	224.91 (10/26)	155.71 (11/20)	1964	766.08 (1/2)	178.81 (1/3)	137.30 (3/31)
1965	969.26 (12/31)	249.55 (12/17)	163.32 (4/20)	1965	840.59 (6/28)	187.29 (6/28)	149.84 (12/20)
1966	995.15 (2/9)	271.72 (2/15)	152.39 (1/12)	1966	744.32 (10/7)	184.34 (10/7)	118.96 (8/29)
1967	943.08 (9/25)	274.49 (8/4)	140.43 (4/20)	1967	786.41 (1/3)	205.16 (1/3)	120.97 (11/8)
1968	985.21 (12/3)	279.48 (12/2)	141.30 (11/19)	1968	825.13 (3/21)	214.58 (3/5)	119.79 (3/25)
1969	968.85 (5/14)	279.88 (2/7)	139.95 (1/31)	1969	769.93 (12/17)	169.03 (12/17)	106.31 (12/9)
1970	842.00 (12/29)	183.31 (1/5)	121.84 (12/31)	1970	631.16 (5/26)	116.69 (7/7)	95.86 (6/30)
1971	950.82 (4/28)	248.33 (9/7)	128.39 (1/19)	1971	797.97 (11/23)	169.70 (1/4)	108.03 (11/24)

* Utilities were not computed until January 1, 1929.

3. Annual Closing Highs-Lows (Monthly)

a. *Industrials*

Month	Highs					Lows				
January	1906 1907 1910 1913 1917 1920 1940 1941 1953 1960 1962				(11)	1905 1918 1922 1927 1936 1943 1945 1950 1951 1954 1955 1958 1961 1963 1964 1967				(16)
February	1903 1931 1934 1966				(4)	1908 1909 1912 1915 1919 1928 1933 1944 1959				(9)
March	1914 1923 1932 1937				(4)	1898 1904 1925 1926 1935 1938 1948 1968				(8)
April	1902 1930 1956 1971				(4)	1897 1916 1939 1942				(4)
May	1946 1969				(2)	1924 1947 1952 1970				(4)
June	1901 1911 1948				(3)	1913 1940 1949 1962 1965				(5)
July	1933 1943 1947 1957				(4)	1906 1910 1932 1934				(4)
August	1898 1926				(2)	1921				(1)
September	1897 1899 1912 1929 1939 1951 1967				(7)	1900 1911 1953				(3)
October	1918 1922				(2)	1923 1946 1957 1960 1966				(5)
November	1908 1909 1916 1919 1925 1935 1936 1938 1950 1964				(10)	1903 1907 1929 1937 1956 1971				(6)
December	1900 1904 1905 1915 1921 1924 1927 1928 1942 1944 1945 1949 1952 1954 1955 1958 1959 1961 1963 1965 1968 1970				(22)	1899 1901 1902 1914 1917 1920 1930 1931 1941 1969				(10)
					75					75

The Averages

b. Rail-Trans.

	Highs					*Lows*				
January	1903	1906	1907	1910		1901	1902	1918	1922	
	1913	1914	1917	1921		1927	1936	1943	1944	
	1932	1940	1949	1953		1945	1952	1954	1955	
	1957	1960	1970		(15)	1958	1961	1963	1964	
						1967	1971			(18)
February	1931	1934	1947	1951		1908	1909	1912	1915	
	1962	1966	1969		(7)	1920	1924	1928	1933	
						1948				(9)
March	1923	1930	1937		(3)	1904	1925	1926	1935	
						1938	1968			(6)
April	1899				(1)	1897	1898	1916	1939	(4)
May	1901	1919	1956		(3)	1905	1906	1940	1947	(4)
June	1946				(1)	1900	1913	1921	1942	
						1949	1950	1951	1965	(8)
July	1911	1933	1943	1948	(5)	1910	1932	1970		(3)
	1959									
August	1909	1941	1967		(3)	1923				(1)
September	1897	1902	1922	1926		1903	1911	1934	1953	
	1929	1939	1971		(7)	1960				(5)
October	1912	1916	1927	1936		1946	1962	1966		(3)
	1961	1964			(6)					
November	1915	1918	1920	1928		1907	1929	1956	1959	(4)
	1942	1955	1958		(7)					
December	1898	1900	1904	1905		1899	1914	1917	1919	
	1908	1924	1925	1935		1930	1931	1937	1941	
	1938	1944	1945	1950		1957	1969			(10)
	1952	1954	1963	1965						
	1968				(17)					
					75					75

c. Utilities *

	Highs					Lows				
January	1937	1940	1941	1942		1943	1944	1945	1949	
	1966	1969	1971		(7)	1951	1952	1954	1956	
						1958	1961	1963		(11)
February	1934	1947			(2)	1948	1960			(2)
March	1931	1953	1959	1962	(4)	1933	1935	1938	1964	
						1968				(5)
April	1930	1965	1967		(3)	1936	1939	1942		(3)
May	1946	1950	1957		(3)	1947				(1)
June	1948				(1)	1940	1953	1962	1970	(4)
July	1933	1943	1955		(3)	1932	1950			(2)
August	1939	1956	1963		(3)	1966				(1)
September	1929	1932			(2)	1959				(1)
October	1936	1938			(2)	1937	1946	1955	1957	(4)
November	1961	1964	1968		(3)	1929	1967	1971		(3)
December	1935	1944	1945	1949		1930	1931	1934	1941	
	1951	1952	1954	1958		1965	1969			(6)
	1960	1970			(10)					
					43					43

* Utility average was not computed until January 1, 1929.

4. Annual Trading Range (Points) *

Year	Inds.	Rail-Trans.	Utils.**	Year	Inds.	Rail-Trans.	Utils.
1897	17.33	19.11		1935	51.73	14.53	15.32
1898	18.97	19.10		1936	41.79	19.23	7.45
1899	19.34	14.56		1937	80.76	35.55	17.89
1900	18.08	22.00		1938	59.46	14.98	10.05
1901	16.74	25.20		1939	34.48	11.76	6.39
1902	8.87	17.63		1940	40.96	10.53	8.42
1903	24.55	32.48		1941	27.25	6.63	7.14
1904	26.82	28.15		1942	26.79	5.97	4.36
1905	27.80	19.02		1943	26.56	10.71	7.61
1906	17.82	18.06		1944	18.31	14.95	4.63
1907	43.37	50.54		1945	44.47	17.86	13.00
1908	29.76	34.01		1946	49.38	23.62	10.54
1909	20.62	20.56		1947	23.64	12.26	5.27
1910	24.72	24.31		1948	27.77	16.82	4.39
1911	14.12	14.06		1949	38.92	13.26	7.95
1912	14.00	9.43		1950	38.66	26.65	6.86
1913	16.46	17.60		1951	37.38	17.69	5.75
1914	30.26	22.03		1952	35.65	30.50	5.11
1915	44.99	20.43		1953	38.30	21.65	6.01
1916	25.19	13.17		1954	124.52	51.39	10.25
1917	33.23	35.01		1955	99.25	29.99	5.29
1918	15.69	15.70		1956	58.70	30.79	8.14
1919	40.47	17.50		1957	100.98	62.00	12.51
1920	43.13	7.54		1958	146.76	58.02	22.06
1921	17.60	12.04		1959	104.90	22.27	9.65
1922	24.84	20.56		1960	119.42	37.06	15.05
1923	19.62	13.85		1961	124.66	21.86	36.15
1924	32.18	19.27		1962	190.25	34.97	27.74
1925	44.39	19.95		1963	120.42	37.43	15.18
1926	31.44	20.92		1964	125.63	46.10	18.41
1927	49.67	25.53		1965	128.67	62.26	13.48
1928	108.67	20.10		1966	250.83	87.38	33.43
1929	182.48	61.04	79.89	1967	156.67	69.33	19.46
1930	136.56	66.29	53.48	1968	160.08	64.90	21.51
1931	120.57	80.16	42.85	1969	198.92	110.85	33.64
1932	47.56	28.07	19.58	1970	210.84	66.62	25.98
1933	58.51	33.10	18.40	1971	152.85	78.63	20.36
1934	21.04	19.78	14.20				

* Based on closing prices.
** Utility average was not computed until January 1, 1929.

5. Review of Over-all Action

a. Industrial Average

Year	Net Adv.	%	Net Dec.	%	Ad-vances	De-clines	Unch.	Tot. Ses-sions
1897	8.67	21.3			164	134	3	302
1898	11.11	22.4			151	145	2	298
1899	5.56	9.2			163	132	1	296
1900	4.63	7.0			151	144	5	300
1901			6.15	8.7	149	141	3	293
1902			0.27	0.4	155	137	6	298
1903			15.18	23.6	139	158	1	298
1904	20.50	41.7			173	124	3	300
1905	26.59	38.2			171	127	3	301
1906			1.85	1.9	157	147	0	304
1907			35.60	37.7	129	171	1	301
1908	27.40	46.6			174	127	0	301
1909	12.90	15.0			163	128	5	296
1910			17.69	17.9	156	139	2	297
1911	0.32	0.4			143	153	2	298
1912	6.19	7.6			163	136	2	301
1913			9.09	10.3	130	165	3	298
1914			24.20	30.7	93	95	3	191
1915	44.57	81.7			181	120	1	302
1916			4.15	4.2	154	143	4	301
1917			20.62	21.7	140	157	1	298
1918	7.82	10.5			145	150	2	297
1919	25.03	30.5			166	126	1	293
1920			35.28	32.9	139	159	1	299
1921	9.85	13.7			152	145	1	298
1922	17.63	21.7			165	133	2	300
1923			3.21	3.3	155	143	2	300
1924	24.99	26.2			177	122	3	302
1925	36.15	30.0			178	123	0	301
1926	0.54	0.3			167	132	0	299
1927	45.20	28.8			183	115	3	301
1928	97.60	48.2			175	120	0	295
1929			51.52	17.2	155	135	1	291
1930			83.90	33.8	159	137	2	298
1931			86.68	52.7	123	177	0	300
1932			17.97	23.1	139	163	0	302
1933	38.74	64.6			146	138	1	285
1934	5.37	5.4			147	154	0	301

Year	Net Adv.	%	Net Dec.	%	Ad-vances	De-clines	Unch.	Tot. Ses-sions
1935	40.09	38.5			176	125	0	301
1936	35.77	24.8			167	133	1	301
1937			59.05	32.2	149	149	1	299
1938	33.91	28.1			153	147	1	301
1939			4.52	2.9	149	150	1	300
1940			19.11	12.7	158	140	4	302
1941			20.17	15.3	138	162	1	301
1942	8.44	7.6			168	130	3	301
1943	16.49	13.8			166	132	3	301
1944	16.43	12.1			171	121	6	298
1945	40.59	26.6			163	122	1	286
1946			15.71	8.1	136	145	0	281
1947	3.96	2.2			147	136	0	283
1948			3.86	2.1	153	127	3	283
1949	22.83	12.9			148	132	2	282
1950	35.28	17.6			164	114	3	281
1951	33.82	14.4			145	134	4	283
1952	22.67	8.4			147	122	2	271
1953			11.00	3.8	128	123	0	251
1954	123.49	44.0			159	91	2	252
1955	84.01	20.08			156	96	0	252
1956	11.07	2.3			126	124	1	251
1957			63.78	12.8	123	126	3	252
1958	147.96	34.0			145	106	1	252
1959	95.71	16.4			144	107	2	253
1960			63.47	9.3	119	132	1	252
1961	115.25	18.7			135	115	0	250
1962			79.04	10.8	118	132	2	252
1963	110.85	17.0			142	108	1	251
1964	111.18	14.6			146	103	0	249
1965	95.13	10.9			140	110	2	252
1966			183.57	18.9	114	137	1	252
1967	119.42	15.2			131	118	2	251
1968	38.64	4.3			117	108	1	226
1969			143.39	15.2	120	129	1	250
1970	38.56	4.8			126	126	2	254
1971	51.28	6.1			132	120	1	253
					11,189	9,927	129	21,246

b. Rail-Trans.

Year	Net Adv.	%	Net Dec.	%	Advances	Declines	Unch.	Tot. Sessions
1897	10.58	20.5			165	136	0	302
1898	12.70	20.4			162	132	4	298
1899	2.74	3.7			159	135	2	296
1900	17.26	22.2			163	134	3	300
1901	19.86	20.9			167	121	5	293
1902	4.13	4.5			163	132	3	298
1903			20.65	17.4	137	159	2	298
1904	19.10	19.4			173	122	5	300
1905	15.83	13.5			167	134	0	301
1906			3.46	2.6	155	148	1	304
1907			41.03	31.6	134	164	3	301
1908	31.28	35.2			174	127	0	301
1909	10.36	8.6			158	134	4	296
1910			16.35	12.5	149	144	4	297
1911	2.77	2.4			147	146	5	298
1912	0.01			unch.	154	145	2	301
1913			13.12	11.2	127	170	1	298
1914			15.19	14.6	86	102	3	191
1915	19.52	22.0			151	149	2	302
1916			2.90	2.7	143	155	3	301
1917			25.42	24.2	138	157	3	298
1918	4.59	5.8			148	145	4	297
1919			9.02	10.7	138	150	5	293
1920	0.66	0.8			139	157	3	299
1921			1.69	2.1	147	149	2	298
1922	11.84	15.9			162	132	6	300
1923			5.25	6.1	157	142	1	300
1924	17.47	21.7			166	136	0	302
1925	14.60	14.8			160	136	5	301
1926	7.93	7.0			153	142	4	299
1927	19.44	16.1			162	137	2	301
1928	10.84	7.7			158	136	1	295
1929			6.42	4.2	150	138	3	291
1930			48.14	33.3	128	169	1	298
1931			62.95	65.2	125	174	1	300
1932			7.73	23.0	133	166	3	302
1933	14.52	56.1			137	145	3	285
1934			3.98	9.8	148	152	1	301
1935	4.04	11.1			151	149	1	301
1936	13.15	32.5			158	139	4	301
1937			24.17	45.1	147	149	3	299

Year	Net Adv.	%	Net Dec.	%	Ad-vances	De-clines	Unch.	Tot. Ses-sions
1938	4.52	15.3			142	152	7	301
1939			2.15	6.3	143	157	0	300
1940			3.70	11.7	155	138	9	302
1941			2.71	9.6	146	145	10	301
1942	1.97	7.7			139	153	9	301
1943	6.17	22.5			161	138	2	301
1944	14.84	44.2			176	119	3	298
1945	14.40	29.8			161	122	3	286
1946			11.67	18.6	131	146	4	281
1947	1.35	2.6			133	143	7	283
1948	0.38	0.7			150	132	1	283
1949			0.10	.2	145	134	3	282
1950	24.88	47.2			152	126	3	281
1951	4.06	5.2			138	139	6	283
1952	29.57	36.2			146	124	1	271
1953			17.24	15.5	115	136	0	251
1954	51.83	55.1			141	110	1	252
1955	17.43	11.9			137	112	3	252
1956			10.06	6.2	114	137	0	251
1957			61.42	40.1	106	144	2	252
1958	60.69	62.6			132	120	0	252
1959			3.60	2.3	116	135	2	253
1960			23.20	15.1	109	138	5	252
1961	12.99	9.9			119	130	1	250
1962			2.80	1.9	120	130	2	252
1963	37.50	26.6			138	111	2	251
1964	26.80	15.0			141	105	3	249
1965	42.14	20.5			137	115	0	252
1966			44.51	18.0	123	129	0	252
1967	30.27	14.9			130	117	4	251
1968	38.36	16.4			111	112	3	226
1969			95.26	35.1	95	150	5	250
1970			4.82	2.7	125	128	1	254
1971	72.20	42.1			142	110	1	253
					10,708	10,326	211	21,246

c. Utilities

Year	Net Adv.	%	Net Dec.	%	Ad-vances	De-clines	Unch.	Tot. Ses-sions
1929 *	2.63	3.1			163	124	3	291
1930			27.47	31.1	154	142	2	298
1931			29.39	48.3	130	169	1	300
1932			3.91	12.4	133	166	3	302
1933			4.21	15.3	128	154	3	285
1934			5.49	23.6	120	176	5	301
1935	11.75	66.0			155	133	13	301
1936	5.28	17.9			152	147	2	301
1937			14.48	41.6	131	164	4	299
1938	2.67	13.1			139	162	0	301
1939	2.56	11.1			154	137	9	300
1940			5.73	22.4	142	150	10	302
1941			5.83	29.4	145	148	8	301
1942	0.52	3.7			147	143	11	301
1943	7.33	50.4			165	130	6	301
1944	4.50	20.6			166	124	8	298
1945	11.76	44.6			177	103	6	286
1946			0.86	2.3	152	125	4	281
1947			3.87	10.4	133	142	8	283
1948	0.15	0.4			153	121	9	283
1949	7.74	23.1			151	115	16	282
1950			0.31	0.8	152	121	8	281
1951	6.24	15.2			152	125	6	283
1952	5.38	11.4			146	115	10	271
1953			0.56	1.1	137	110	4	251
1954	10.43	20.0			150	96	6	252
1955	1.69	2.7			147	102	3	252
1956	4.38	6.8			131	117	3	251
1957	0.04	unch.			130	121	1	252
1958	22.42	32.7			161	85	6	252
1959			3.17	3.5	123	122	8	253
1960	12.19	13.7			145	104	3	252
1961	29.14	29.1			152	95	3	250
1962	0.07	unch.			136	112	4	252
1963	9.76	7.6			137	110	4	251
1964	16.18	11.6			134	106	9	249
1965			2.54	1.6	124	124	4	252
1966			16.45	10.8	100	145	7	252
1967			8.27	6.1	115	133	3	251
1968	9.26	7.2			101	122	3	226
1969			27.09	27.0	105	142	3	250
1970	11.76	10.7			125	124	5	254
1971			4.09	3.4	113	134	6	253
					6,006	5,540	240	11,787

* Utilities were not computed until 1929.

B. RECORDS OF THE DOW

1. Trading Sessions

Number of Trading Sessions (1897–1971)   21,246

Number of Advancing Sessions (Industrials)   11,189
Number of Declining Sessions (Industrials)   9,927

Number of Advancing Sessions (Rail-Trans.)   10,708
Number of Declining Sessions (Rail-Trans.)   10,326

Number of Advancing Sessions (Utilities) *   6,006
Number of Declining Sessions (Utilities) *   5,540
Number of Trading Sessions (1929–1971) *   11,787

Industrials Closed Unchanged   129
Rail-Trans. Closed Unchanged   211
Utilities Closed Unchanged   240

* Utility Average was not computed until January 1, 1929.

2. Monthly Record

	Industrials		Rail-Trans.		Utilities	
	Up	Down	Up	Down	Up	Down
January	48	27	47	28	26	16 **
February	37	38	34	41	22	21
March	44	31	42	33	22	20 **
April	41	34	38	37	21	22
May	38	37	40	35	19	23 **
June	36	39	41	34	22	21
July	50	25	50	25	28	15
August	52	22	45	28 *	27	16
September	33	41	30	44	18	25
October	40	34	37	37	25	18
November	43	31	39	35	21	22
December	54	21	45	30	28	15
	516	380	488	407	279	234

* Rail-Trans. Average closed unchanged from preceding month in August, 1968.
** Utility Average closed unchanged from preceding month in January, 1942; March, 1969; May, 1956.

3. Daily Advances-Declines

	Industrials		Rail-Trans.		Utilities	
	Up	Down	Up	Down	Up	Down
Monday	1,669	1,959	1,559	2,062	923	1,144
Tuesday	1,984	1,742	1,862	1,849	1,050	1,069
Wednesday	2,022	1,758	1,969	1,798	1,156	978
Thursday	1,944	1,778	1,893	1,807	1,123	994
Friday	2,107	1,604	2,032	1,676	1,172	933
Saturday *	1,463	1,086	1,393	1,134	582	422
	11,189	9,927	10,708	10,326	6,006	5,540

* N.Y. Stock Exchange has been closed on Saturdays since September 29, 1952.

Weekdays When Dow Averages Reached Closing Annual Highs-Lows

	Industrials		Rail-Trans.		Utilities	
	High	Low	High	Low	High	Low
Monday	12	18	14	21	6	12
Tuesday	16	21	8	17	9	14
Wednesday	14	12	13	12	9	8
Thursday	8	9	9	12	6	3
Friday	18	8	17	7	6	4
Saturday	7	7	14	6	7	2
	75	75	75	75	43	43

4. High-Low Records

a. Industrials

Record closing high (1897–1971) ...... 995.15 ...... February 9, 1966
Record closing low (1897–1971) ...... 38.49 ...... April 23, 1897

First time closed above 100 ...... June 12, 1906
First time closed above 200 ...... December 19, 1927
First time closed above 300 ...... January 2, 1929
First time closed above 400 ...... December 29, 1954
First time closed above 500 ...... March 12, 1956
First time closed above 600 ...... February 20, 1959
First time closed above 700 ...... May 17, 1961
First time closed above 800 ...... February 28, 1964
First time closed above 900 ...... January 28, 1965

First time carried above 1,000 (intraday) ...... January 18, 1966
Closed above 1929 high (381.17) ...... November 23, 1954
Closed above Rail-Transportation Average ...... November 15, 1916

b. Rail-Trans.

Record closing high (1897–1971) ...... 279.88 ...... February 7, 1969
Record closing low (1897–1971) ...... 13.23 ...... July 8, 1932

First time closed above 100 ...... March 13, 1901
First time closed above 150 ...... November 20, 1928
First time closed above 200 ...... May 12, 1964
First time closed above 250 ...... January 10, 1966

Closed above 1929 high (189.11) ...... February 25, 1964

c. Utilities

Record closing high (1929–1971) ...... 163.32 ...... April 20, 1965
Record closing low (1929–1971) ...... 10.58 ...... April 28, 1942

First time closed above 100 ...... June 6, 1929
First time closed above 125 ...... July 20, 1929
First time closed above 150 ...... August 3, 1964

Closed above 1929 high (144.61) ...... July 7, 1964

5. Biggest One-Day Advances-Declines (1900–1971)

	INDUSTRIALS						*RAIL-TRANS.*					
	Advances			*Declines*			*Advances*			*Declines*		
Year	*Pts.*	*%*	*Date*	*Pts.*	*%*	*Date*	*Pts.*	*%*	*Date*	*Pts.*	*%*	*Date*
1900	2.05	3.1	1/2	2.85	4.4	4/16	1.67	2.1	11/7	1.50	1.9	5/8
1901	4.29	6.4	5/10	4.34	6.1	5/9	6.69	6.5	5/10	8.25	7.3	5/9
1902	2.08	3.2	9/30	2.21	3.3	9/29	4.37	3.6	9/30	4.57	3.7	9/29
1903	2.16	5.1	10/16	2.18	4.1	8/19	2.78	2.8	6/11	3.16	2.8	4/13
1904	2.11	3.2	12/16	4.24	6.1	12/12	1.79	2.0	3/15	3.78	3.2	12/12
1905	2.49	2.9	11/27	2.73	3.4	4/27	2.64	2.1	8/11	3.16	2.5	4/27
1906	2.63	3.0	5/4	2.52	2.7	4/27	2.99	2.5	5/4	3.36	2.7	5/1
1907	2.39	3.2	3/26	6.89	8.3	3/14	6.24	6.2	3/15	7.81	7.3	3/14
1908	1.97	2.4	11/4	1.89	2.2	12/17	2.91	2.9	6/1	2.24	2.2	5/23
1909	1.81	2.1	1/7	2.91	3.5	2/23	2.82	2.2	9/10	3.25	2.8	2/23
1910	2.45	3.0	6/7	3.04	3.4	2/7	2.79	2.4	6/7	2.67	2.1	1/14
1911	2.28	2.9	11/9	2.32	3.0	10/27	1.73	1.5	5/16	2.16	2.6	2/24
1912	1.65	1.8	11/6	2.01	2.2	7/5	2.03	1.7	11/6	1.82	1.4	5/3
1913	2.17	3.0	6/12	4.20	4.9	1/20	2.68	2.7	6/12	1.86	1.7	6/2
1914	2.04	3.7	12/14	16.70	23.4	12/12	2.08	2.3	12/14	4.71	5.0	7/30
1915	2.58	4.2	5/11	3.10	4.5	5/7	2.50	2.8	7/27	1.80	1.9	5/7
1916	4.93	5.5	12/22	5.10	5.4	12/21	2.38	2.3	12/22	3.40	3.1	10/5
1917	3.03	3.2	2/3	6.91	7.2	2/1	6.41	9.0	12/27	3.40	3.3	2/1
1918	2.82	3.7	1/31	2.51	3.1	5/27	2.16	2.4	11/7	2.88	3.3	9/3
1919	3.72	3.7	6/17	5.17	4.8	8/4	2.33	2.9	11/14	3.41	3.9	8/4
1920	3.12	4.3	11/22	3.85	4.2	5/19	3.15	4.5	2/17	3.24	4.0	11/12
1921	3.93	5.0	5/2	2.35	3.5	6/20	2.42	3.6	4/15	2.33	3.4	6/20
1922	2.27	2.4	11/2	2.47	2.6	6/12	2.92	3.4	7/6	1.87	2.0	10/30
1923	2.62	3.0	10/31	2.69	3.0	7/27	1.79	2.2	5/24	3.64	4.3	5/7
1924	2.49	2.1	12/31	3.42	3.4	2/15	2.17	2.4	11/7	1.77	2.2	1/15
1925	2.86	1.9	11/25	5.83	3.7	11/10	2.35	2.2	11/13	1.69	1.7	3/23
1926	6.32	4.4	3/4	4.15	2.7	10/15	3.14	3.0	3/4	2.74	2.6	3/30
1927	5.65	3.0	9/6	7.21	3.7	10/8	2.85	2.0	12/2	2.68	2.0	10/28
1928	9.81	3.5	11/22	13.72	5.1	12/8	2.85	2.1	6/13	3.29	2.2	12/6
1929	28.40	12.3	10/30	38.33	12.8	10/28	7.68	6.0	11/14	10.91	6.6	10/28
1930	10.13	4.6	6/19	14.20	5.8	6/16	3.88	4.0	12/19	4.40	3.0	5/1
1931	12.86	14.9	10/6	8.20	7.1	9/24	7.59	11.4	9/23	6.28	10.2	9/24
1932	7.67	11.4	9/21	5.79	8.4	8/12	4.13	11.6	2/13	3.94	11.8	10/5
1933	8.26	15.3	3/15	7.55	7.8	7/21	4.43	17.9	3/15	4.74	9.6	7/21
1934	4.53	4.6	1/15	6.06	6.6	7/26	2.64	6.3	1/15	3.30	8.8	7/26
1935	2.86	2.0	12/3	3.45	2.6	10/2	1.88	5.8	2/18	1.55	4.5	10/2
1936	3.99	2.3	11/4	4.88	3.2	4/27	1.66	3.3	7/14	1.92	4.3	4/27
1937	7.71	6.1	10/20	10.57	7.8	10/18	2.56	8.5	10/20	3.06	6.5	9/7
1938	5.75	5.2	4/9	6.07	5.3	3/25	2.14	9.5	6/23	2.04	9.3	3/25
1939	10.03	7.3	9/5	5.44	3.7	1/23	2.78	10.7	9/5	2.33	8.0	3/31
1940	5.77	4.4	11/7	9.36	6.8	5/14	1.47	6.2	6/12	1.98	6.6	5/13
1941	3.76	3.5	12/30	4.08	3.5	12/8	1.03	3.5	7/21	1.51	5.6	12/8

| | INDUSTRIALS | | | | | | RAIL-TRANS. | | | | | |
| | Advances | | | Declines | | | Advances | | | Declines | | |
Year	Pts.	%	Date	Pts.	%	Date	Pts.	%	Date	Pts.	%	Date
1942	2.18	2.1	7/8	2.45	2.3	3/6	1.24	4.9	1/2	0.72	2.9	4/14
1943	2.60	2.0	3/25	4.30	3.2	4/9	1.07	3.1	4/5	1.75	5.2	11/8
1944	1.76	1.2	12/28	2.14	1.5	9/6	1.20	2.6	12/14	1.36	3.4	9/6
1945	3.10	1.9	8/23	3.39	2.0	7/17	1.70	2.7	11/15	2.31	3.7	6/28
1946	6.08	3.6	10/15	10.51	5.6	9/3	2.42	5.2	10/31	4.68	8.2	9/3
1947	3.58	2.1	6/11	5.07	3.0	4/14	1.29	3.0	6/11	1.73	3.4	3/7
1948	3.78	2.0	5/14	7.30	3.8	11/3	2.33	3.9	5/14	3.45	5.6	11/3
1949	3.14	1.8	1/6	3.38	1.9	9/20	1.36	3.0	9/13	1.83	4.0	5/31
1950	4.56	2.0	12/27	10.44	4.7	6/26	2.44	3.6	10/2	3.46	6.2	6/26
1951	4.51	2.0	1/2	5.13	1.9	10/22	2.25	2.8	4/5	2.72	3.5	6/25
1952	3.87	1.5	3/4	3.98	1.5	2/19	2.90	3.0	6/4	2.27	2.3	10/15
1953	3.71	1.4	10/15	5.93	2.1	4/6	6.02	6.6	12/17	4.78	5.0	12/16
1954	7.54	2.1	11/3	6.96	2.1	6/8	3.04	2.2	12/16	3.56	3.2	6/8
1955	10.37	2.3	9/27	31.89	6.4	9/26	4.41	2.7	11/25	11.15	6.8	9/26
1956	8.87	1.9	5/29	8.48	1.6	4/10	4.12	2.5	5/29	3.96	2.4	5/28
1957	17.34	4.1	10/23	13.04	2.9	11/26	5.91	5.5	10/23	6.28	5.5	10/21
1958	8.63	1.6	11/26	14.68	2.6	11/24	3.81	2.8	9/19	4.58	3.0	11/24
1959	9.72	1.5	12/8	14.78	2.2	8/10	4.73	3.0	8/20	3.10	1.9	8/10
1960	11.06	1.8	7/29	9.32	1.5	3/3	3.25	2.1	1/5	3.92	2.7	3/3
1961	11.24	1.8	1/4	12.60	1.8	4/24	5.40	3.7	10/4	2.22	1.5	3/23
1962	27.03	4.7	5/29	34.95	5.7	5/28	4.66	3.7	5/31	6.88	5.3	5/28
1963	32.03	4.5	11/26	21.16	2.9	11/22	4.39	2.6	11/26	3.28	1.9	11/22
1964	7.63	0.9	8/11	11.00	1.3	12/1	4.42	2.2	5/20	3.40	1.6	11/9
1965	16.63	2.0	6/30	13.77	1.6	6/28	4.95	2.6	6/30	3.53	1.8	7/20
1966	19.54	2.6	10/12	16.32	1.9	7/25	5.40	2.4	5/18	5.62	2.2	3/14
1967	14.94	1.8	6/6	15.54	1.8	6/5	5.36	2.2	6/1	8.79	3.2	8/8
1968	20.58	2.4	4/1	13.60	1.5	7/22	5.53	2.1	6/7	3.59	1.4	7/22
1969	16.08	1.7	4/30	15.23	1.6	1/6	4.16	2.4	12/24	4.50	2.3	11/24
1970	32.04	5.1	5/27	20.81	3.1	5/25	8.22	6.2	5/27	5.38	3.9	5/25
1971	32.93	3.8	8/16	17.09	1.9	6/18	10.99	5.1	8/16	5.89	2.6	11/1

Industrials

Biggest Daily Gains (Points)	*Reasons*
32.93 – August 16, 1971	Nixon revealed Phase I of new economic program.
32.04 – May 27, 1970	Market more confident after Nixon conferred with 40 business leaders.
32.03 – November 26, 1963	Relief from worry about consequences of JFK's assassination.
28.40 – October 30, 1929	Technical recovery after panic-type selling smash.
27.03 – May 29, 1962	Snapback rally, following a 73.77 (11.3%) drop in 6 previous trading sessions.

Biggest Daily Losses (Points)	*Reasons*
38.33 – October 28, 1929	A day in the 1929 panic.
34.95 – May 28, 1962	Climax selling extended the drop triggered by JFK's remarks about steel industry.
31.89 – September 26, 1955	Eisenhower's heart attack.
30.57 – October 29, 1929	16.4 million shares traded in selling avalanche.
25.55 – November 6, 1929	Renewed panic liquidation.

Rail-Trans.

Biggest Daily Gains (Points)	*Reasons*
10.99 – August 16, 1971	Bullish interpretation of Nixon's Phase I announcement.
8.22 – May 27, 1970	Both Dow Averages recover from oversold positions around their May lows.
7.68 – November 14, 1929	Discount rate cut spurred technical recovery.
7.59 – September 23, 1931	NYSE lifted ban on short selling.
6.69 – May 10, 1901	General market (Rails, especially) rebounded after Northern Pacific Panic of May 9.

Biggest Daily Losses (Points)	*Reasons*
11.15 – September 26, 1955	The one-day "Heart Attack" sell off.
10.91 – October 28, 1929	Part of the 1929 panic.
10.73 – November 6, 1929	Another day of panic selling.
8.79 – August 8, 1967	Profit taking, after posting new high for 1967 on August 4.
8.54 – November 12, 1929	Further evidence of the 1929 debacle.

Industrials

Biggest Daily Gain (Percentage)	*Reasons*
15.3% – March 15, 1933	End of the banking holiday.

Biggest Daily Loss (Percentage)	Market reopened after being closed since
23.4% – December 12, 1914	July 30 because of war.

Rail-Trans.

Biggest Daily Gain (Percentage)	*Reasons*
17.9% – March 15, 1933	End of the banking holiday.

Biggest Daily Loss (Percentage)	Pre-election profit taking, after scoring
11.8% – October 5, 1932	good gains from rock-bottom depression closing lows: Industrials, 41.22; Rails, 13.23.

Utilities

Year	Advances			Declines		
	Pts.	%	Date	Pts.	%	Date
1929 *	13.44	18.1	10/30	17.79	17.0	10/28
1930	4.30	5.4	6/19	5.70	6.4	6/16
1931	4.60	13.2	10/6	3.36	7.4	9/24
1932	3.59	12.2	9/21	2.33	7.3	10/5
1933	3.38	15.9	4/20	3.28	9.1	7/20
1934	1.81	7.4	1/15	1.32	4.3	2/7
1935	1.11	4.6	8/3	1.33	5.0	8/24
1936	1.13	3.7	3/14	1.19	3.9	4/27
1937	2.00	10.2	10/20	1.49	5.5	9/7
1938	1.33	7.2	5/6	1.00	4.6	7/27
1939	0.99	4.8	1/14	1.38	6.0	3/31
1940	1.10	5.1	6/24	1.77	7.6	11/6
1941	0.60	3.2	2/28	0.89	5.5	12/8
1942	0.45	4.1	5/1	0.66	4.9	3/5
1943	0.62	3.4	4/14	0.97	4.6	11/8
1944	0.56	2.6	1/4	0.62	2.5	9/6
1945	1.01	3.6	4/13	0.93	2.4	12/17
1946	1.15	3.2	9/5	2.71	6.9	9/3
1947	0.58	1.6	1/17	0.78	2.1	3/7
1948	0.55	1.6	8/17	1.46	4.1	11/3
1949	0.47	1.4	1/6	0.44	1.3	2/5
1950	0.96	2.5	12/21	1.64	3.7	6/26
1951	0.55	1.3	3/16	0.48	1.1	3/13
1952	0.82	1.7	2/18	1.01	2.1	2/16
1953	0.68	1.3	4/8	0.96	1.8	4/6
1954	1.16	2.0	11/3	0.69	1.2	6/8
1955	0.68	1.1	3/3	2.46	3.8	9/26
1956	1.01	1.6	2/6	0.78	1.2	5/28
1957	1.45	2.3	10/23	1.67	2.6	10/21
1958	1.04	1.2	12/29	1.26	1.5	11/25
1959	1.09	1.2	2/10	1.35	1.6	6/9
1960	0.81	0.9	6/7	1.35	1.5	10/24
1961	1.88	1.5	10/19	1.76	1.3	12/20
1962	5.38	5.2	5/29	8.22	7.3	5/28
1963	1.52	1.1	11/26	1.95	1.4	11/22
1964	1.06	0.7	10/16	1.19	0.8	10/15
1965	3.22	2.1	6/30	1.88	1.2	6/28
1966	2.54	1.9	10/18	2.54	2.0	8/22
1967	1.25	0.9	1/6	1.57	1.3	11/20
1968	3.26	2.5	6/20	2.01	1.6	3/14
1969	2.49	2.2	10/14	1.69	1.3	7/22
1970	2.87	2.4	3/25	1.92	1.7	4/23
1971	2.14	1.9	8/16	1.73	1.5	5/25

* Utilities were not computed until 1929.

Dow Utilities

Biggest Daily Gains (Points)	*Reasons*
13.44 – October 30, 1929	Sharp technical rebound, following loss of 31.93 in three straight days.
8.85 – November 14, 1929	Another rebound following 16.69 drop in four sessions.
7.59 – October 31, 1929	An extension of the preceding day's recovery.
6.29 – October 5, 1929	Snapback recovery after losing 10.42 in two days.
5.38 – May 29, 1962	Technical recovery in a bear market.

Biggest Daily Losses (Points)	*Reasons*
17.79 – October 28, 1929	Panic liquidation.
12.65 – October 29, 1929	Extension of previous day's drop.
10.92 – November 6, 1929	Downdrive resumed after late October recovery.
8.75 – October 3, 1929	The first big fall after reaching 1929 closing high of 144.61 in September.
8.22 – May 28, 1962	Culmination of a spring selling drive that carried from a high of 125.57 (5/2) to a closing low for the month reached this day at 104.35.

6. Biggest Monthly Advances-Declines

Year	INDUSTRIALS						RAIL-TRANS.					
	Advances			Declines			Advances			Declines		
	Month	Pts.	%	Month	Pts.	%	Month	Pts.	%	Month	Pts.	%
1900	Nov.	7.55	12.8	Apr.	4.69	7.1	Nov.	9.33	11.7	June	4.66	5.9
1901	Apr.	5.88	8.0	Sept.	6.81	9.3	Apr.	11.32	10.8	July	9.82	8.4
1902	Mar.	2.38	3.8	Nov.	4.01	6.1	July	5.47	4.5	Nov.	4.20	3.5
1903	Dec.	4.78	10.7	July	8.32	14.1	Dec.	4.53	4.8	Sept.	8.30	8.5
1904	Nov.	8.99	14.0	Dec.	2.41	3.3	Nov.	5.57	4.9	Feb.	5.62	5.6
1905	Dec.	6.31	7.0	Apr.	3.94	4.9	July	3.71	3.0	Apr.	7.08	5.7
1906	July	5.40	6.2	Feb.	6.75	6.7	Aug.	6.09	4.7	Apr.	8.67	6.5
1907	Apr.	4.15	5.2	Mar.	10.39	11.5	June	4.14	4.1	Oct.	14.33	14.6
1908	July	7.75	10.7	Sept.	4.73	5.6	Nov.	7.53	6.9	Feb.	5.67	6.2
1909	July	4.51	4.9	Nov.	3.05	3.1	Mar.	5.28	4.5	Nov.	3.56	2.7
1910	Oct.	5.05	6.3	Jan.	7.14	7.2	Aug.	2.91	2.7	June	7.99	6.7
1911	Nov.	5.18	6.8	Aug.	6.77	7.9	Jan.	4.76	4.2	Aug.	10.09	8.2
1912	Mar.	6.87	8.4	Dec.	3.53	3.9	Mar.	3.53	3.1	Dec.	3.91	3.2
1913	July	3.59	4.8	Jan.	4.15	4.7	July	2.16	2.1	Feb.	4.55	3.9
1914	Jan.	4.07	5.2	Dec.	16.84	23.6	Jan.	5.71	5.5	July	13.00	12.7
1915	Apr.	10.95	18.0	May	7.11	9.9	Oct.	9.11	9.3	May	5.29	5.4
1916	Sept.	10.65	11.5	Dec.	10.97	10.4	Sept.	5.00	4.8	Jan.	7.30	6.8
1917	May	4.15	4.5	Oct.	9.31	11.1	Dec.	3.93	4.9	Oct.	6.94	8.0
1918	Jan.	5.42	7.3	Nov.	4.38	5.1	May	4.20	5.3	Dec.	2.76	3.2
1919	May	12.62	13.6	Nov.	15.32	13.0	May	6.05	7.2	Aug.	5.29	6.1

INDUSTRIALS

RAIL-TRANS.

Year	Advances			Declines			Advances			Declines		
	Month	Pts.	%	Month	Pts.	%	Month	Pts.	%	Month	Pts.	%
1920	Mar.	11.50	12.6	Feb.	12.51	12.0	Aug.	4.47	6.1	Nov.	5.07	6.1
1921	Jan.	4.18	5.8	May	5.40	6.8	Nov.	3.77	5.2	Feb.	2.85	3.7
1922	Feb.	4.16	5.1	Sept.	4.48	4.4	July	4.53	5.4	Nov.	4.69	5.3
1923	Aug.	6.55	7.5	June	9.68	9.9	Feb.	3.30	3.8	June	6.19	7.5
1924	Dec.	9.13	8.2	Mar.	4.21	4.3	Nov.	7.07	7.9	Feb.	1.09	1.3
1925	Oct.	13.06	9.1	Mar.	5.96	4.9	Dec.	5.41	5.0	Mar.	5.94	5.9
1926	June	9.61	6.7	Mar.	13.99	9.1	Aug.	5.04	4.3	Oct.	3.66	3.0
1927	Nov.	16.48	9.1	Oct.	15.86	8.0	July	7.54	5.6	Oct.	7.78	5.5
1928	Nov.	41.22	16.3	June	9.26	4.2	Nov.	10.12	7.1	June	5.89	4.1
1929	June	36.38	12.2	Oct.	69.94	20.4	Aug.	15.33	8.8	Sept.	14.98	7.9
1930	Jan.	18.66	7.5	June	48.73	17.7	Mar.	4.94	3.2	Apr.	12.20	7.8
1931	Feb.	22.11	13.2	Sept.	42.80	30.7	June	12.30	16.9	May	16.08	18.2
1932	Aug.	18.90	34.8	May	11.37	20.3	Aug.	14.79	68.0	Apr.	8.13	27.4
1933	Apr.	22.26	40.0	Feb.	9.51	15.6	May	10.05	31.0	Sept.	11.51	21.9
1934	Nov.	9.58	10.3	July	7.67	8.0	Jan.	8.97	21.9	July	9.30	21.1
1935	Apr.	8.64	8.6	Jan.	2.65	2.5	Nov.	4.59	13.3	Feb.	3.38	10.0
1936	Oct.	9.37	5.6	Apr.	10.67	6.8	Jan.	5.72	14.1	Apr.	3.65	7.8
1937	July	16.29	9.6	Sept.	22.84	12.9	Mar.	3.72	6.4	Sept.	8.35	16.8
1938	June	26.14	24.3	Mar.	30.69	23.7	June	5.71	28.1	Mar.	10.90	36.5
1939	Sept.	18.13	13.5	Mar.	15.46	10.5	Sept.	9.51	36.4	Mar.	6.10	18.8
1940	June	5.65	4.9	May	32.21	21.7	June	3.03	13.5	May	7.54	24.6
1941	June	7.38	6.4	Oct.	9.00	7.1	July	2.20	7.7	Dec.	1.54	5.7
1942	May	5.53	5.8	Mar.	7.26	6.8	Jan.	2.82	11.1	Mar.	2.65	9.6
1943	May	6.58	4.9	Nov.	8.70	6.3	Feb.	2.85	9.8	Nov.	3.74	10.6

Year	Month			Month			Month			Month		
1944	June	6.14	4.3	Apr.	2.61	1.9	Dec.	5.52	12.9	Apr.	0.73	1.8
1945	Aug.	11.41	7.0	Mar.	5.99	3.7	Apr.	6.37	12.6	July	3.50	5.8
1946	Jan.	11.76	6.1	Sept.	16.77	8.9	Jan.	4.82	7.7	Sept.	9.57	16.7
1947	June	8.05	4.8	Apr.	6.56	3.7	Dec.	5.36	11.4	Apr.	3.42	7.0
1948	Oct.	10.32	5.8	July	8.13	4.3	Mar.	4.46	9.1	Nov.	9.43	15.4
1949	Dec.	8.58	4.5	Feb.	6.06	3.4	Dec.	4.65	9.7	Feb.	4.86	9.2
1950	Sept.	9.49	4.4	June	14.31	6.4	Dec.	9.11	13.3	June	4.04	7.2
1951	July	15.22	6.3	May	9.48	3.7	Jan.	8.94	11.5	June	7.25	9.1
1952	Nov.	14.43	5.4	Apr.	11.83	4.4	Mar.	9.49	11.2	Sept.	2.96	2.9
1953	Oct.	11.77	4.5	Aug.	14.16	5.1	Oct.	3.36	3.6	Aug.	10.23	9.7
1954	Nov.	34.63	9.8	Aug.	12.12	3.5	Dec.	14.39	10.9	Aug.	7.11	5.9
1955	Nov.	28.39	6.2	Oct.	11.75	2.5	Nov.	17.12	11.4	Oct.	5.52	3.6
1956	Mar.	28.14	5.8	May	38.07	7.4	Mar.	12.20	7.6	May	11.53	6.5
1957	Apr.	19.55	4.1	Sept.	28.05	5.8	July	3.33	2.3	Sept.	13.79	10.0
1958	Dec.	26.19	4.7	Feb.	10.10	2.2	Apr.	12.92	10.9	Feb.	6.09	5.6
1959	July	31.28	4.9	Sept.	32.73	4.9	Nov.	8.17	5.1	Sept.	6.05	3.7
1960	May	23.80	4.0	Jan.	56.74	8.4	Jan.	4.27	3.4	Sept.	11.30	8.3
1961	Jan.	32.31	5.3	Sept.	18.73	2.6	Nov.	10.86	8.3	June	5.44	3.8
1962	Nov.	59.53	10.1	June	52.08	8.5	Apr.	18.26	15.1	June	10.56	8.2
1963	Apr.	35.18	5.2	June	20.08	2.8	Sept.	10.86	7.1	July	6.70	3.9
1964	Aug.	36.89	4.4	Aug.	2.62	0.3	July	11.92	5.8	Aug.	11.55	5.3
1965	Sept.	37.48	4.2	June	50.01	5.4	Jan.	14.04	7.2	June	11.35	5.5
1966	Oct.	32.85	4.2	Aug.	58.97	7.0	Jan.	14.21	5.7	May	26.40	10.4
1967	Jan.	64.20	8.2	Oct.	46.92	5.1	May	25.04	12.3	Oct.	24.38	9.3
1968	Apr.	71.55	8.5	Jan.	49.64	5.5	Aug.	18.66	7.9	July	10.66	4.1
1969	Oct.	42.90	5.3	June	64.37	6.9	Dec.	5.30	2.7	June	21.41	9.1
1970	July	50.59	7.4	Jan.	56.30	7.0	Aug.	18.16	11.8	June	23.89	16.5
1971	Dec.	58.86	7.1	Oct.	48.19	5.0	Aug.	33.12	16.1	July	9.21	4.3

Industrials

Biggest monthly advance (pts.)......71.55......April, 1968
Biggest monthly advance (%)........40.0........April, 1933

Biggest monthly decline (pts.).......69.94......October, 1929
Biggest monthly decline (%).........30.7........September, 1931

Rail-Trans.

Biggest monthly advance (pts.)......33.12......August, 1971
Biggest monthly advance (%)........68.0........August, 1932

Biggest monthly decline (pts.).......26.40......May, 1966
Biggest monthly decline (%).........36.5........March, 1938

Utilities *

	Advances			Declines		
Year	Month	Pts.	%	Month	Pts.	%
1929	June	21.55	22.2	Oct.	44.27	31.7
1930	Feb.	8.41	9.1	June	20.16	19.6
1931	Feb.	9.20	14.7	Sept.	19.42	33.9
1932	Aug.	10.31	45.2	May	6.48	26.8
1933	Apr.	5.76	29.8	Sept.	5.25	17.0
1934	Jan.	3.76	16.1	July	3.86	16.2
1935	Oct.	2.50	9.9	Feb.	1.37	7.9
1936	Jan.	2.69	9.1	Apr.	2.74	8.6
1937	July	3.78	14.4	Sept.	3.23	11.8
1938	Oct.	4.91	25.3	Mar.	4.68	23.6
1939	July	2.98	13.0	Mar.	4.15	16.1
1940	June	3.77	20.0	May	6.20	24.7
1941	June	0.90	5.3	Apr.	1.79	9.1
1942	Oct.	1.89	15.4	Mar.	2.18	16.0
1943	Jan.	2.06	14.2	Nov.	1.12	5.1
1944	Aug.	1.39	5.8	Apr.	0.66	2.9
1945	Apr.	2.82	10.2	Mar.	0.83	2.9
1946	Jan.	3.12	8.2	Sept.	4.59	11.8
1947	June	1.36	4.1	Nov.	1.94	5.6
1948	May	1.75	5.1	Nov.	2.80	7.9
1949	Dec.	2.03	5.2	June	0.64	1.8
1950	Sept.	1.67	4.3	June	3.16	7.2
1951	July	2.78	6.6	Mar.	1.37	3.1
1952	Mar.	1.78	3.7	Apr.	1.78	3.5

	Advances			Declines		
Year	Month	Pts.	%	Month	Pts.	%
1953	Oct.	1.66	3.4	June	2.29	4.5
1954	Nov.	2.94	5.1	Oct.	3.23	5.3
1955	Nov.	2.55	4.0	Sept.	2.96	4.5
1956	July	3.77	5.6	Aug.	2.52	3.5
1957	Jan.	2.39	3.5	June	4.19	5.7
1958	Dec.	5.75	6.7	Aug.	1.61	2.2
1959	July	2.69	3.1	Sept.	3.20	3.5
1960	June	5.39	6.1	Sept.	4.41	4.6
1961	Oct.	7.63	6.2	Dec.	5.06	3.8
1962	July	9.04	8.3	May	13.42	10.6
1963	Jan.	6.44	4.2	Sept.	4.01	2.8
1964	July	6.49	4.5	Mar.	2.74	2.0
1965	Jan.	5.51	3.6	June	6.02	3.8
1966	Oct.	12.00	9.6	Aug.	11.09	8.4
1967	Dec.	3.39	2.7	Oct.	7.23	5.5
1968	June	9.58	7.8	Mar.	6.26	4.9
1969	Oct.	7.86	7.1	Nov.	7.63	6.4
1970	Feb.	10.06	9.6	Apr.	9.08	8.6
1971	Dec.	7.38	6.7	May	5.37	4.5

Biggest monthly advance (pts.) ...... 21.55 ...... June, 1929
Biggest monthly advance (%) ...... 45.2 ...... August, 1932

Biggest monthly decline (pts.) ...... 44.27 ...... October, 1929
Biggest monthly decline (%) ...... 33.9 ...... September, 1931

* Utilities were not computed until 1929.

7. Most Consecutive Advancing-Declining Days

a. Industrials

Year	No. of Days	Advances Dates	Pts.	%	No. of Days	Declines Dates	Pts.	%
1900	9	11/1–11/12	8.29	14.0	6	2/20–2/27	2.90	4.4
					6	4/27–5/3	2.03	3.2
1901	8	3/27–4/8	3.49	5.1	8	1/11–1/19	3.12	4.6
1902	6	7/14–7/19	1.59	2.5	8	11/1–11/11	5.10	7.7
	6	12/16–12/22	3.10	5.2				
1903	7	5/14–5/21	3.77	6.2	8	9/16–9/24	3.68	7.3
	7	8/10–8/17	6.50	11.6	8	10/7–10/15	4.98	10.5
1904	8	8/31–9/10	2.99	5.5	7	2/16–2/24	2.15	4.4
	8	10/7–10/15	4.48	7.8				
1905	9	2/10–2/21	3.25	4.4	6	1/19–1/25	2.22	3.1
	9	3/29–4/7	4.99	6.4	6	5/16–5/22	5.33	4.4
1906	7	5/4–5/11	6.96	8.1	6	6/12–6/18	3.72	4.0
1907	7	4/3–4/10	2.94	3.6	8	9/7–9/16	5.75	7.8
1908	7	7/1–7/9	3.78	5.2	5	11/18–11/23	1.52	1.7
	7	7/28–8/4	3.03	3.8	5	12/10–12/15	2.27	2.6
1909	8	4/30–5/7	3.37	3.8	6	2/16–2/23	6.81	7.9
1910	10	10/6–10/18	5.26	6.5	7	5/25–6/2	3.81	4.3
1911	7	4/24–5/1	2.82	3.5	7	9/18–9/23	5.25	6.7
	7	12/9–12/16	3.29	4.2				
1912	9	9/14–9/24	2.91	3.2	5	7/8–7/12	2.36	2.6
1913	6	12/19–12/26	3.07	4.1	8	5/26–6/5	4.81	6.0
1914	7	6/3–6/10	1.34	1.6	8	4/8–4/17	2.46	3.0
1915	9	7/20–7/29	4.95	7.0	9	2/13–2/24	3.61	6.2
1916	11	9/2–9/15	7.20	7.9	6	4/15–4/22	6.67	7.3
1917	7	3/13–3/20	3.17	3.3	6	4/3–4/10	5.86	4.0
	7	5/19–5/26	5.62	6.1	6	8/27–9/4	7.86	8.8
1918	5	6/11–6/15	2.28	2.9	8	11/16–11/23	4.32	5.0
	5	8/23–8/28	1.57	1.9				
	5	11/4–11/9	2.83	3.3				
1919	7	5/1–5/9	5.73	6.2	7	6/9–6/16	7.99	7.4
					7	11/5–11/12	12.47	10.4
1920	6	6/30–7/8	4.15	4.6	7	7/9–7/16	4.56	4.8
1921	11	10/18–10/29	4.47	6.4	8	5/6–5/14	2.84	3.5
1922	7	8/15–8/22	4.54	2.7	8	6/3–6/12	5.63	5.8
1923	6	2/1–2/7	3.62	3.7	8	10/22–10/27	2.07	2.4
	6	12/4–12/10	1.22	1.3				
1924	9	12/12–12/22	6.00	5.5	9	3/20–3/29	4.35	4.5
1925	8	7/11–7/18	3.67	2.8	4	1/23–1/27	2.07	1.7
					4	7/28–7/31	2.69	2.0
					4	12/15–12/18	2.03	1.3

		Advances					Declines		
Year	No. of Days	Dates	Pts.	%	No. of Days	Dates	Pts.	%
1926	8	5/20–5/28	6.27	4.6	8	2/23–3/3	16.49	10.2
1927	10	7/9–7/20	6.33	3.7	4	1/11–1/14	1.65	1.1
	10	7/22–8/2	7.80	4.4	4	10/19–10/22	7.54	4.0
					4	10/26–10/29	4.99	2.7
					4	12/5–12/8	3.76	1.9
1928	7	8/15–8/22	15.63	7.3	6	2/14–2/20	7.83	3.9
	7	11/5–11/13	15.73	6.2	6	6/6–6/12	15.15	7.0
1929	11	6/25–7/8	25.40	7.9	8	3/18–3/26	23.49	7.3
1930	8	1/18–1/27	14.60	5.9	6	9/24–9/30	21.85	9.6
1931	5	2/6–2/11	12.50	7.4	8	3/25–4/2	16.11	8.7
	5	2/18–2/24	15.81	8.8	8	5/12–5/20	13.82	9.1
	5	11/4–11/9	12.29	11.8				
1932	5	7/20–7/25	5.99	13.7	8	3/31–4/8	14.25	18.5
	5	7/27–8/1	5.90	12.0				
	5	8/3–8/8	14.55	27.4				
	5	12/5–12/9	5.75	10.3				
1933	7	6/5–6/12	6.73	7.5	5	3/17–3/22	6.09	9.7
1934	8	3/28–4/6	5.19	5.3	5	1/3–1/8	3.63	3.6
					5	4/21–4/26	2.99	2.8
					5	5/9–5/14	5.35	5.1
					5	7/19–7/24	7.25	7.4
					5	9/6–9/11	4.40	5.7
1935	8	6/7–6/15	5.63	5.0	6	2/19–2/26	4.93	4.6
1936	10	10/1–10/13	8.47	5.0	5	9/11–9/16	3.84	2.4
					5	12/16–12/21	6.12	3.4
1937	6	6/29–7/7	11.23	6.7	7	10/7–10/15	11.70	7.9
1938	11	6/14–6/25	20.07	17.9	8	1/21–1/29	12.19	9.2
1939	6	5/24–5/31	6.41	4.9	5	3/15–3/20	9.82	6.5
					5	8/16–8/21	8.48	6.0
1940	8	8/14–8/23	7.36	5.8	7	8/6–8/13	6.36	4.7
·1941	5	5/16–5/21	2.09	1.8	14	7/29–8/13	4.41	3.4
	5	6/7–6/12	4.98	4.2				
	5	7/2–7/8	4.79	3.9				
	5	12/24–12/30	4.98	4.7				
1942	8	8/10–8/18	2.65	2.5	5	1/6–1/10	3.68	3.2
1943	8	3/22–3/30	7.69	6.0	7	9/21–9/28	2.48	1.7
1944	11	4/25–5/6	3.87	2.9	5	9/5–9/9	3.85	2.6
1945	7	1/31–2/7	2.26	1.5	6	1/18–1/24	3.98	2.6
	7	4/10–4/18	7.73	5.0				
	7	9/5–9/12	5.09	2.9				
1946	8	7/24–8/2	8.88	4.5	8	10/22–10/30	7.73	4.5
1947	6	5/19–5/24	3.76	2.3	7	11/21–11/29	3.77	2.1
	6	10/9–10/16	4.76	2.7				
	6	11/14–11/20	3.17	1.8				
1948	10	5/6–5/17	9.50	5.3	7	11/22–11/30	6.22	3.5

205

	Advances				Declines			
Year	No. of Days	Dates	Pts.	%	No. of Days	Dates	Pts.	%
1949	6	6/29–7/7	5.26	3.2	6	2/2–2/8	6.68	4.1
					6	2/18–2/25	3.72	1.6
1950	9	1/26–2/4	6.74	3.4	5	2/10–2/16	2.11	1.0
					5	7/7–7/13	13.39	6.4
1951	8	4/25–5/2	8.94	3.5	6	6/18–6/25	8.73	3.4
					6	10/16–10/20	13.45	4.8
1952	6	1/16–1/22	4.94	1.8	6	4/1–4/7	6.08	2.3
	6	6/24–7/1	5.96	2.2	6	8/12–8/19	6.15	2.1
	6	7/28–8/4	2.16	0.8				
	6	10/30–11/7	8.01	3.0				
1953	7	6/30–7/8	3.93	1.5	6	2/4–2/11	8.62	3.0
1954	9	9/1–9/14	15.98	4.8	7	10/7–10/15	11.23	3.8
1955	11	1/18–2/1	21.50	5.5	5	1/11–1/17	12.69	3.2
1956	7	11/29–12/7	28.69	6.1	8	5/7–5/16	23.75	4.6
1957	5	4/17–4/24	9.34	1.9	5	6/18–6/24	16.11	3.1
	5	5/15–5/21	6.04	1.3	5	7/31–8/6	14.80	3.0
	5	6/11–6/17	9.43	1.9	5	8/8–8/14	12.55	2.5
					5	9/4–9/10	15.90	3.3
					5	10/16–10/22	28.11	6.3
1958	8	2/28–3/11	18.12	4.1	9	3/25–4/7	13.66	3.0
	8	6/25–7/7	11.42	2.4				
1959	10	6/24–7/8	32.83	5.2	7	6/1–6/9	26.17	4.1
	10	11/17–12/1	29.92	4.7				
1960	8	5/11–5/20	20.42	3.4	11	7/11–7/25	45.23	7.0
	8	10/31–11/10	34.09	5.9				
1961	8	2/23–3/6	22.06	3.3	7	2/3–2/13	16.58	2.5
1962	7	10/29–11/7	46.73	8.2	7	6/18–6/26	42.42	7.3
1963	8	3/4–3/13	17.94	2.7	10	7/10–7/23	26.25	3.7
1964	9	3/6–3/18	16.48	2.0	6	8/19–8/26	13.62	1.6
					6	11/23–12/1	26.29	3.0
1965	9	1/22–2/3	13.04	1.5	6	7/15–7/22	21.46	2.4
1966	6	3/31–4/7	26.00	2.8	8	4/26–5/5	50.78	5.3
	6	5/20–5/27	24.05	2.8				
	6	12/5–12/12	31.07	3.9				
1967	9	1/3–1/13	49.44	6.3	8	10/27–11/8	41.32	4.6
	9	4/13–4/25	46.55	5.5				
1968	9	4/23–5/3	27.22	3.1	12	1/9–1/24	46.69	5.1
1969	6	2/5–2/13	3.98	0.4	7	2/14–2/25	52.90	5.6
					7	7/18–7/29	51.13	6.0
1970	12	11/19–12/7	64.42	6.5	7	1/9–1/19	26.00	3.0
					7	4/16–4/28	51.61	6.7
1971	10	4/5–4/19	45.81	5.1	11	10/13–10/27	57.17	6.4

b. Rail-Trans.

	Advances				Declines			
Year	No. of Days	Dates	Pts.	%	No. of Days	Dates	Pts.	%
1900	9	12/19–12/31	4.52	5.0	6	6/14–6/20	3.22	4.2
1901	9	3/26–4/4	5.17	5.0	6	1/14–1/19	4.29	4.4
1902	9	3/12–3/21	2.71	2.4	6	10/1–10/7	4.80	3.8
	9	7/11–7/19	3.52	2.9				
1903	8	12/18–12/29	3.04	3.2	7	7/29–8/5	5.15	5.3
1904	10	10/7–10/18	4.35	4.0	8	1/28–2/5	4.00	4.0
1905	7	7/24–7/31	3.33	2.7	6	5/16–5/22	5.33	4.4
1906	7	5/4–5/11	7.86	6.5	6	6/12–6/18	4.28	3.3
1907	5	3/26–4/1	9.43	9.6	7	5/14–5/21	5.59	5.2
	5	4/18–4/23	3.13	2.9				
	5	7/11–7/16	2.48	2.4				
	5	11/26–12/2	6.56	8.0				
1908	6	3/19–3/25	2.95	3.2	5	1/20–1/24	4.09	4.3
					5	2/5–2/10	5.28	5.8
1909	7	7/27–8/3	2.80	2.2	6	2/16–2/23	6.00	5.0
1910	7	10/10–10/18	3.38	2.9	6	7/20–7/26	4.40	3.9
1911	7	1/26–2/2	2.97	2.5	6	6/12–6/17	0.95	0.8
	7	4/24–5/1	3.11	2.7	6	8/21–8/26	2.96	2.6
1912	5	5/10–5/15	1.90	1.6	7	12/2–12/9	4.10	3.4
	5	6/1–6/6	2.29	1.9				
	5	6/15–6/20	1.11	0.9				
	5	8/9–8/14	2.10	1.7				
	5	10/30–11/6	3.22	2.8				
1913	4	7/24–7/28	1.33	1.3	8	4/22–4/30	4.16	3.7
					8	5/26–6/5	5.95	5.4
1914	5	1/10–1/15	2.54	2.4	8	4/8–4/17	2.96	2.8
1915	9	3/19–3/29	3.92	4.4	7	7/1–7/9	4.30	4.6
1916	6	6/3–6/9	2.17	2.0	8	1/22–1/31	4.80	4.5
	6	9/2–9/9	1.85	1.8	8	3/24–4/1	1.59	1.5
1917	5	2/16–2/21	2.15	2.2	8	1/25–2/2	7.37	7.0
	5	3/15–3/20	3.23	3.3				
	5	6/21–6/26	2.04	2.2				
1918	6	8/7–8/13	2.44	3.0	7	11/16–11/23	3.37	3.7
	6	10/16–10/22	4.60	5.2				
1919	8	2/14–2/24	2.38	2.9	7	6/9–6/16	4.34	4.8
1920	6	7/2–7/10	3.46	4.9	6	3/19–3/25	2.15	2.9
	6	8/28–9/3	2.43	3.2	6	3/27–4/5	1.52	2.0
	6	9/28–10/4	4.60	5.8	6	12/15–12/21	3.83	5.2

	Advances				Declines			
Year	No. of Days	Dates	Pts.	%	No. of Days	Dates	Pts.	%
1921	8	7/16–7/25	2.77	3.9	8	8/3–8/11	3.91	5.2
1922	8	1/10–1/18	3.15	4.3	6	5/31–6/6	2.05	2.4
					6	11/21–11/27	3.94	4.6
1923	7	6/2–6/9	3.50	4.3	6	3/5–3/10	1.65	1.8
					6	5/15–5/21	2.58	3.1
1924	8	7/18–7/26	2.41	2.7	6	10/2–10/8	2.02	2.2
	8	10/30–11/8	5.24	5.9	6	12/5–12/11	2.27	2.3
1925	7	5/15–5/22	2.20	2.3	8	8/25–9/2	3.60	3.5
	7	12/22–12/31	2.83	2.6				
1926	5	6/2–6/7	1.45	1.3	6	3/13–3/19	4.82	4.3
	5	6/28–7/2	0.96	0.8	6	9/7–9/13	3.35	2.7
	5	8/30–9/3	4.73	4.0				
1927	7	2/10–2/18	4.89	3.9	5	8/14–8/19	1.75	1.2
1928	9	7/21–7/31	3.93	2.9	9	11/28–12/8	9.45	6.2
1929	7	4/20–4/27	1.71	1.2	6	3/20–3/26	6.59	4.3
1930	7	8/23–9/2	4.14	3.2	12	12/3–12/16	15.51	14.5
1931	7	1/19–1/26	6.14	5.9	10	12/7–12/17	8.95	22.2
1932	7	7/9–7/16	2.50	18.9	8	3/31–4/8	7.95	25.3
					8	12/15–12/23	4.11	14.7
1933	6	6/30–7/7	9.58	20.4	7	3/29–4/5	4.19	15.1
1934	7	5/14–5/21	2.66	6.5	10	4/21–5/2	4.72	9.3
	7	7/3–7/11	1.40	3.2				
1935	7	9/4–9/11	2.18	6.2	6	2/19–2/26	4.29	12.4
1936	6	7/8–7/14	5.26	11.1	6	12/16–12/22	3.32	6.0
1937	7	6/29–7/8	4.54	9.0	7	10/11–10/19	7.30	19.5
1938	11	9/27–10/8	7.88	34.2	9	3/2–3/11	4.36	14.5
1939	8	8/2–8/12	6.92	26.7	8	1/5–1/13	3.39	9.9
	8	8/19–8/27	5.09	16.5	8	11/21–11/30	2.38	7.0
1940	6	12/24–12/31	1.03	3.8	9	3/7–3/16	1.23	4.0
1941	6	11/14–11/21	1.18	4.3	7	4/4–4/12	1.86	6.3
					7	12/3–12/10	3.25	11.8
1942	6	8/13–8/19	1.36	5.3	6	8/4–8/10	0.71	2.7
	6	12/15–12/21	1.40	5.4				
1943	7	2/19–2/27	2.83	9.7	6	2/2–2/8	0.49	1.7
					6	11/1–11/8	3.44	9.8
					6	11/23–11/30	2.90	8.7
1944	9	6/9–6/19	2.59	6.7	4	1/24–1/27	0.94	2.5
					4	3/25–3/29	1.07	2.7
					4	6/5–6/8	1.34	3.3
					4	8/31–9/6	1.83	4.5
1945	7	3/10–3/17	3.04	6.1	5	1/11–1/16	2.08	4.1
	7	10/4–10/11	1.32	2.2	5	1/18–1/23	2.63	5.3

	Advances				Declines			
Year	No. of Days	Dates	Pts.	%	No. of Days	Dates	Pts.	%
	7	10/30–11/7	4.31	7.3	5	8/10–8/20	6.32	10.9
1946	8	7/24–8/2	2.22	3.7	8	7/5–7/16	2.59	4.0
1947	6	11/14–11/20	2.20	4.7	6	2/13–2/19	1.66	3.2
1948	10	3/30–4/9	2.88	5.5	7	11/22–11/30	3.24	5.9
					7	12/14–12/21	1.40	2.6
1949	5	12/12–12/16	1.43	2.9	7	11/5–11/15	2.08	4.2
1950	9	7/13–7/25	7.76	14.5	7	10/19–10/26	3.97	5.6
	9	11/8–11/18	5.93	8.4				
1951	9	1/26–2/5	8.28	10.1	7	10/15–10/22	5.33	6.1
	9	7/17–7/27	6.09	8.1				
1952	6	11/17–11/24	4.28	4.2	6	7/2–7/10	2.26	2.1
					6	9/3–9/10	5.14	5.0
1953	5	1/26–1/30	3.10	2.8	11	12/2–12/16	7.96	8.0
	5	2/18–2/25	2.75	2.6				
	5	6/17–6/23	4.95	4.9				
	5	11/24–12/1	2.69	2.8				
1954	8	12/10–12/21	8.92	6.6	5	10/25–10/29	2.86	2.4
1955	6	3/22–3/29	5.98	4.1	6	7/25–8/1	3.88	2.4
	6	4/5–4/13	6.73	4.5				
	6	8/17–8/24	4.17	2.7				
	6	11/1–11/9	6.66	4.5				
1956	6	3/8–3/15	6.35	3.9	7	5/18–5/28	13.97	8.0
1957	11	6/25–7/10	9.01	6.3	7	1/11–1/18	8.22	5.2
1958	10	7/15–7/28	10.98	8.3	9	2/17–2/27	5.00	4.6
					9	3/25–4/7	5.89	5.5
1959	8	11/27–12/8	7.99	5.4	9	5/25–6/4	6.76	4.0
1960	10	8/4–8/17	6.50	4.9	8	2/26–3/8	13.30	8.8
1961	8	9/27–10/6	9.01	6.4	10	5/18–6/2	4.13	2.8
1962	10	11/16–11/30	9.22	7.1	7	4/19–4/30	5.83	4.0
					7	5/4–5/14	7.70	5.4
					7	5/18–5/28	13.87	10.2
1963	10	12/5–12/18	6.97	4.0	9	7/11–7/23	10.12	5.8
1964	11	6/19–7/6	12.13	5.9	9	7/27–8/6	8.85	4.0
1965	7	1/11–1/19	13.67	1.6	5	3/26–4/1	5.71	2.6
	7	7/27–8/4	13.94	7.1	5	4/14–4/21	2.92	1.4
					5	7/16–7/22	5.61	2.8
					5	11/16–11/22	2.56	1.1
1966	9	2/3–2/15	13.81	5.4	12	8/8–8/23	21.63	9.8
1967	10	1/11–1/23	14.76	6.9	12	10/3–10/18	15.11	5.7
					12	10/20–11/6	20.55	8.3
1968	7	3/27–4/4	6.39	2.9	11	10/21–11/7	8.05	3.0
	7	4/8–4/18	13.31	5.9				
	7	9/24–10/4	12.39	4.8				
1969	7	1/30–2/7	6.71	2.5	12	2/13–3/3	27.03	9.7
1970	10	11/20–12/4	13.15	9.0	7	1/22–1/30	8.69	5.0
					7	6/22–6/30	19.30	13.7
1971	14	3/26–4/15	21.40	10.8	7	3/17–3/25	6.41	3.1

8. Annual Closing Highs-Lows (by Months) Dow Jones Industrial Stocks (1969–1971)

Month	1969 High	1969 Low	1970 High	1970 Low	1971 High	1971 Low
January	ACD, AC, A, C, JM, WX	IP, S	ACD, AC, A, C, IP, OI, UA, Z	WX	GF, N	ACD, C, DD, EK, GE, PG, S, J, SWX, WX, Z
February	AMB, OI, X, DD, SWX, HR, UK	PG	EK	DD, J	T, HR, JM	–0–
March	–0–	Z, EK	AA, T, X	–0–	AMB, AC	–0–
April	AA, IP, GE, UA	–0–	BS, SWX	–0–	C, GM, IP, OI, SD, J, TX, X, Z	–0–
May	T, GF, GT, SD, TX, BS, GM, S, J	–0–	–0–	ACD, AMB, AC, EK, GE, GF, GM, GT, N, IP, JM, OI, PG, S, TX, UK, Z	AA, A, UK, UA	–0–
June	–0–	–0–	–0–	T, C	–0–	BS

July	-0-	AA, AMB, GF, GT, N, SWX	-0-	HR, SD, UA	SWX	-0-
August	-0-	-0-	-0-	AA, SWX	-0-	-0-
September	-0-	-0-	UK	-0-	ACD, DD, GT	-0-
October	PG, Z	A	-0-	A	WX	GF
November	-0-	-0-	-0-	BS, X	-0-	AA, AMB, AC, A, GM, GT, HR, N, IP, JM, OI, SD, TX, UK, UA, X
December	EK, N	ACD, AC, T, BS, C, DD, GE, GM, HR, JM, OI, SD, J, TX, UK, UA, X, WX	AMB, DD, GE, GF, GM, GT, HR, N, JM, PG, S, SD, J, TX, WX	-0-	BS, EK, GE, PG, S	T

Stock & Symbol		1969				1970				1971			
		High	Date	Low	Date	High	Date	Low	Date	High	Date	Low	Date
Allied Chem.	(ACD)	37³/₈	1/3	23⁵/₈	12/16	27¹/₄	1/21	16¹/₈	5/25	34⁵/₈	9/7	23³/₈	1/4
Alum. of Amer.	(AA)	84	4/30	64³/₈	7/28	73⁵/₈	3/6	47¹/₄	8/13	70	5/12	36³/₄	11/10
Amer. Brands	(AMB)	41¹/₂	2/5	32⁷/₈	7/30	45³/₄	12/29	29⁵/₈	5/26	49⁵/₈	3/16	37¹/₄	11/12
Amer. Can	(AC)	58	1/3	37⁵/₈	12/17	44³/₄	1/23	35	5/26	45⁵/₈	3/22	29⁷/₈	11/12
Amer. T&T	(T)	57³/₄	5/14	48¹/₂	12/17	53³/₈	3/25	40³/₈	6/25	53⁵/₈	2/1	40⁷/₈	12/7
Anaconda	(A)	64⁵/₈	1/10	27	10/1	32	1/5	19³/₈	10/29	23¹/₂	5/13	11¹/₂	11/24
Beth. Steel	(BS)	36¹/₂	5/14	26	12/17	30³/₈	4/9	19³/₄	11/25	30¹/₈	12/28	20³/₈	6/21
Chrysler	(C)	57¹/₄	1/2	32¹/₈	12/16	35¹/₄	1/2	16¹/₂	6/23	33	4/23	25	1/15
Du Pont	(DD)	165⁵/₈	2/13	102¹/₄	12/17	133¹/₂	12/30	93¹/₂	2/17	157³/₄	9/8	129³/₄	1/18
East. Kodak	(EK)	82⁵/₈	12/30	68⁷/₈	3/17	84	2/11	57⁵/₈	5/26	99¹/₄	12/20	72¹/₄	1/7
Gen. Elec.*	(GE)	48⁷/₈	4/30	37³/₈	12/17	47	12/31	30¹/₄	5/26	66¹/₂	12/20	46³/₄	1/6
Gen. Foods *	(GF)	42⁷/₈	5/26	36¹/₄	7/29	44³/₈	12/22	33³/₈	5/26	44¹/₄	1/6	31¹/₄	10/28
Gen. Motors	(GM)	83¹/₄	5/8	66	12/17	81³/₈	12/30	59¹/₂	5/26	90³/₄	4/29	74⁵/₈	11/12
Goodyear*	(GT)	33⁵/₈	5/14	25⁵/₈	7/28	32¹/₄	12/29	21¹/₂	5/26	35	9/3	27⁵/₈	11/23
Int. Harv.	(HR)	37⁵/₈	2/7	24¹/₄	12/18	29¹/₄	12/7	22	7/7	33³/₄	2/16	23³/₈	11/1
Int. Nick.	(N)	43³/₄	12/15	32⁵/₈	7/28	47⁵/₈	12/10	33³/₄	5/26	46³/₈	1/19	25¹/₄	11/1
Int. Paper	(IP)	45³/₄	4/29	34⁷/₈	1/8	39⁵/₈	1/5	28³/₈	5/26	40	4/29	28³/₄	11/17
Johns-Manv.*	(JM)	43⁵/₈	1/3	28	12/18	40⁵/₈	12/18	26³/₄	5/26	45⁷/₈	2/17	37³/₈	11/11
Owens-Ill.	(OI)	77³/₄	2/3	60³/₈	12/10	63	1/14	38³/₄	5/26	65⁵/₈	4/28	41	11/24
Pr. & Gamble *	(PG)	55⁷/₈	10/24	41¹/₄	2/26	60¹/₂	12/8	40¹/₄	5/26	81	12/21	56³/₈	1/22
Sears, R'buck	(S)	74¹/₂	5/21	60⁵/₈	1/23	76³/₈	12/10	51³/₈	5/26	103⁵/₈	12/29	75¹/₈	1/5
Cal. Std.	(SD)	74⁵/₈	5/14	48³/₄	12/10	54³/₄	12/30	38¹/₂	5/26	62⁷/₈	4/19	50¹/₂	11/10
Jersey Std.	(J)	85¹/₈	5/14	60³/₄	12/3	73³/₈	12/31	50¹/₈	7/7	81⁷/₈	4/12	67¹/₂	1/15
Swift	(SWX)	34⁷/₈	2/13	22	7/29	32⁵/₈	4/10	22¹/₂	2/17	45	7/20	29³/₄	1/11
Texaco *	(TX)	44	5/14	27⁷/₈	12/10	35¹/₄	12/4	24	8/26	39	4/27	29⁷/₈	11/24
Un. Carbide	(UK)	47	2/13	35³/₄	12/22	40³/₈	9/9	29¹/₂	5/21	50¹/₈	5/14	39	11/23
Un. Aircraft	(UA)	80¹/₈	4/30	39	12/30	40¹/₄	1/2	24	5/26	45	5/14	24⁵/₈	11/24
U.S. Steel	(X)	48³/₈	2/6	33	12/17	39	3/4	28¹/₂	7/7	35⁵/₈	4/19	25³/₈	11/23
West. Elec.*	(WX)	35³/₄	1/3	27¹/₈	12/16	34¹/₂	12/29	26⁷/₈	11/25	48⁵/₈	10/7	32³/₄	1/11
Woolworth	(Z)	43¹/₂	10/24	28⁵/₈	3/25	38¹/₄	1/2	25¹/₂	1/29	55⁵/₈	4/29	35⁵/₈	1/4

* Adjusted for stock split.

C. MAJOR PRICE MOVEMENTS (1897–1971)

1. Industrials

From	To	Industrials	Points *	%	No. Tdg. Sess.
April 23, 1897	September 5, 1899	38.49 to 77.61	P 39.12	101	709
September 5, 1899	September 24, 1900	77.61 to 52.96	M 24.65	32	314
September 24, 1900	June 17, 1901	52.96 to 78.26	P 25.30	48	214
June 17, 1901	November 9, 1903	78.26 to 42.15	M 36.11	46	513
November 9, 1903	January 19, 1906	42.15 to 103.00	P 60.85	144	659
January 19, 1906	November 15, 1907	103.00 to 53.00	M 50.00	49	552
November 15, 1907	November 19, 1909	53.00 to 100.53	P 47.53	90	600
November 19, 1909	September 25, 1911	100.53 to 72.94	M 27.59	27	551
September 25, 1911	September 30, 1912	72.94 to 94.15	P 21.21	29	305
September 30, 1912	December 24, 1914 **	94.15 to 53.17	M 40.98	44	558 **
December 24, 1914	November 21, 1916	53.17 to 110.15	P 56.98	107	577
November 21, 1916	December 19, 1917	110.15 to 65.95	M 44.20	40	320
December 19, 1917	November 3, 1919	65.95 to 119.62	P 53.67	81	552
November 3, 1919	August 24, 1921	119.62 to 63.90	M 55.72	47	540
August 24, 1921	September 3, 1929	63.90 to 381.17	P 317.27	497	2,402
September 3, 1929	July 8, 1932	381.17 to 41.22	M 339.95	89	845
July 8, 1932	March 10, 1937	41.22 to 194.40	P 153.18	372	1,390
March 10, 1937	March 31, 1938	194.40 to 98.95	M 95.45	49	317
March 31, 1938	November 12, 1938	98.95 to 158.41	P 59.46	60	187
November 12, 1938	April 8, 1939	158.41 to 121.44	M 36.97	23	120
April 8, 1939	September 12, 1939	121.44 to 155.92	P 34.48	28	131
September 12, 1939	April 28, 1942	155.92 to 92.92	M 63.00	40	789
April 28, 1942	May 29, 1946	92.92 to 212.50	P 119.58	129	1,211
May 29, 1946	June 13, 1949	212.50 to 161.60	M 50.90	24	857
June 13, 1949	April 6, 1956	161.60 to 521.05	P 359.45	222	1,807
April 3, 1956	October 22, 1957	521.05 to 419.79	M 101.26	19	389
October 22, 1957	January 5, 1960	419.79 to 685.47	P 265.68	63	554
January 5, 1960	October 25, 1960	685.47 to 566.05	M 119.42	17	205
October 25, 1960	December 13, 1961	566.05 to 734.91	P 168.86	30	284
December 13, 1961	June 26, 1962	734.91 to 535.76	M 119.15	28	134

* P — Plus
  M — Minus
** NYSE closed from July 30, 1914, to December 12, 1914, on account of World War I.

From	To	Industrials	Points *	%	No. Tdg. Sess.
June 26, 1962	February 9, 1966	535.76 to 995.15	P 459.39	86	909
February 9, 1966	October 7, 1966	995.15 to 744.32	M 250.83	25	167
October 7, 1966	December 3, 1968	744.32 to 985.21	P 240.89	32	500
December 3, 1968	May 26, 1970	985.21 to 631.16	M 354.05	36	367
May 26, 1970	......	631.16 to	......	.....	......
April 28, 1971	......	950.82 to	......	.....	......

Average advance (points)	......	146
Average decline (points)	......	106
Average advance (percent)	......	124%
Average decline (percent)	......	37%
Average no. advancing sessions	......	764
Average no. declining sessions	......	443

2. Rail-Trans.

From	To	Rail-Trans.	Points *	%	No. Tdg. Sess.
April 19, 1897	September 9, 1902	48.12 to 129.36	P 81.24	169	1,604
September 9, 1902	September 28, 1903	129.36 to 88.80	M 40.56	31	315
September 28, 1903	January 22, 1906	88.80 to 138.36	P 49.56	56	696
January 22, 1906	November 21, 1907	138.36 to 81.41	M 56.95	42	555
November 21, 1907	August 14, 1909	81.41 to 134.46	P 53.05	65	517
August 14, 1909	July 26, 1910	134.46 to 105.59	M 28.87	21	280
July 26, 1910	October 5, 1912	105.59 to 124.35	P 18.76	18	664
October 5, 1912	December 24, 1914 **	124.35 to 87.40	M 36.95	30	553 **
December 24, 1914	October 4, 1916	87.40 to 112.28	P 24.88	28	538
October 4, 1916	December 19, 1917	112.28 to 70.75	M 41.53	37	359
December 19, 1917	November 9, 1918	70.75 to 92.91	P 22.16	31	265
November 9, 1918	June 20, 1921	92.91 to 65.52	M 27.39	29	773
June 20, 1921	September 11, 1922	65.52 to 93.99	P 28.47	43	368
September 11, 1922	August 4, 1923	93.99 to 76.78	M 17.21	18	269
August 4, 1923	September 3, 1929	76.78 to 189.11	P 112.33	146	1,819
September 3, 1929	July 8, 1932	189.11 to 13.23	M 175.88	93	845
July 8, 1932	July 7, 1933	13.23 to 56.53	P 43.30	376	291
July 7, 1933	March 12, 1935	56.53 to 27.31	M 29.22	52	499

* P — Plus
  M — Minus
** NYSE closed from July 30, 1914 to December 12, 1914 on account of World War I.

From	*To*	*Industrials*	*Points* *	*%*	*No. Tdg. Sess.*
March 12, 1935	March 17, 1937	27.31 to 64.46	P 37.15	136	606
March 17, 1937	March 31, 1938	64.46 to 19.00	M 45.46	71	311
March 31, 1938	September 27, 1939	19.00 to 35.90	P 16.90	89	451
September 27, 1939	May 21, 1940	35.90 to 22.14	M 13.76	38	194
May 21, 1940	August 1, 1941	22.14 to 30.88	P 8.74	39	361
August 1, 1941	June 2, 1942	30.88 to 23.31	M 7.57	25	249
June 2, 1942	June 13, 1946	23.31 to 68.31	P 45.00	193	1,192
June 13, 1946	May 19, 1947	68.31 to 41.16	M 27.14	40	264
May 19, 1947	July 14, 1948	41.16 to 64.95	P 23.79	58	322
July 14, 1948	June 13, 1949	64.95 to 41.03	M 23.92	37	261
June 13, 1949	December 22, 1952	41.03 to 112.53	P 71.50	174	979
December 22, 1952	September 14, 1953	112.53 to 90.56	M 21.97	20	184
September 14, 1953	May 9, 1956	90.56 to 181.23	P 90.67	100	667
May 9, 1956	December 24, 1957	181.23 to 95.67	M 85.56	47	409
December 24, 1957	July 8, 1959	95.67 to 173.56	P 77.89	81	385
July 8, 1959	September 29, 1960	173.56 to 123.37	M 50.19	29	311
September 29, 1960	October 11, 1961	123.37 to 152.92	P 29.55	24	259
October 11, 1961	October 1, 1962	152.92 to 114.86	M 38.06	25	244
October 1, 1962	February 15, 1966	114.86 to 271.72	P 156.86	137	846
February 15, 1966	October 7, 1966	271.72 to 184.34	M 87.38	32	163
October 7, 1966	February 7, 1969	184.34 to 279.88	P 95.54	51	561
February 7, 1969	July 7, 1970	279.88 to 116.69	M 163.19	58	353
July 7, 1970	......	116.69 to	......	.....	......

Average advance (points)	......	54
Average decline (points)	......	51
Average advance (percent)	......	101
Average decline (percent)	......	39
Average no. advancing sessions	......	670
Average no. declining sessions	......	370

D. BULLISH ACTION—EPISODES

1812   Speculation rampant for first time during War of 1812.

1819   Five-year depression ended. Stocks turned upward.

1825   Opening of Erie Canal created craze for speculation.

1831   Market moved forward as rush of foreign goods turned tide of gold outward.

1838 Order restored after 1837 panic.

1840 Rails paced upward trend.

1843 Depression ended, market recovered. Foreign commerce showed net balance of $40.4 million—best showing to date.

1864 Wild speculation, especially in rails. Gold also active on upside. Stocks were bulled to levels not duplicated for many years during the spring and summer.

1865 Tight money checked market's rise.

1871 A period of heavy speculation at rising prices.

1874 Agriculture pulled U.S. out of doldrums after 1873 panic, helped turn market upward.

1878 Strong bull year; good crops, large rail earnings.

1879 Bull market topped out temporarily in October.

1880 Generally an upward year. Immense crops, record rail earnings, booming business, rail mergers, and high dividends all helped market.

1881 Bull market topped out in June.

1882 Accord reached in railway war in Northwest enabled market to close year on strength.

1884 Market rallied abruptly from oversold position reached June 27.

1885 Low for year was reached in April. June–December was period of strength. Building prosperous, rail industry harmonious.

1890 Market scored sharp December recovery after November selling smash.

1891 Market closed year around peak prices.

1895 Stocks spiraled after banking syndicate arranged with President Cleveland to provide Treasury with gold equal to $65 million.

1896 Market snapped back sharply from August low. Bumper crops, high wheat exports, McKinley's election.

1897 *April 23–September 10*. DJI rose 17.33 (4.5%). Main bullish factor: McKinley signing Dingley Tariff Bill.

1898 *April 21–August 26*. DJI rose 17.70 (41%). Victory and peace after war with Spain.

1899 *February 7–April 25*. DJI rose 15.33 (24.7%). Continuation of postwar boom.

1900 *September 24–November 20*. DJI rose 18.11 (34.2%). Low interest rates, plentiful money, record rail earnings, McKinley's reelection.

1901 1. *March 13–April 19.* DJI rose 8.71 (11.5%). Industrials climbed in sympathy with outstanding rail strength.

2. *May 9–June 17.* DJI rose 10.88 (16.1%). Recovery after Northern Pacific panic.

1902 *December 15–February 16, 1903.* DJI rose 8.13 (13.6%). Token recovery in a bear market.

1903 1. *August 8–17.* DJI rose 6.50 (13.7%). Temporary rally during a panic.

2. *November 9–January 27, 1904.* DJI rose 8.35 (19.8%). First upward leg in a new bull market.

1904 *March 12–December 5.* DJI rose 26.82 (57.8%). Bulls had their own way after Supreme Court ordered Northern Securities dissolved for being a monopoly.

1905 1. *January 25–April 14.* DJI rose 14.99 (21.8%).

2. *November 13–January 19, 1906.* DJI rose 22.17 (36.5%).

1906 1. *May 3–June 6.* DJI rose 8.76 (10.3%). Recovery from sell off after San Francisco earthquake-fire.

2. *July 13–January 7, 1907.* DJI rose 11.19 (13.1%). Advance resumed after reaching year's low of 85.18.

1907 Brief trading rallies in panic year:

1. *March 25–April 10.* DJI rose 9.39 (12.5%).

2. *June 21–July 6.* DJI rose 5.09 (6.6%).

3. *August 24–September 6.* DJI rose 4.64 (6.7%).

4. *November 15–December 6.* DJI rose 8.77 (16.5%).

5. *December 17–January 14, 1908.* DJI rose 8.99 (15.8%).

1908 1. *February 13–March 25.* DJI rose 11.30 (19.3%). First upward leg of bull market.

2. *April 6–May 18.* DJI rose 8.08 (12.1%).

3. *July 1–August 10.* DJI rose 12.64 (17.4%).

4. *September 22–November 13.* DJI rose 11.31 (14.7%).

1909 1. *February 23–June 5.* DJI rose 14.55 (18.2%). Market topped out temporarily in anticipation of Hughes Committee's report on investigation of NYSE after 1907 panic.

2. *June 21–November 19.* DJI rose 10.87 (12.1%).

1910 1. *February 8–March 8.* DJI rose 9.53 (11.2%).

2. *July 26–October 18.* DJI rose 12.40 (16.8%).

1911 *September 25–December 16.* DJI rose 9.54 (13.1%).

1912 *February 10–September 30.* DJI rose 14.00 (17.5%).

1913 *June 11–September 13.* DJI rose 11.32 (15.7%).

1915   1. *February 24–April 30.* DJI rose 17.56 (32.4%). First good recovery of the war.

2. *May 14–December 27.* DJI rose 38.83 (64.3%).

1916   Two "soda pop" rallies ran into resistance at 96–97 DJ and caused double top formation:

1. *January 31–February 11.* DJI rose 5.57 (6.1%).

2. *March 2–16.* DJI rose 5.56 (6.1%).

3. *April 22–November 21.* DJI rose 25.19 (30%). After market overcame selling resistance at double top area of 96–97 DJ in September, it carried forward to year's closing peak.

1917   1. *February 2–March 10.* DJI rose 11.19 (12.9%). First rally after the drop caused by break in U.S.-German relations.

2. *May 9–June 9.* DJI rose 10.00 (11.2%). First meaningful recovery after U.S. entered war. Thereafter market dropped with few rallies to wartime low of 65.95 (12/19).

3. *December 19–February 19, 1918.* DJI rose 16.13 (24.5%). Initial recovery from World War I low.

1918   1. *April 11–May 15.* DJI rose 8.46 (11.2%). Strikes outlawed for war duration.

2. *June 1–October 18.* DJI rose 11.14 (14.3%). Market anticipated end of war.

1919   1. *February 18–July 14.* DJI rose 37.04 (49.3%). Idea of inflation fueled market in peacetime boom. Scandals rocked Wall Street. Many corners, attempted corners.

2. *August 20–November 3.* DJI rose 21.16 (21.5%). Final leg of post-Armistice advance.

1920   1. *February 25–April 8.* DJI rose 15.67 (17.4%). Government relinquished control of railroads. ICC granted major rate increase.

2. *May 19–July 8.* DJI rose 7.15 (8.2%). A minor trading recovery after decline from April high.

3. *August 10–September 17.* DJI rose 6.75 (8.1%). Another snapback rally. Market mostly in professional hands.

1921–1929   *August 24, 1921–September 3, 1929.* DJI rose 317.27 (497%). In 1929, four small probing tests preceded the final upward thrust:

1. *January 8–February 5.* DJI rose 25.08 (8.4%), from 296.98 to 322.06;

2. *February 16–March 1*. DJI rose 25.33 (8.6%), from 295.85 to 321.18;

3. *March 6–16*. DJI rose 14.80 (4.8%), from 305.20 to 320.00.

4. *March 26–May 4*. DJI rose 30.57 (10.3%), from 296.51 to 327.08. This penetrated a triple top previously formed at 320–323 DJ.

Following a 33.66-point reaction to 293.42 (5/27), the DJI climbed to 355.62 (8/3), then dropped back to 337.99 (8/9) before spurting 43.18 (12.8%) to the final peak.

1929   1. *October 4–10*. DJI rose 27.69 (8.5%). First snapback rally after initial 56-point drop.

2. *November 13–December 7*. DJI rose 64.77 (32.6%). Recovery was sparked by a discount rate cut from 5% to 4½%.

3. *December 20–April 17, 1930*. DJI rose 63.18 (27.4%). A most deceptive "Baby Bull" market. Those who followed it lost heavily.

1930   1. *May 3–29*. DJI rose 16.76 (6.5%). Hoover: "I am convinced we have now passed the worst . . . we shall rapidly recover."

2. *June 24–September 10*. DJI rose 33.25 (15.7%).

3. *December 16–February 24, 1931*. DJI rose 36.85 (23.4%).

1931   1. *June 2–27*. DJI rose 35.23 (28.9%). Hoover announced moratorium on intergovernmental debts.

2. *October 5–November 9*. DJI rose 30.31 (35%). Hoover called meeting with financial leaders to discuss ways to handle crisis.

3. *December 17–March 8, 1932*. DJI rose 14.99 (20.3%).

1932   *July 8–September 7*. DJI rose 38.71 (9.4%). In trying to establish a base, market climbed slowly from rock-bottom depression low of 41.22 DJ.

1933   1. *February 27–July 18*. DJI rose 58.51 (116.6%). U.S. off gold standard. NRA established. FDR's first "fireside chat."

2. *July 22–September 19*. DJI rose 17.25 (19.5%).

3. *October 21–February 5, 1934*. DJI rose 27.10 (32.4%).

1934   *July 26–April 6, 1936*. DJI rose 76.48 (89.4%).

1936   *April 29–March 10, 1937*. DJI rose 50.75 (35.3%).

1937   1. *June 14–August 14*. DJI rose 24.51 (14.8%). Final advance before crash.

2. *November 24–January 11, 1938*. DJI rose 20.71 (18.2%). Rally from temporarily oversold position.

1938   Three-stage recovery from 1937 panic:

1. *March 31–April 16*. DJI rose 22.05 (22.3%). More "pump priming" reported, government bonds strong, London stock market advanced 7 straight days.

2. *May 31–August 6*. DJI rose 37.93 (35.2%). Evidence of moderate unseasonal pickup in several business lines.

3. *September 26–November 12*. DJI rose 28.50 (21.7%). Hitler called for 4-power conference. Chamberlain vowed: "Peace in our time." FDR suggested truce between U.S. labor, industry, government.

1939   April 8–September 12. DJI rose 34.48 (28.4%). Peace hopes, good business news supported market, until World War II erupted over Labor Day weekend.

1940   June 10–January 10, 1941. DJI rose 21.75 (19.4%). A slow and cautious recovery after spring selling smash, despite bad war news.

1942   April 28–July 14, 1943. DJI rose 52.90 (56.9%). Market improved steadily after reaching low for war years at 92.92.

1944   February 7–May 29, 1946. DJI rose 78.28 (58.3%).

1946   October 9–February 8, 1947. DJI rose 21.37 (13.1%). Gradual improvement after liquidation dried up.

1947   May 17–July 24. DJI rose 23.64 (14.5%). Technical recovery encouraged by market testing and holding above 1946 panic bottom.

1948   1. *March 16–June 15*. DJI rose 27.77 (16.8%).

2. *September 27–October 23*. DJI rose 14.20 (8.3%). Market met heavy resistance around June high area.

1949   June 13–June 12, 1950. DJI rose 66.78 (41.3%). A breakdown on June 13 below 1946 panic bottom was false. Thereafter recovery became more forceful despite labor strikes.

1950   1. *July 13–November 24*. DJI rose 38.01 (19.2%). Recovery after the setback caused by Korean War eruption.

2. *December 4–February 13, 1951*. DJI rose 33.38 (15%).

1951   1. *March 14–May 3*. DJI rose 19.18 (7.9%), carried well above February high.

2. *June 29–September 13*. DJI rose 33.73 (13.8%).

3. *November 24–January 22, 1952*. DJI rose 29.45 (11.5%).

1952   Market was flat and dull during most of year.

1. *February 20–March 31*. DJI rose 10.97 (4.2%).

2. *May 1–August 11*. DJI rose 23.94 (9.3%).

3. *October 22–January 1, 1953*. DJI rose 30.73 (11.7%).

1953 Until September, trend was generally downward, punctuated only by minor rallies.

1. *February 18–March 17*. DJI rose 9.50 (3.4%).

2. *April 23–May 11*. DJI rose 8.06 (3.0%).

3. *June 16–August 13*. DJI rose 13.86 (5.3%).

4. *September 14–June 1, 1954*. DJI rose 73.18 (28.6%).

1954 Strong bull year with only temporary hesitation.

1. *June 9–August 20*. DJI rose 31.11 (9.7%).

2. *August 31–October 6*. DJI rose 28.63 (8.1%).

3. *October 29–December 31*. DJI rose 52.25 (14.8%).

1955 1. *January 17–March 4*. DJI rose 31.48 (8.1%).

2. *March 14–April 26*. DJI rose 39.28 (10.0%).

3. *May 17–July 27*. DJI rose 54.33 (13.1%).

4. *August 9–September 23*. DJI rose 38.64 (8.6%).

5. *October 11–December 30*. DJI rose 49.81 (11.4%), in rally from "Heart Attack" market low.

1956 1. *January 23–April 6*. DJI rose 58.70 (12.7%).

2. *May 28–August 2*. DJI rose 52.14 (11.1%), helped by successful Eisenhower operation.

3. *October 1–November 5*. DJI rose 26.67 (5.7%).

4. *November 28–December 31*. DJI rose 33.37 (7.2%).

1957 1. *February 12–July 12*. DJI rose 65.95 (14.5%).

2. *October 22–November 29*. DJI rose 30.08 (7.2%).

3. *December 17–February 4, 1958*. DJI rose 33.00 (7.8%), sparked by January margin cut.

1958 1. *February 25–November 17*. DJI rose 130.55 (29.9%). Advance only briefly interrupted by two margin rate hikes.

2. *November 25–January 21, 1959*. DJI rose 57.14 (10.0%).

1959 1. *February 9–August 3*. DJI rose 103.64 (18.0%).

2. *September 22–December 31*. DJI rose 62.91 (10.2%). End of record-long steel strike triggered push to all-time high.

1960 1. *March 8–April 18*. DJI rose 31.67 (5.3%).

2. *May 2–June 9*. DJI rose 56.81 (9.5%).

3. *July 25–August 24*. DJI rose 39.88 (6.6%).

4. *September 28–October 14*. DJI rose 27.39 (4.8%).

5. *October 25–November 10*. DJI rose 45.96 (8.1%).

6. *December 5–May 19, 1961*. DJI rose 112.47 (19.0%).

1961 1. *July 18–September 17*. DJI rose 47.23 (7.0%).

2. *September 25–December 13.* DJI rose 43.05 (6.2%).

1962   1. *January 29–March 15.* DJI rose 33.62 (4.9%).

2. *June 26–August 23.* DJI rose 80.24 (15.0%). JFK promised "across-the-board, top to bottom" corporate and personal tax cuts.

3. *October 23–February 18, 1963.* DJI rose 130.90 (23.5%). Recovery from Cuban missile crisis.

1963   1. *March 1–May 31.* DJI rose 67.24 (10.9%).

2. *July 25–October 29.* DJI rose 72.79 (10.6%).

3. *November 22–May 7, 1964.* DJI rose 118.68 (16.7%). Market encouraged by LBJ signing tax-cut bill.

1964   1. *June 8–November 18.* DJI rose 91.40 (11.4%).

2. *December 15–May 14, 1965.* DJI rose 82.17 (9.6%).

1965   *June 28–February 9, 1966.* DJI rose 154.56 (18.4%). Climactic decline on 10½ million shares (largest since 5/31/62) preceded this recovery.

1966   1. *October 7–December 12.* DJI rose 76.22 (10.2%). Bonds strong. LBJ said business never better. DJ Rails reversed bearish pattern of declining tops and bottoms.

2. *December 30–May 8, 1967.* DJI rose 123.94 (15.8%). Interest rates eased. Banks cut prime rate. Martin of Federal Reserve said economy might soon resume rapid growth.

1967   1. *June 5–September 25.* DJI rose 95.31 (11.2%). Middle East shooting war ended quickly. Short position at record high.

2. *November 8–January 8, 1968.* DJI rose 59.35 (7.0%).

1968   1. *March 21–July 15.* DJI rose 98.59 (11.9%). LBJ declined to run for presidency. North Vietnam bombing curtailed, peace talks agreed upon.

2. *July 30–December 3.* DJI rose 102.21 (11.6%). Steel strike averted. Federal Reserve eased credit reins.

1969   1. *February 25–May 14.* DJI rose 69.05 (7.7%). Peace hopes, good first quarter earnings supported market.

2. *July 29–November 10.* DJI rose 61.09 (7.6%). Senate cleared bill to extend income tax surcharge. Martin of FRB said "less inflationary momentum in the economy." Possibility of more troop removals from Vietnam.

1970   1. *May 26–June 19.* DJI rose 89.27 (14.1%). Initial recovery from bear market low.

2. *July 7–September 8.* DJI rose 103.78 (15.5%). Peace hopes

brightened. FRB eased monetary pressure in area of bank reserve requirements.

3. *September 22–April 28, 1971.* DJI rose 203.35 (27.2%). Prime-discount rates cut. Interest rates fell. Government indicated it would shore up economy.

1971 1. *August 10–September 8.* DJI rose 81.34 (9.7%). Wages, prices, rents temporarily frozen.

2. *November 23–January 18, 1972.* DJI rose 119.25 (14.9%). Taxes cut, margin lowered, dollar devalued, import surcharge removed.

BEARISH ACTION—EPISODES

1792 Panic in April caused by tight money, adverse trade conditions, and the failure for $3 million of Colonel William Duer, who tried unsuccessfully to corner "when issued" stock of the U.S. Bank.

1814 Exports fell to $7 million, hundreds of businesses failed. Cash was scarce. State banks had too little capital to carry states through the crisis.

1826 Overexpansion, tight money triggered panic.

1830 July was great period of financial distress; caused by excessive imports, a deranged currency.

1836 Credit almost at breaking point early this year. Small panic in Wall Street, October 23.

1837 First really major panic; sparked by falling land prices. Other bearish factors: overexpansion of banking and credit, real estate speculation, mania for canal building.

1848 Crisis in Europe in 1847 extended to U.S. banks overburdened with loans.

1851 Depression stemmed from bad credit system, lower-than-expected trade with California, unfavorable export-import balance, declining European commodities. It reached a peak in August, but there was panic in October over value of state money.

1853 Brief panic in July when banks called in majority of loans preparatory to publishing an initial weekly statement of their condition in *The N.Y. Times,* as decreed by state legislature.

1854 California defaulted interest payments; heavy failures followed. Stock market collapsed in July after banks suspended payments, due to fraud and deception of government officials.

1855   The failure in San Francisco of many prominent bankers caused panic in September.

1856   Market peaked out in December, some time before the coming crisis. But cash became scarce and the high prices attained by rail stocks were not soon matched.

1857   "Bankers' Panic" touched off by failure of Ohio Life Insurance Co. Also called the "Western Blizzard," it stemmed from an influx of gold from California (which caused a vast expansion of the banking system), a bad crop year, and the rapid construction of railroads on borrowed capital. Business generally was prostrated for 6 to 7 months.

1860   Stocks declined 7 to 16 points in a month's time after Lincoln was elected.

1861   Semipanic on Exchange when the Civil War erupted.

1867   The market broke badly in January and there were many failures when money was tied up by bear operators.

1869   "Black Friday," a day of panic resulting from unsuccessful attempt by Jay Gould and James Fisk, Jr. to corner gold.

1873   First panic to harm the public. Failure of Jay Cooke & Co. (September 18) was principal factor. Also, the collapse of rail speculation, due to a lack of capital. NYSE closed for 12 days.

1876   All financial fundamentals were bearish.

1877   Bear raiders drove market to a 20-year low in June, erasing all gains since 1861.

1879   Bull market topped out in October.

1880   Market trended generally upward until December, when tight money triggered a break.

1881   Market fell abruptly after Garfield was shot July 2.

1882   A 3-year depression began.

1883   Business worsened steadily. Rail speculators suffered huge losses.

1884   Bank runs, lack of confidence in Government's silver policy, and, especially, failure of Grant & Ward (involving prestige of General Grant) launched panic in May.

1886   Heavy liquidation in December due to tight money. Market depressed also by new high for labor strikes.

1888   Market retarded by unfavorable rail traffic and rate wars. Stocks advanced moderately after Harrison elected, but too much silver legislation prompted downside reversal in December.

1890 British sold American securities after Baring crisis in London, but New York market recovered strongly when the selling dried up.

1892 Generally a bear year despite record earnings.

1893 Unfavorable trade balance, overspeculation, overcapitalization, bad agricultural conditions, lack of confidence in monetary system carried market to year's low in July. Improvement began in fourth quarter after prices stabilized.

1894 A bear year. NYSE seats lost value as volume contracted. Several important strikes and many other depressing factors.

1895 Virtual run on Treasury began as everyone hoarded gold.

1896 "Silver Panic" in July–August drove market to 10-year low.

1897 *September 10–March 25, 1898.* DJI fell 13.82 (24.8%), including 5.37-point (10.7%) drop when "Maine" was blown up.

1899 *September 5–December 18.* DJI fell 19.34 (24.9%). Higher interest rates, tight money, falling surplus deposits. N.Y. Produce Exchange Co. failed. Call money quoted at 186%.

1901 1. *May 8–9.* DJI fell 7.64 (10.1%); Rails, 13.68 (11.7%) in "Nipper Panic" caused by corner in Northern Pacific Railroad stock. Those who were short of NP sold other stocks heavily to protect short positions, or to pay their losses. NP vaulted to $1,000 a share before settlement was effected.

2. *June 17–December 24.* DJI fell 16.74 (21.4%). McKinley shot and died in September. Bear market began October 1.

1902 *April 24–December 15.* DJI fell 8.87 (43.0%) in downward leg of bear market.

1903 *February 16–November 9.* DJI fell 25.55 (37.7%). "Rich Man's Panic" caused by nation's inability to digest more securities. Interest rates were high, banking situation bad all year.

1904 *December 5–12.* DJI fell 7.46 (10.2%). Reaction in bull market.

1906 *January 19–July 13.* DJI fell 17.82 (17.3%). San Francisco earthquake-fire in April spurred this along.

1907 1. *January 7–March 25.* DJI fell 20.98 (21.8%).

2. *April 10–November 15.* DJI fell 31.78 (37.5%). A credit crisis arising from inflation. All of the advance since 1900 was wiped out.

1910 1. *January 3–February 8.* DJI fell 13.31 (13.5%).

2. *March 8–May 3.* DJI fell 9.84 (10.4%).

3. *May 21–July 26.* DJI fell 16.04 (17.9%) to 73.62, where bear market ended.

1911   June 19–September 25. DJI fell 14.12 (16.2%).

1912   September 30–June 11, 1913. DJI fell 22.04 (23.4%). Weakness in the winter due mostly to anticipation of Pujo Committee's report on wrongdoings of the "Money Trust."

1914   DJI fell 9.41 (11.6%) in 7 sessions preceding closing of NYSE (7/31), on account of war in Europe. Dow Rails fell 9.36 (9.5%) in 8 sessions.

1915   1. April 30–May 14. DJI fell 11.40 (15.8%). A temporary interruption in war boom year, caused by concern over U.S.-German relations and sinking of "Lusitania."

2. *December 27–April 22, 1916.* DJI fell 14.25 (14.4%).

1916   November 21–December 21. DJI fell 19.99 (18.1%). Sudden crash sparked by peace overtures. "War Babies" the main selling targets.

1917   1. January 3–February 2. DJI fell 12.17 (12.3%). Anticipation of U.S. entering war.

2. *June 9–December 19.* DJI fell 33.13 (33.4%). A brief rally after U.S. entered war ran into panic liquidation.

1918   October 18–November 25. DJI fell 9.20 (10.3%). Post-Armistice reaction.

1919   1. July 14–August 20. DJI fell 13.77 (11.4%). Federal Reserve Board's observations about "speculative tendency of the times." Increasing signs of industrial unrest.

2. *November 3–December 22.* DJI fell 16.07 (13.4%). Increase in discount rate by N.Y. Reserve Bank reversed market's inflationary boom.

1920   1. January 3–February 25. DJI fell 19.90 (18.1%). Weakness in raw-material prices.

2. *April 8–December 21.* DJI fell 38.90 (36.9%). Gradual credit tightening, nationwide buyers' strikes.

1926   1. February 11–March 30. DJI fell 27.11 (16.7%). Profit taking after long and virtually uncorrected rise, plus unfavorable decision about rail merger program.

2. *August 14–October 19.* DJI fell 20.98 (12.6%).

1927   1. August 3–8. DJI fell 5.28 (2.8%). Coolidge declared: "I do not choose to run."

2. *October 3–22.* DJI fell 20.00 (10.0%). Normal profit taking following sharp advance.

1928   November 28–December 8. DJI fell 38.29 (13.0%). After this decline the Federal Reserve issued a statement designed to halt re-loaning of Reserve funds to brokers.

1929 Four brief selling squalls interrupted final drive to record highs before the Great Crash:

1. *February 5–16.* DJI fell 26.21 (8.1%).
2. *March 1–6.* DJI fell 15.98 (5.0%).
3. *March 16–26.* DJI fell 23.49 (7.3%).
4. *May 4–27.* DJI fell 33.66 (10.0%).

Crash Phases:

1. *September 3–October 4.* DJI fell 56.00 (14.7%).
2. *October 10–November 13.* DJI fell 154.17 (40.9%).
3. *April 17–June 24, 1930.* DJI fell 82.23 (28.0%).
4. *September 10–December 16, 1930.* DJI fell 87.57 (35.7%).
5. *February 24, 1931–July 8, 1932.* DJI fell 153.14 (78.8%), as German-Austrian agreement for customs union plunged U.S. into more critical depression phase.

1933   1. July 19–22. DJI fell 20.18 (18.6%). Top-heavy specula-tive structure collapsed. Commodities and alcohol stocks especially weak. Liquor stocks had formerly been strong in anticipation of Repeal. Prohibition ended December 5.

2. *September 19–October 21.* DJI fell 22.10 (20.9%).

1934   February 5–July 26. DJI fell 25.23 (22.8%). Market worried about business, discouraging foreign news.

1935   May 28–June 1. DJI fell 7.00 (6.0%). Supreme Court ruled NRA unconstitutional.

1936   April 6–29. DJI fell 18.34 (11.3%). More bad news from Europe.

1937   1. March 10–June 14. DJI fell 28.89 (14.9%). Government warnings about inflation, plus indications of a business letdown and auto-labor negotiations.

2. *August 14–November 24.* DJI fell 76.38 (40.1%). Collapse of production and bearish European developments induced panic selling, especially October 18 when U.S. Steel dropped 7½ points, Chrysler 11, Westinghouse Electric 9½, American Smelting 7½.

1938   January 1–March 31. DJI fell 35.40 (26.3%). European developments (Germany's annexation of Austria), plus Richard Whitney's expulsion from NYSE, contributed to pessimism, but 1937–1938 bear market low was reached March 31 at 98.95.

1939   March 10–April 8. DJI fell 30.84 (20.3%). Further international tension, including Far East.

1940   May 9–June 10. DJI fell 36.33 (24.5%). "Sitzkrieg" ended. Germans invaded Low Countries, blitzed across France.

1941   January 10–April 28, 1942. DJI fell 40.67 (30.4%). Disturbing Far East reports. Uncertainty about when German attack on Britain would begin. Steady price erosion on very low volume featured this period, which carried the market to its low for the war years—92.92 on 4/28/42. Pearl Harbor and early war reverses.

1943   July 14–February 7, 1944. DJI fell 11.60 (8.0%).

1945   December 11–February 26, 1946. DJI fell 9.80 (5.0%). Strikes, 100% margin requirement, and Chester Bowles' pushing for further wage/price controls.

1946   May 29–October 9. DJI fell 49.38 (23.2%), including 10½-point drop in panic session after Labor Day. But decline was brief; public not heavily in market.

1947   1. February 8–May 17. DJI fell 21.28 (11.5%).

2. *July 24–March 16, 1948.* DJI fell 21.46 (11.5%).

1948   October 23–June 13, 1949. DJI fell 28.59 (15.0%). Truman beat Dewey—a presidential election setback that developed into a brief penetration of the 1946 crash low in June, 1949.

1950   1. June 12–July 13. DJI fell 30.92 (13.5%). Korean War.

2. *November 24–December 4.* DJI fell 13.14 (5.6%). U.S. forces clashed with Chinese "volunteers."

1951   1. May 3–June 29. DJI fell 20.49 (7.8%).

2. *September 13–November 24.* DJI fell 20.42 (7.4%).

1953   January 5–September 14. DJI fell 38.30 (13.0%). Seesaw downward action punctuated by intermediate drops of 4.0%, 6.9%, 5.7%, 7.3%.

1954   Minor setbacks in June, August, October; otherwise, trend was upward.

1955   Three profit taking reactions:

1. *March 4–14.* DJI fell 28.32 (6.7%).

2. *April 26–May 17.* DJI fell 16.52 (3.8%).

3. *July 27–August 9.* DJI fell 19.64 (4.2%), followed by "Heart Attack Market" decline *(September 23–October 11)*, when DJI fell 48.86 (10.0%).

1956 1. *May 4–28.* DJI fell 47.63 (9.2%). Uncertainty about Eisenhower's operation.

2. *August 2–October 1.* DJI fell 52.25 (10.0%). Tension in Middle East.

3. *November 5–28.* DJI fell 29.27 (5.9%). Fighting in Egypt.

4. *December 31–February 12, 1957.* DJI fell 44.65 (8.9%).

1957 *July 12–October 22.* DJI fell 100.98 (19.4%). Decline took place from triple top formed at 520–522 DJ and ended with climactic turnaround (10/23). Market scored biggest daily gain since 1929 on 4.6-million-share volume.

1958 Dow Industrials closed lower in only one month (February) during entire year.

1959 *August 3–September 22.* DJI fell 61.65 (9.1%). Market reacted from typical "Head and Shoulders" pattern, after the DJI reached record closing high of 678.10 early in August. Left shoulder: 663.56 (7/10); Head: 678.10 (8/3); Right shoulder: 664.41 (8/31). Main reason: steel strike.

1960 1. *January 5–29.* DJI fell 62.85 (9.1%). Worry about Quemoy and Matsu Islands.

2. *August 24–September 28.* DJI fell 72.48 (11.3%). Uncertainty about Cuba.

1961 *December 13, 1961–June 26, 1962.* DJI fell 199.15 (27.1%). Dominican Government overthrown, labor troubles, and, especially, JFK's hassle with steel industry. Market declined from double top formed (11/15 and 12/13/61) at 734–735 DJ.

1962 Decline from double top ended June 26 at 535.76 DJ.

August 23–October 27. DJI fell 57.94 (9.5%). Cuban missile crisis low reached October 23 at 558.06.

1963 *October 29–November 22.* DJI fell 49.01 (6.4%). JFK assassination, margin rate boost to 70%.

1964 1. *July 17–August 6.* DJI fell 27.95 (3.3%). Tonkin Gulf incidents carried market down to August 6 low of 823.40 DJ.

2. *November 18–December 15.* DJI fell 34.26 (3.8%).

1965 *May 14–June 28.* DJI fell 99.03 (10.5%). LBJ stroke rumor,

FRB Chairman Martin's warning about "disquieting similarities" with 1929.

1966 1. *February 9–March 15*. DJI fell 84.07 (8.4%). Renewed bombing North Vietnam bases, worry about tighter credit/higher taxes.

2. *April 21–May 17*. DJI fell 90.59 (9.5%). Martin of FRB said tax hikes needed to curb inflation. Dow Theory signaled bear market.

3. *June 14–October 7*. DJI fell 158.85 (17.6%). Higher interest rates, prime rate boosts, concern over Vietnam.

1967 1. *May 8–June 5*. DJI fell 61.86 (6.8%). Overloaded speculative position, war in Middle East.

2. *September 25–November 8*. DJI fell 93.15 (9.9%). Credit tightening, decline in U.S. gold stocks, unfavorable yield relationship between bonds-common stocks, Israel-Egypt tension.

1968 1. *January 8–March 21*. DJI fell 83.79 (9.2%). "Pueblo" seizure, discount rate increases, Tet offensive, sharp drop in gold supply.

2. *July 15–July 30*. DJI fell 40.72 (4.4%). Crisis between Russia-Czechoslovakia.

3. *December 3–January 8, 1969*. DJI fell 63.96 (6.5%). Credit squeeze.

1969 1. *February 13–25*. DJI fell 52.90 (5.6%). Uncertainty about struggle between inflation/deflation.

2. *May 14–July 29*. DJI fell 166.89 (17.2%). Credit clamps tightened further, threat of price controls, peace hopes punctured.

3. *November 10–December 17*. DJI fell 93.12 (10.8%). Signs the economy was slipping.

1970 1. *January 5–30*. DJI fell 67.25 (8.3%). IBM's poor earnings, disappointment over State of Union speech.

2. *April 9–May 26*. DJI fell 161.34 (20.4%). Cambodia, strikes, Middle East turmoil, campus unrest, fear psychology.

1971 1. *April 28–August 10*. DJI fell 111.23 (17.0%). World monetary developments, prime-discount rate hikes, crisis facing U.S. dollar.

2. *September 8–November 23*. DJI fell 122.96 (13.4%). Record mutual-fund redemptions, uncertainty/confusion over Phase 2.

PART 2

Other Leading Averages

A. STANDARD & POOR'S 500-STOCK PRICE INDEX

An important indicator of stock price changes, computed by Standard & Poor's Corporation and determined by the market action of 500 leading issues: 425 Industrials, 20 Rails, 55 Utilities.

1. The Index (calculated back to 1926) is based on the relationship between average prices of these stocks during a certain base period (1941–1943) and their average hourly or closing prices today.

2. Aggregate value is determined by multiplying the prevailing market price of each stock by its number of shares outstanding.

3. The result is then divided by the aggregate value of the base period and multiplied by ten.

4. Consistency is maintained by adjusting the base year price of any stock used in the average whenever it is split or a stock dividend is paid.

PERFORMANCE OF THE 500-STOCK PRICE INDEX

Year	High	Date	Low	Date	Aver- age Pr.	Closing Pr. (12/31)	Change	
1926	13.66	12/24	10.93	3/30	12.59	13.49	......	
1927	17.71	12/31	13.18	1/27	15.34	17.66	Plus	4.18
1928	24.35	12/31	16.95	2/20	19.95	24.35	Plus	6.69
1929	31.92	9/7	17.66	11/13	26.02	21.45	Minus	2.90
1930	25.92	4/10	14.44	12/16	21.03	15.34	Minus	6.11
1931	18.17	2/24	7.72	12/17	13.66	8.12	Minus	7.22
1932	9.31	9/7	4.40	6/1	6.93	6.89	Minus	1.23
1933	12.20	7/18	5.53	2/27	8.96	10.10	Plus	3.21
1934	11.82	2/6	8.36	7/26	9.84	9.50	Minus	0.60
1935	13.46	11/19	8.06	3/14	10.60	13.43	Plus	3.93
1936	17.69	11/9	13.40	1/2	15.47	17.18	Plus	3.75
1937	18.68	3/6	10.17	11/24	15.41	10.55	Minus	6.63
1938	13.79	11/9	8.50	3/31	11.49	13.21	Plus	2.66
1939	13.23	1/4	10.18	4/8	12.06	12.49	Minus	0.72
1940	12.77	1/3	8.99	6/10	11.02	10.58	Minus	1.91
1941	10.86	1/10	8.37	12/29	9.82	8.69	Minus	1.89
1942	9.77	12/31	7.47	4/28	8.67	9.77	Plus	1.08
1943	12.64	7/14	9.84	1/2	11.50	11.67	Plus	1.90
1944	13.29	12/16	11.56	2/7	12.47	13.28	Plus	1.61
1945	17.68	12/10	13.21	1/23	15.16	17.36	Plus	4.08
1946	19.25	5/29	14.12	10/9	17.08	15.30	Minus	2.06
1947	16.20	2/8	13.71	5/17	15.17	15.30	Unchanged	
1948	17.06	6/15	13.84	2/14	15.53	15.20	Minus	0.10
1949	16.79	12/30	13.55	6/13	15.23	16.76	Plus	1.56
1950	20.43	12/29	16.65	1/14	18.40	20.41	Plus	3.65
1951	23.85	10/15	20.69	1/3	22.34	23.77	Plus	3.36
1952	26.59	12/30	23.09	2/20	24.50	26.57	Plus	2.80
1953	26.66	1/5	22.71	9/14	24.73	24.81	Minus	1.76
1954	35.98	12/31	24.80	1/11	29.69	35.98	Plus	11.17
1955	46.41	11/14	34.58	1/17	40.49	45.48	Plus	9.50
1956	49.74	8/2	43.11	1/23	46.62	46.67	Plus	1.19
1957	49.13	7/15	38.98	10/22	44.38	39.99	Minus	6.68
1958	55.21	12/31	40.33	1/2	46.24	55.21	Plus	5.22
1959	60.71	8/3	53.58	2/9	57.38	59.89	Plus	4.68
1960	60.39	1/5	52.30	10/25	55.85	58.11	Minus	1.78
1961	72.64	12/12	57.57	1/3	66.27	71.55	Plus	13.44
1962	71.13	1/3	52.32	6/26	62.38	63.10	Minus	8.45
1963	75.02	12/31	62.69	1/2	69.87	75.02	Plus	11.92
1964	86.28	11/20	75.43	1/2	81.37	84.75	Plus	9.73

Year	High	Date	Low	Date	Aver-age Pr.	Closing Pr. (12/31)	Change	
1965	92.63	11/15	81.60	6/28	88.17	92.43	Plus	4.26
1966	94.06	2/9	73.20	10/7	85.26	80.33	Minus	12.10
1967	97.59	9/25	80.38	1/3	91.93	96.47	Plus	16.14
1968	108.37	11/29	87.72	3/5	98.70	103.86	Plus	7.39
1969	106.16	5/14	89.20	12/17	97.84	92.06	Minus	11.80
1970	93.46	1/5	69.29	5/26	83.22	92.15	Plus	0.09
1971	104.77	4/28	90.16	11/23	98.29	102.09	Plus	9.94

Record closing high: 108.37 (11/29/68)
Record closing low: 4.40 (6/1/32)

Biggest advancing year: 1967 (16.14 points)
Biggest declining year: 1966 (12.10 points)

B. NEW YORK STOCK EXCHANGE INDEX (COMPOSITE)

A major market indicator established in 1966 and calculated back to 1939 to maintain continuity, which measures by computer the daily, hourly, and even minute-by-minute price changes of all Exchange-listed common stocks. Specific stock group indexes furnished also by the Exchange are Industrial, Transportation, Utility, Finance & Real Estate.

The indexes are adjustable to compensate for possible stock splits, stock dividends, et cetera, and are calculated by multiplying the price of each stock by the number of shares listed. Whenever a stock reaches 100 it is adjusted by splitting the price, or selecting a new base, to make it approximate in value the average price of listed shares.

Year	High	Date	Low	Date	Close	Change	
1939	7.64	10/21	6.06	4/8	7.38	......	
1940	7.56	4/6	5.66	5/25	6.43	Minus	0.95
1941	6.61	1/11	5.27	12/27	5.27	Minus	1.16
1942	5.93	12/26	4.64	4/25	5.93	Plus	0.66
1943	7.64	7/17	5.99	1/2	7.14	Plus	1.21
1944	8.14	12/16	7.11	2/5	8.14	Plus	1.00
1945	10.86	12/8	8.22	1/20	10.67	Plus	2.53
1946	11.89	6/3	8.85	11/23	9.44	Minus	1.23
1947	9.91	2/8	8.33	5/17	9.25	Minus	0.19
1948	10.25	6/11	8.46	2/14	8.99	Minus	0.26
1949	9.91	12/30	8.22	6/10	9.91	Plus	0.92
1950	12.01	12/30	9.85	1/14	12.01	Plus	2.10
1951	13.89	9/14	12.28	1/6	13.60	Plus	1.59
1952	14.49	12/26	13.31	10/24	14.49	Plus	0.89
1953	14.65	1/2	12.62	9/18	13.60	Minus	0.89
1954	19.40	12/31	13.70	1/8	19.40	Plus	5.80
1955	23.71	12/9	19.05	1/7	23.71	Plus	4.31
1956	25.90	8/3	22.55	1/20	24.35	Plus	0.64
1957	26.30	7/12	20.92	12/20	21.11	Minus	3.24
1958	28.85	12/24	21.45	1/10	28.85	Plus	7.74
1959	32.39	7/31	28.94	2/6	32.15	Plus	3.30
1960	31.99	1/8	28.38	10/21	30.94	Minus	1.21
1961	38.60	12/8	31.17	1/6	38.39	Plus	7.45
1962	38.02	3/16	28.20	6/22	33.81	Minus	4.58
1963	39.92	12/27	34.41	1/4	39.92	Plus	6.11
1964	46.49	11/18	40.47	1/3	45.65	Plus	5.73
1965	50.00	12/31	43.64	6/28	50.00	Plus	4.35
1966	51.06	2/9	39.37	10/7	43.72	Minus	6.28
1967	54.16	10/9	43.74	1/3	53.83	Plus	10.11
1968	61.27	11/29	48.70	3/5	58.90	Plus	5.07
1969	59.32	5/14	49.31	7/29	51.53	Minus	7.37
1970	52.36	1/5	37.69	5/26	50.23	Minus	1.30
1971	57.76	4/28	49.60	11/23	56.43	Plus	6.20

Source: Fact Book, New York Stock Exchange, Inc.

C. AMERICAN STOCK EXCHANGE INDEXES

The system consists of three market indicators designed to help assess price trends and conditions on the Exchange:

1. The Price Change Index, computed regularly, reflects the current price level of all common stocks and warrants traded.

2. The Breadth-of-Market Summary, computed daily at the close of trading, reveals the extent in which price changes are spread broadly across the market or concentrated in only a few issues.

3. The Price/Earnings Profile, computed monthly, shows the price level of ASE stocks relative to their current earnings.

PRICE CHANGE INDEX

Year	High	Low	Last	Change	
1962 *	7.51 Dec.	6.06 Oct.	7.18	......	
1963	9.24 Oct.	7.24 Jan.	8.92	Plus	1.74
1964	11.03 Dec.	8.99 Jan.	11.03	Plus	2.11
1965	14.61 Dec.	10.39 Jan.	14.45	Plus	3.42
1966	17.00 Apr.	12.07 Oct.	13.69	Minus	0.76
1967	24.52 Dec.	13.78 Jan.	24.52	Plus	10.83
1968	33.25 Dec.	21.58 Mar.	32.72	Plus	8.20
1969	32.91 Jan.	25.02 July	26.27	Minus	6.45
1970	27.02 Jan.	19.36 May	22.75	Minus	3.52
1971	26.95 Apr.	22.61 Jan.	25.59	Plus	2.84

* October, November, December.

Source: Amex Databook 1971 (American Stock Exchange, Inc.)

SECTION 4

Market Influences

PART 1

Federal Reserve Board and the Banks

A. MARGIN RATE CHANGES

The amount of money and/or securities a client must deposit with his broker to finance part of the cost of purchasing listed securities is regulated by the Board of Governors of the Federal Reserve Board, under the Securities Act of 1934. The New York Stock Exchange also has its own regulations, supplementing those of the Federal Reserve; individual brokerage firms have special rules.

Prior to 1934, this requirement, called margin, was negotiated by brokers and their clients. It sometimes dropped as low as 10% before the crash in 1929, when stock market credit topped $8.5 billion. Since then, it has ranged from a high of 100% (all cash) after World War II to a low of 40% in the 1937–1945 era. Forty % margin means that $100 worth of a listed stock can be bought for $40 down. Margins have been changed 20 times since October 15, 1934, when the initial rate was set at 45%.

239

MARGIN CHANGES AND PRICE MOVEMENTS

Dow Jones Industrials

	Effective Date	Same Day	Day Later	Week Later	Month Later	6 Mos. Later
Initial Margin 45%	(10/15/34)	94.16	95.25	94.78	99.52	105.93
Raised to 55	(2/1/36)	149.58	150.62	150.40	154.08	165.42
Lowered to 40	(11/1/37)	135.94	130.14	123.98	122.11	110.09
Raised to 50	(2/5/45)	155.35	155.50	156.34	160.68	163.19
Raised to 75	(7/5/45)	164.26	164.67	166.85	163.19	191.47
Raised to 100	(1/21/46)	196.63	197.35	204.62	195.62	200.54
Lowered to 75	(2/1/47)	180.88	181.92	184.49	179.29	183.81
Lowered to 50	(3/30/49)	178.45	177.10	176.71	174.16	182.51
Raised to 75	(1/17/51)	248.01	247.39	244.36	254.70	253.89
Lowered to 50	(2/20/53)	281.89	282.99	284.27	289.69	271.73
Raised to 60	(1/4/55)	406.17	397.24	400.25	409.76	459.42
Raised to 70	(4/23/55)	426.86	430.64	426.30	420.32	460.82
Lowered to 50	(1/16/58)	445.23	444.12	447.93	442.27	481.00
Raised to 70	(8/5/58)	506.95	503.11	508.19	512.77	586.12
Raised to 90	(10/16/58)	540.11	546.36	540.72	567.44	617.58
Lowered to 70	(7/28/60)	605.67	616.73	609.23	634.46	650.64
Lowered to 50	(7/10/62)	586.01	589.06	577.85	592.32	669.51
Raised to 70	(11/6/63)	744.03	745.66	751.11	760.25	828.18
Raised to 80	(6/10/68)	913.38	917.95	903.45	922.82	977.69
Lowered to 65	(5/6/70)	718.39	723.07	693.84	700.23	771.97
Lowered to 55	(12/6/71)	855.72	857.40	858.79	908.49	951.46

B. DISCOUNT RATE CHANGES (New York Reserve Bank)

Increases and decreases in the United States' money supply are regulated by 12 voting members of the Federal Open Market Committee: 7 from the Board of Governors of the Federal Reserve System, plus 5 of the 12 Federal Reserve bank presidents. Their principal controlling instruments are open-market operations, changes in reserve requirements, and discount rate changes.

The discount rate (often used synonymously with rediscount rate and bank rate) represents the amount of interest the Federal Reserve charges its member banks for loans. It has been raised 41 times and lowered

48 times since its inception in 1914 through 1971. The all-time high was 7% in 1920–1921; the record low was ½% to 1% from October, 1942, to April, 1946. Low or declining interest rates have a favorable influence on stock prices.

RATE CHANGES—MARKET PRICES

Dow Jones Industrials

	Date	Day Later	Week Later	Month Later	3 Mos. Later	6 Mos. Later
Initial Rate 6% *	11/16/14	Market	Closed	55.35	56.64	63.41
Lowered to 5	12/23/14	53.17	54.55	58.52	59.10	71.28
Lowered to 4½	2/3/15	56.83	57.05	55.88	69.54	76.71
Lowered to 4	2/18/15	55.38	54.61	56.57	62.70	81.86
Raised to 4½	12/21/17	68.23	72.13	76.11	78.71	81.65
Raised to 4¾	4/6/18	77.69	76.01	79.36	83.20	84.35
Raised to 6	1/23/20	102.65	104.21	92.98	95.46	89.63
Raised to 7	6/1/20	90.65	91.46	91.26	86.34	76.50
Lowered to 6½	5/5/21	79.68	77.60	71.18	68.61	73.91
Lowered to 6	6/16/21	67.57	65.36	67.44	70.95	80.95
Lowered to 5½	7/21/21	68.27	68.18	64.50	71.00	82.53
Lowered to 5	9/22/21	70.90	71.19	71.11	78.76	87.26
Lowered to 4½	11/3/21	73.94	75.61	79.00	82.93	93.81
Lowered to 4	6/22/22	93.07	92.06	95.78	98.55	98.62
Raised to 4½	2/23/23	102.85	104.51	103.98	93.90	92.04
Lowered to 4	5/1/24	91.68	92.04	90.15	102.12	104.17
Lowered to 3½	6/12/24	91.23	90.15	96.38	104.95	110.71
Lowered to 3	8/8/24	102.08	104.01	101.26	105.53	122.37
Raised to 3½	2/27/25	122.71	125.68	117.48	129.13	141.54
Raised to 4	1/8/26	159.10	155.10	159.10	140.67	155.66
Lowered to 3½	4/23/26	144.83	143.71	141.16	155.43	149.56
Raised to 4	8/13/26	166.64	162.06	158.97	154.58	157.56
Lowered to 3½	8/5/27	182.51	177.13	196.91	188.47	196.63
Raised to 4	2/23/28	196.53	199.02	195.43	214.62	216.15

		Date	Day Later	Week Later	Month Later	3 Mos. Later	6 Mos. Later
Raised	to 4½%	5/18/28	214.33	217.74	201.96	223.61	278.78
Raised	to 5	7/13/28	207.77	209.95	215.53	249.13	304.06
Raised	to 6	8/9/29	344.84	361.49	374.93	220.39	268.56
Lowered	to 5	11/1/29	257.68	236.53	241.70	268.41	274.59
Lowered	to 4½	11/15/29	227.56	245.74	245.88	269.25	269.91
Lowered	to 4	2/7/30	269.78	271.52	275.57	263.69	232.69
Lowered	to 3½	3/14/30	270.25	280.55	293.18	244.25	236.62
Lowered	to 3	5/2/30	258.31	267.29	274.45	234.50	185.39
Lowered	to 2½	6/20/30	215.30	218.78	229.29	229.85	169.42
Lowered	to 2	12/24/30	161.18	164.58	169.80	186.00	151.60
Lowered	to 1½	5/8/31	151.31	144.49	135.92	134.94	116.79
Raised	to 2½	10/9/31	105.61	102.49	116.79	79.98	64.48
Raised	to 3½	10/16/31	102.28	108.88	104.76	84.44	63.39
Lowered	to 3	2/26/32	82.02	86.11	75.69	49.99	74.43
Lowered	to 2½	6/24/32	44.76	44.39	49.78	74.83	57.98
Raised	to 3½	3/3/33	**	**	55.69	90.02	100.22
Lowered	to 3	4/7/33	59.30	62.88	76.63	105.35	98.20
Lowered	to 2½	5/26/33	89.61	92.21	98.49	104.72	95.77
Lowered	to 2	10/20/33	83.64	93.22	101.28	105.52	106.55
Lowered	to 1½	2/2/34	109.41	106.09	105.79	98.82	90.87
Lowered	to 1	8/27/37	175.93	172.17	152.03	123.71	129.64
Lowered	to ½***−1	10/30/42	114.07	116.12	114.50	125.58	135.48
Raised	to 1	4/25/46	204.59	204.98	209.42	196.25	165.23
Raised	to 1¼	1/12/48	177.49	175.95	166.33	179.05	191.47
Raised	to 1½	8/13/48	180.30	183.60	179.38	174.32	172.16
Raised	to 1¾	8/21/50	219.79	218.55	226.01	231.16	252.28
Raised	to 2	1/16/53	286.97	286.89	282.18	276.74	269.41
Lowered	to 1¾	2/5/54	293.58	293.99	299.45	317.93	347.79
Lowered	to 1½	4/16/54	311.78	314.54	323.33	339.96	354.35
Raised	to 1¾	4/15/55	428.42	425.52	415.01	460.23	446.13
Raised	to 2	8/5/55	454.05	457.01	476.24	470.58	478.57
Raised	to 2¼	9/9/55	476.51	483.67	441.14	487.64	497.84
Raised	to 2½	11/18/55	477.30	482.88	481.80	476.46	496.39
Raised	to 2¾	4/13/56	509.15	507.20	497.28	511.10	489.40
Raised	to 3	8/24/56	505.70	502.04	487.70	470.29	466.90
Raised	to 3½	8/23/57	470.14	484.35	458.96	448.38	437.19

* 1914–1921, inclusive, is the rate on 61 to 90-day commercial, agricultural, and live-stock paper; various rates prevailed on other maturities and other classes of paper during this period.
** Market closed from 3/4 to 3/14 for banking holiday.
*** ½% on advances to member banks, secured by direct and fully guaranteed obligations of the U.S. which have one year or less to run to call date, or to maturity if no call date.

	Date	Day Later	Week Later	Month Later	3 Mos. Later	6 Mos. Later
Lowered to 3%	11/15/57	434.96	442.68	433.40	442.27	457.86
Lowered to 2¾	1/24/58	448.46	450.02	437.19	453.42	497.12
Lowered to 2¼	3/7/58	451.90	453.04	440.09	469.46	515.23
Lowered to 1¾	4/18/58	450.72	454.92	455.98	486.55	544.19
Raised to 2	9/12/58	523.40	526.48	545.95	562.27	613.75
Raised to 2½	11/7/58	557.72	564.68	556.08	574.46	615.64
Raised to 3	3/6/59	609.96	614.69	611.16	621.62	642.69
Raised to 3½	5/29/59	643.51	629.98	643.06	664.41	659.18
Raised to 4	9/11/59	633.79	625.78	638.55	670.50	605.83
Lowered to 3½	6/10/60	655.85	650.89	640.44	609.35	612.09
Lowered to 3	8/12/60	624.17	629.27	609.35	604.80	637.04
Raised to 3½	7/17/63	695.90	690.88	718.81	750.77	775.69
Raised to 4	11/24/64	882.40	864.43	868.16	897.84	914.21
Raised to 4½	12/6/65	951.33	951.55	985.46	917.76	881.68
Lowered to 4	4/7/67	842.43	859.74	909.63	869.05	933.31
Raised to 4½	11/20/67	870.95	882.11	886.90	843.10	894.19
Raised to 5	3/22/68	827.27	840.67	891.99	901.83	930.45
Raised to 5½	4/19/68	891.99	906.03	894.19	913.92	967.49
Lowered to 5¼	8/30/68	900.36	921.25	935.79	985.09	905.21
Raised to 5½	12/18/68	975.14	954.25	931.25	907.38	887.09
Raised to 6	4/4/69	918.78	932.64	958.95	883.21	809.40
Lowered to 5¾	11/30/70	760.13	761.57	823.18	890.06	936.34
Lowered to 5½	12/4/70	818.66	825.92	830.57	891.36	922.15
Lowered to 5¼	1/8/71	837.21	845.70	882.12	920.39	900.99
Lowered to 5	1/22/71	865.62	868.50	868.98	940.63	886.68
Lowered to 4¾	2/19/71	868.98	878.83	912.92	920.04	880.77
Raised to 5	7/16/71	886.39	887.78	888.95	872.44	911.12
Lowered to 4¾	11/19/71	803.15	816.59	885.01	913.46	961.54
Lowered to 4½	12/17/71	885.01	881.47	911.12	942.88	945.06

Most consecutive rate increases: 7 (from 1½% to 3½%) April 15, 1955–August 23, 1957.

Most consecutive rate decreases: 8 (from 6% to 1½%) November 11, 1929–May 8, 1931.

Biggest consecutive rate increase: 3% (from 4% to 7%) December 21, 1917–June 1, 1920.

Biggest consecutive rate decrease: 4½% (from 6% to 1½%) November 1, 1929–May 8, 1931.

Biggest single rate increase: 1¼% (from 4¾% to 6%) January 23, 1920.

Biggest single rate decrease: 1% twice (from 6% to 5%) December 23, 1914 and November 1, 1929.

Most rate changes in a calendar year: 6 in 1971.

Longest time no rate change: 62 months (August 27, 1937–October 30, 1942).

C. PRIME RATE CHANGES

The lending rate set generally by big New York City banks, upon which the lending rates of commercial banks throughout the country are based, is called the prime rate. Rate changes are influenced mostly by overall business conditions, the supply and demand for credit, and knowledge and expectations about Treasury and Federal Reserve Board policy.

The prime rate conception was initiated during the Depression, as a floor below which the major banks agreed they could not operate profitably. It stood at $1\frac{1}{2}\%$ from the latter part of 1933 until December, 1947. Since then it has ranged from a low of 2% in August, 1948, to a record peak of $8\frac{1}{2}\%$ in June, 1969.

Year	High	Low	Year	High	Low
1919	6%	$5\frac{1}{4}\%$	1928	$5\frac{1}{2}\%$	$4\frac{1}{4}\%$
1920	7	6	1929	6	$5\frac{1}{2}$
1921	7	$5\frac{1}{2}$	1930	6	$3\frac{1}{2}$
1922	$5\frac{1}{2}$	$4\frac{1}{2}$	1931	5	$2\frac{3}{4}$
1923	$5\frac{1}{2}$	$4\frac{3}{4}$	1932	4	$3\frac{1}{4}$
1924	$5\frac{1}{2}$	$3\frac{1}{2}$	1933	4	$1\frac{1}{2}$
1925	5	$4\frac{1}{2}$	1934 (to November, 1947)		$1\frac{1}{2}$
1926	5	$4\frac{1}{2}$	1947 (December)		$1\frac{3}{4}$
1927	$4\frac{1}{2}$	$4\frac{1}{4}$	1948 (August)		2

Dow Jones Industrials

			Date	Day Later	Week Later	Month Later	3 Mos. Later
Raised	to	2¼%	9/22/50	226.06	228.94	230.62	231.54
Raised	to	2½	1/8/51	243.50	245.02	253.34	250.57
Raised	to	2¾	10/17/51	273.51	264.95	260.82	271.91
Raised	to	3	12/19/51	267.45	264.06	272.93	264.37
Raised	to	3¼	4/27/53	273.96	278.34	273.96	268.46
Lowered to		3	3/17/54	300.10	296.89	311.78	327.21
Raised	to	3¼	8/4/55	456.40	455.18	476.24	467.35
Raised	to	3½	10/14/55	446.13	458.47	484.88	476.24
Raised	to	3¾	4/13/56	509.15	507.20	497.28	511.10
Raised	to	4	8/21/56	502.34	503.05	490.33	467.91
Raised	to	4½	8/6/57	498.48	492.14	478.63	435.82
Lowered to		4	1/22/58	447.93	451.16	437.19	449.55
Lowered to		3½	4/21/58	449.55	454.51	458.50	493.36
Raised	to	4	9/11/58	519.43	522.34	545.95	563.07
Raised	to	4½	5/18/59	635.44	632.35	629.41	650.79
Raised	to	5	9/1/59	655.80	642.69	633.60	664.38
Lowered to		4½	8/23/60	641.56	626.40	585.20	602.47
Raised	to	5	12/6/65	951.33	951.55	985.46	917.76
Raised	to	5½	3/10/66	927.95	919.32	942.42	891.75
Raised	to	5¾	6/29/66	870.10	888.86	847.38	772.66
Raised	to	6	8/16/66	819.59	790.14	814.30	820.87
Lowered to 5½–¾			1/26–27/67	844.04	857.46	836.64	894.82
Lowered to		5½	3/22–23/67	876.67	869.99	887.53	877.37
Raised	to	6	11/22/67	877.60	883.15	887.37	849.80
Raised	to	6½	4/19/68	891.99	906.03	894.19	913.92
Lowered to		6–6¼	9/25/68	933.24	949.47	961.28	954.25
Raised	to	6¼	11/13/68	963.89	965.13	981.29	952.70
Raised	to	6½	12/2/68	985.21	979.36	947.73	908.63
Raised	to	6¾	12/18/68	975.14	954.25	931.25	907.38
Raised	to	7	1/7/69	921.25	928.33	947.85	918.78
Raised	to	7½	3/17/69	907.38	917.08	924.12	885.73
Raised	to	8½	6/9/69	912.49	891.16	861.62	783.79
Lowered to		8	3/25/70	791.05	792.04	735.15	693.59
Lowered to		7½[a]	8/27/70	765.81	765.27	758.97	781.35
Lowered to		7¼	11/12/70	759.79	755.82	823.18	888.83
Lowered to		7	11/23/70	772.73	794.09	823.11	870.00
Lowered to		6¾	12/22/70	823.11	842.00	861.31	910.60

[a] Rate cut—initiated by Canal National Bank, Portland, Maine—followed by other small banks and finally by Morgan Guaranty and remaining holdouts on September 21.

	Date	*Day* *Later*	*Week* *Later*	*Month* *Later*	*3 Mos.* *Later*
Lowered to 6½% [b]	1/5/71	837.97	844.19	876.57	905.07
Lowered to 6¼	1/15/71	847.82	861.31	890.06	938.17
Lowered to 6 [c]	1/18/71	849.47	865.62	885.06	948.85
Lowered to 5¾	2/9/71	881.09	890.06	899.10	932.55
Lowered to 5¼	3/17/71	916.83	899.37	948.85	906.25
Raised to 5½	4/23/71	944.00	941.75	913.15	887.78
Raised to 5¾ [d]	6/15/71	908.59	874.42	888.87	904.86
Raised to 6 [e]	6/21/71	874.42	873.10	890.84	903.40
Raised to 6½ [f]	8/3/71	844.92	839.59	912.75	842.58
Lowered to 5¾ [g]	10/20/71	854.85	836.38	803.15	910.30
Lowered to 5½	11/4/71	840.39	814.91	855.72	906.68
Lowered to 5¼	12/20–21/71	888.32	889.98	907.44	934.00

[b] Initiated by 1st Pennsylvania Banking & Trust; followed by Chemical, Bank of America, Wells Fargo—January 7–8.

[c] Initiated by Morgan, Chemical, Chase. Rate became effective January 22.

[d] By 1st Pennsylvania Banking & Trust.

[e] By Bank of California.

[f] By The Michigan Bank.

[g] On October 21, First National City Bank and Irving Trust began calculating a weekly "floating rate." Banker's Trust adopted this floating rate system December 29.

Most consecutive rate increases: 7 (from 1½% to 3¼%) December, 1947–April 27, 1953.

Most consecutive rate decreases: 10 (from 8½% to 5¼%) March 25, 1970–March 17, 1971.

Biggest consecutive rate increase: 2¼% (from 6–6¼% to 8½%) September 25, 1968–June 9, 1969.

Biggest consecutive rate decrease: 3¼% (from 8½% to 5¼%) June 9, 1969–March 17, 1971.

Biggest single rate increase: 1% (from 7½% to 8½%) June 9, 1969.

Biggest single rate decrease: ¾% (from 6½% to 5¾%) October 20, 1971.

Most rate changes in calendar year: Twelve in 1971.

Longest time no rate change: 63½ months (August 23, 1960–December 6, 1965).

PART 2

Presidential Elections

A. DOW JONES INDUSTRIALS IN PRE-PRESIDENTIAL ELECTION YEARS

(P – Plus; M – Minus)

Year	J	F	M	A	M	J	J	A	S	O	N	D	Mos. Up	Mos. Down	Chg. Prev. Yr.
1903	P	P	M	M	M	M	M	M	M	M	M	P	5	7	M 15.18
1907	M	M	M	M	M	M	M	P	P	P	P	P	4	8	M 35.60
1911	P	P	M	P	P	P	P	M	P	M	M	P	8	4	P 0.32
1915	P	M	P	M	P	P	P	P	P	P	P	P	10	2	P 44.57
1919	M	P	P	P	P	M	P	P	M	P	P	P	9	3	P 25.03
1923	M	P	M	M	M	M	P	M	P	P	M	P	5	7	M 3.21
1927	M	P	M	P	P	M	M	P	P	M	P	P	8	4	P 45.20
1931	P	P	M	M	M	M	M	M	P	P	M	M	5	7	M 86.68
1935	M	P	M	P	P	P	M	M	P	M	M	M	10	2	P 40.09
1939	M	P	M	M	P	M	P	P	M	M	P	P	5	7	M 4.52
1943	P	P	P	M	P	P	P	P	P	M	M	P	9	3	P 16.49
1947	P	M	M	M	M	P	M	M	P	P	M	P	5	7	P 3.96
1951	P	P	M	M	M	M	P	M	M	M	M	P	7	5	P 33.82
1955	P	P	M	P	M	P	M	M	M	P	P	P	8	4	P 84.01
1959	P	P	P	M	P	M	P	M	M	P	P	P	8	4	P 95.71
1963	P	P	P	P	M	P	M	P	P	P	M	P	8	4	P 110.85
1967	P	M	P	M	P	M	M	P	M	M	M	P	7	5	P 119.42
1971	P	P	P	P	M	M	M	P	M	M	M	P	6	6	P 51.28
P:	12	13	6	13	8	10	12	11	9	8	10	17			
M:	6	5	12	5	10	8	6	7	9	10	8	1			

Months in Pre-election Years When DJI Posted Closing Highs-Lows

	Jan.	Feb.	Mar.	Apr.	May	June	July	Aug.	Sept.	Oct.	Nov.	Dec.
Highs:	1907	1903 1931	1923	1971	0	1911	1943 1947	0	1939 1951 1955 1967	0	1919 1935	1915 1927 1959 1963
Lows:	1927 1943 1951 1955 1963 1967	1915 1919 1959	1935	1939	1947	0	0	0	1911	1923	1903 1907 1971	1931

B. DOW JONES INDUSTRIALS IN PRESIDENTIAL ELECTION YEARS

(P – Plus; M – Minus)

Year	J	F	M	A	M	J	J	A	S	O	N	D	Mos. Up	Mos. Down	Chg. Prev. Yr.
1900	P	P	P	M	M	M	P	P	M	P	P	P	8	4	P 4.63
1904	M	M	P	M	M	P	P	P	P	P	P	M	7	5	P 20.50
1908	P	M	P	P	P	P	M	M	P	P	P	M	8	4	P 27.40
1912	M	P	P	P	M	M	M	P	P	M	P	P	7	5	P 6.19
1916	M	P	P	P	P	M	M	P	P	P	M	M	7	5	M 4.15
1920	M	M	M	M	M	M	P	M	M	P	M	M	2	10	M 35.28
1924	P	M	M	P	M	P	P	M	P	P	M	P	7	5	P 24.99
1928	M	M	P	P	P	M	M	M	P	P	P	P	7	5	P 97.60
1932	M	M	P	M	M	P	P	M	M	M	M	P	4	8	M 17.97
1936	P	P	P	M	P	P	P	P	P	P	P	M	10	2	P 35.77
1940	M	P	P	P	P	P	P	P	P	M	M	P	9	3	M 19.11
1944	P	M	P	P	M	M	M	P	M	P	P	P	7	5	P 16.43
1948	M	M	P	P	P	P	M	M	M	M	P	P	6	6	M 3.86
1952	P	M	P	P	P	P	M	M	M	M	P	P	7	5	P 22.67
1956	M	M	M	P	P	P	M	P	M	P	P	P	7	5	P 11.07
1960	M	M	P	P	M	P	M	P	M	P	P	P	7	5	M 63.47
1964	P	P	P	P	P	M	M	M	P	P	P	M	8	4	P 111.18
1968	M	M	P	P	M	M	P	P	P	P	M	M	6	6	P 38.64
P:	7	9	15	6	9	10	11	14	7	13	13	10			
M:	11	9	3	12	9	8	7	4	11	5	5	8			

Months in Election Years When DJI Posted Closing Highs-Lows

	Jan.	Feb.	Mar.	Apr.	May	June	July	Aug.	Sept.	Oct.	Nov.	Dec.
Highs:	1920	0	1932	1956	0	1948	0	0	1912	0	1908	1900
	1940										1916	1904
	1960										1936	1924
											1964	1928
												1944
												1952
												1968
Lows:	1936	1908	1904	1916	1924	1940	1932	0	1900	1960	0	1920
	1956	1912	1948		1952							
	1964	1928	1968									
		1944										

251

C. DOW JONES INDUSTRIALS IN POST-PRESIDENTIAL ELECTION YEARS
(P – Plus; M – Minus)

Year	J	F	M	A	M	J	J	A	S	O	N	D	Mos. Up	Mos. Down	Chg. Prev. Yr.
1901	M	P	P	P	M	P	M	P	M	M	P	M	6	6	M 6.15
1905	P	P	P	M	M	P	P	M	P	P	P	P	9	3	P 26.59
1909	M	M	P	P	P	P	P	P	P	M	M	P	8	4	P 12.90
1913	M	M	P	M	M	M	P	P	M	M	M	P	4	8	M 9.09
1917	P	M	P	M	P	M	M	M	M	M	M	P	5	7	M 20.62
1921	P	M	P	P	M	M	P	M	P	P	P	P	8	4	P 9.15
1925	P	M	M	P	M	P	P	M	P	P	M	P	9	3	P 36.15
1929	P	M	M	P	P	P	P	P	M	M	M	P	6	6	M 51.52
1933	P	M	P	P	P	P	M	P	M	M	P	P	8	4	P 39.97
1937	P	P	M	M	M	M	M	M	M	M	M	M	4	8	M 59.05
1941	M	M	P	P	P	P	M	M	M	M	P	M	4	8	M 20.17
1945	P	P	M	M	M	P	P	P	P	P	P	P	9	3	P 40.59
1949	P	M	P	M	M	M	P	P	M	P	P	P	8	4	P 22.83
1953	M	M	P	P	P	P	P	M	M	M	P	M	4	8	M 11.00
1957	M	M	P	P	M	M	M	M	M	M	P	M	5	7	M 63.78
1961	P	P	P	P	P	P	P	P	P	P	P	P	10	2	P 115.25
1965	P	P	M	P	P	P	P	P	M	M	M	P	8	4	P 95.13
1969	P	M	P	P	M	M	M	M	M	P	M	M	5	7	M 143.39
P:	12	6	12	11	9	7	13	11	9	9	9	12			
M:	6	12	6	7	9	11	5	7	9	9	9	6			

Months in Post-election Years When DJI Posted Closing Highs-Lows

	Jan.	Feb.	Mar.	Apr.	May	June	July	Aug.	Sept.	Oct.	Nov.	Dec.
Highs:	1913 1917 1941 1953	0	1937	0	1969	1901	1933 1957	0	1929	0	1909 1925	1905 1921 1945 1949 1961 1965
Lows:	1905 1945 1961	1909 1933	1925	0	0	1913 1949 1965	0	1921	1953	1957	1929 1937	1901 1917 1941 1969

253

PART 3

Miscellaneous Forces

A. ACCIDENTS—ACTS OF GOD

September 21, 1776: Fire destroyed 500 homes—about one-eighth of New York—including wall from which Wall Street derived its name.

December 16–17, 1835: Nearly everything south of Wall Street, east of Broadway, destroyed by fire.

October 8–11, 1871: Chicago fire. Stocks dropped 4–10 points.

November 11, 1872: Boston fire. Market declined abruptly.

March, 1888: Blizzard of '88. Only 32 brokers on NYSE trading floor. Volume dropped to 15,800 shares.

May 31, 1889: Johnstown Flood. No important market influence. Stock prices reached a 5-year high in the late summer months, before reacting.

September 8, 1900: Galveston, Texas, hurricane and flood. DJI closed at 57.88; week later, 56.56; following week, 53.43—prior to reaching year's low of 52.96 on the 24th.

Spring of 1904: Baltimore fire—depressant the market did not fully overcome until new bull uptrend got underway from lows reached in May of 47.43 on DJI and 93.55 DJR.

April 18–19, 1906: San Francisco earthquake and fire. San Francisco Stock Exchange closed until May 28. DJI fell 2.61 in 2 days on way to April 28 low of 88.70.

April 15, 1912: "Titanic" sank. No apparent market influence, although prices eroded slowly to a low of 88.72 on April 22 from 89.71 on the 15th.

September 16, 1920: Explosion on Wall Street outside J. P. Morgan & Co. No influence on market. DJI posted month's closing high (89.95) the following day.

August 4, 1933: Gas bombs exploded near NYSE trading floor. Market ignored the incident.

September 21, 1938: New England hurricane. DJI fell 1.94 to 137.35 the following day.

February 15–16, 1958: Blizzard in Northeast. Occurred over weekend, but DJI fell 2.17 to 442.27 in Monday's session.

March 27, 1964: Alaska earthquake. Market was closed for Good Friday holiday.

November 10, 1965: Massive power failure (Northeast and part of Canada) delayed opening of exchanges. Big Board volume sank to 4.9 million shares. DJI fell 0.50 to 951.22.

B. DEATHS—ILLNESSES: WORLD LEADERS

April 14, 1865: President Lincoln shot (died April 15). National victory converted to national mourning. *The N.Y. Times* columned in black. N.Y. Stock Board adjourned at 10:30 A.M.

July 2, 1881: President Garfield shot (died September 19). Market down abruptly; panic averted only by intervention of Sunday and July 4 holiday.

September 6, 1901: President McKinley shot (died September 14). Following day DJI fell 3.20 to 69.03 and did not fully regain ground lost from September 6 level until November 28, 1904.

June 28, 1914: Assassination of Archduke Ferdinand led to World War I. DJI closed off fractionally at 80.00 the following session, then rallied to high of 81.79 on July 8—a level not duplicated for 14 months.

August 2, 1923: President Harding died in office. DJI dropped 1.00 to month's low of 87.20 next day. Year's closing low was 85.76 (October 27)—a bottom not broken until December 9, 1931.

February 15, 1933: President-elect Roosevelt escaped, but Chicago Mayor Cermak was assassinated. DJI declined 1.26 to 55.49 on the

16th and to 50.16 (low for February and for 1933) on the 27th. Thereafter, new bull market began, which lasted until August, 1937.

February 24, 1943: Churchill ill with pneumonia. DJI rose fractionally to 129.58. Bull market that began when DJI reached low for war years at 92.92 (4/28/42) remained intact.

March 12, 1943: Hitler's nervous breakdown. DJI closed at 130.73, continued moving forward to high of 136.82 in March.

April 12, 1945: President Roosevelt died in office. No special market influence. Investors sensed end of war and DJI continued rising to year's closing high of 195.80 on December 11.

January 30, 1948: Gandhi assassinated. No apparent influence on U.S. markets, although DJI declined into February–March, where double bottom formed at 165–166 for advance to year's high of 196.16 on June 15.

November 1, 1950: Truman escaped assassination attempt. DJI rose 0.68 to 225.69; week later 224.25, after posting November low of 222.52 on the 6th.

March 5, 1953: Stalin died. DJI closed 0.16 higher at 283.86 and continued rising in virtually a straight line to month's high of 290.64 on the 17th. Low for year was reached September 14 at 255.49.

September 24, 1955: Eisenhower heart attack. DJI dropped 31.89 from 1955 closing high of 487.45 reached on 23rd to 455.56, rallied in two sessions to 472.61, then melted slowly to an October low of 438.59 before recovering again. The initial setback represented a one-day loss of 6.5%.

June 9, 1956: Eisenhower operation. DJI declined 7.70 to month's low of 475.29 on day preceding operation. Announcement of its success boosted confidence and sparked recovery to June closing peak of 488.26 on the 21st, where stage was set for summer strength carrying to closing high of 520.95 (August 2).

May 30, 1961: Trujillo assassinated. Market was closed for Memorial Day, but event had no discernible effect on stocks. Except for setback in September, DJI moved mostly forward to 1961 closing high of 734.91 on December 13.

November 22, 1963: President Kennedy assassinated. DJI dropped to 710.83 intraday, closed at 711.49 down 21.16. Exchanges halted trading to prevent panic. Public confidence was restored over weekend, including day of national mourning—Monday the 25th. DJI rose 32.03

to 743.52 in first session following assassination. Year's high posted at 767.21 on December 18.

June 9, 1965: Rumors of Johnson stroke or heart attack. DJI fell 25.66 to 876.49 in 3 days (June 8–10) and reached month's low at 840.59 on the 28th. However, majority of weakness appeared to have been caused by possible steel strike, marines ordered to Dominican Republic, war rumblings from Red China, decline in U.S. gold stocks, and, especially, FRB Chairman Martin's remarks about "disquieting similarities" with 1929. DJI bottomed out around 840 area, preparatory to rising to year's closing high (969.26) in final trading session.

October 6, 1965: LBJ to be operated upon. DJI fell 4.28 to 934.42 in 2 days.

November 4, 1966: LBJ surgery taken in stride. DJI rose 0.72 to 805.06; week later, 819.09.

April 4, 1968: Martin Luther King assassinated. DJI fell 6.71 on worry about race riots, but rallied 18.61 in following session and continued uptrending to an April 30 high of 912.22.

June 5, 1968: Robert F. Kennedy shot (died June 6). Market's reaction to second assassination of a leading figure in two months was negative; basic price trends were not affected.

August 8, 1968: LBJ ill. DJI fell 6.66 to 870.37 and posted low for month the next day (869.65). Once fears were allayed, the market resumed uptrend toward year's closing high of 985.21 (12/3).

September 3, 1969: Ho Chi Minh died. Possibility of important change in North Vietnam war strategy sparked sell off from closing high of 837.78 on the 2nd to a low for month of 811.64 on the 8th. Recovery into October reached 868.00 intraday before another decline began. But this was caused mainly by tighter money/credit, continued Middle East tension.

September 28, 1970: Nasser died. DJI dropped 2.80 to 758.97, but death of Egypt's leader had little market influence.

C. WARS—BATTLES; INTERNATIONAL CRISES—INCIDENTS

War of 1812: Gave speculation its first real impetus.

August 28, 1814: British captured Washington. Baltimore, Philadelphia, New York banks suspended specie payments.

War with Mexico (1846–1848): Had little effect on nation or stock market.

April 12–13, 1861: Civil War began with cannonading at Fort Sumter. Semipanic on the Exchange. Money unobtainable; distrust everywhere. Thirteen leading stocks tobogganed an average 20% in 3 days. Government bonds joined the parade downward; those of the seceded states shed 30% in value.

Then the speculators took over. They had discovered a way to make money by selling the dollar short and buying future options on gold at rising prices. Trading in gold and Greenbacks (government scrip issued to finance the war) was the fad of the war years. A rise in gold and a fall in Greenbacks followed Confederate triumphs; Union victories were accompanied by a fall in gold. And each new battle heaped more frosting on the speculative cake.

April 9, 1865: Lee surrendered at Appomattox. Confederacy and the war ended.

February 15, 1898: Battleship "Maine" blew up in Havana harbor. DJI declined from 49.15 this date to low of 48.00 on the 24th.

April 25–December 10, 1898: War with Spain. DJI advanced 16.09 points from 44.02 to 60.11 in this period. Year's closing high was posted August 26 at 60.97.

March 15, 1911: Troops to Mexico under General Pershing. DJI fell 1.75 during the month, but basic uptrend remained intact; trouble with Mexico was not a market factor.

July 28, 1914: Austria declared war on Serbia. DJI fell 2.79 to 76.28 this day and to 71.42 (month's low) on July 30. Thereafter, until December 12, when trading in certain stocks was resumed at pegged prices, the Exchange was shuttered for first time since Panic of 1873. An outlaw market flourished outside on New Street, while it was closed.

February 18, 1915: Germany declared unrestricted submarine warfare in waters surrounding British Isles. DJI fell 0.17 to 55.53 (fifth straight declining session); carried to low of 54.22 on the 24th.

May 7, 1915: "Lusitania" sunk. DJI fell 3.10 to 65.13; thence to May closing low of 60.38.

February 1–2, 1917: U.S. broke relations with Germany. DJI fell 8.42 to 87.01.

April 2, 1917: Wilson asked Congress to declare war. DJI fell 5.86 in 6 sessions to 91.20.

April 6, 1917: U.S. entered war. DJI continued to drop with few rallies to low for month of 90.66 on the 24th.

July 18, 1918: Marshal Foch launched big offensive shortly before DJI reached July closing low of 80.51.

October 6, 1918: Germany asked for peace terms. DJI dropped 3 straight days to October closing low of 83.36 on the 9th, before rallying strongly.

November 11, 1918: War ended; Armistice signed. Market trended mostly lower immediately following peace, on theory that corporate earnings would decline.

January 11, 1923: French-Belgian troops occupied Ruhr. DJI rose 0.83 to 98.12; week later, 98.09.

January 6, 1927: Marines to Nicaragua to guard U.S. property. DJI fell 0.38 to 155.16; week later, 155.68.

March 24, 1927: Marines to China. DJI rose 1.45 to 160.30; week later, 160.08.

September 18, 1931: Japan annexed Manchuria. DJI fell 6.68 to 115.08; week later, 109.86.

October 14, 1933: Germany withdrew from League of Nations. DJI rose 0.23 to 95.59; week later, 83.64.

March 10, 1935: Hitler rejected Versailles Treaty, revived military training. DJI fell 1.79 to 99.39; week later, 97.01.

October 3, 1935: Italy invaded Ethiopia. DJI rose 0.99 to 129.05. Invasion already discounted by 3.45 drop previous day; week later, 132.99.

March 7, 1936: Hitler reoccupied Rhineland. DJI fell 0.89 to 157.86; week later, 154.07.

July 17, 1936: Spanish Civil War began. DJI fell 0.09 to 163.55; week later, 164.37.

October 27, 1936: Rome-Berlin Axis established. DJI rose 2.06 to 174.36; week later, 180.66, due to election results.

December 11, 1937: Italy quit League of Nations. DJI rose 0.11 to 126.83; week later, 126.63.

December 12, 1937: Japanese planes sank U.S. gunboat "Panay." DJI fell 4.00 to 122.83; week later, 129.08.

March 12, 1938: Germany annexed Austria. DJI rose 0.14 to 122.58; week later, 120.43.

September 29–30, 1938: Munich Pact signed. Idea of "peace in our time" sparked 18-point rise to 148.32 by DJI in 7 sessions.

March 15–18, 1939: Germany annexed Czechoslovakia. DJI fell 9.82 in 5 days to 141.28; week later, 141.14.

May 22, 1939: Germany-Italy signed military alliance. DJI rose 1.23 to 132.45; week later, 137.80.

August 23, 1939: Lloyd's of London upped war-risk rates. DJI fell 3.25 to 131.82; week later, 136.16.

August 24, 1939: Germany-Russia signed nonaggression pact. DJI fell 0.49 to 131.33; week later, 134.41, on eve of World War II.

September 1, 1939: Germany attacked Poland. DJI rose 0.84 to 135.25; week later, 150.04.

September 3, 1939: England, France declared war on Germany. DJI rose 10.03 to 148.12 after Labor Day holiday; week later, 155.92.

September 8, 1939: FDR declared limited national emergency. DJI rose 1.72 to 150.04; week later, 154.03.

September 17, 1939: Russia invaded Poland. DJI fell 4.37 to 147.78; week later, 152.64.

November 30, 1939: Russia attacked Finland. DJI fell 1.20 to 145.69; week later, 148.70.

May 10, 1940: Germany invaded Low Countries. DJI fell 3.40 to 144.77; week later, 124.20.

May 12–14, 1940: Germans blitzed across France. DJI continued declining to month's closing low of 113.94 on the 24th.

May 26–June 3, 1940: Evacuation at Dunkerque. DJI moved over relatively narrow range and closed June 3 at 114.73.

June 10, 1940: Italy entered war, invaded France. DJI fell 3.52 to 111.84, their June low.

June 14, 1940: Fall of Paris. Event had been discounted. DJI rose 2.36 to 122.27.

July 14, 1940: Estonia, Latvia, Lithuania annexed by Russia. No market influence. DJI rose 0.24 to 121.72; week later, 122.06.

August 13, 1940: Battle of Britain began. DJI fell 4.28 to 122.98; week later, 123.17.

October 8, 1940: Americans advised to leave Far East. DJI fell 2.20 to 131.31; week later, 131.48.

November 14, 1940: Luftwaffe bombed Coventry. DJI rose 0.36 to 136.97; week later, 131.74.

January 30, 1941: Hitler said ships aiding Britain would be sunk. DJI fell 1.95 to January closing low of 124.05; week later, 124.76.

April 7, 1941: Yugoslavia surrendered. DJI fell 0.68 to 123.64 on idea Germany was winning in Balkans; week later, 118.89.

April 27, 1941: Fall of Athens. DJI rose 0.20 to 116.63; week later, 115.84.

May 10, 1941: Rudolph Hess parachuted into Scotland. DJI rose 1.08 to 117.54; week later, 116.11.

May 27, 1941: FDR declared unlimited national emergency. Market took news in stride. DJI rose 0.22 to 115.95; week later, 117.38.

June 22, 1941: Germany attacked Russia. DJI rose 1.46 to 123.97; week later, 123.14.

December 7, 1941: Japan attacked Pearl Harbor. DJI fell 4.08 to 112.52 in Monday trading session; week later, 111.15.

December 8, 1941: War formally declared on Japan. Market concerned over heavy fleet damage.

February 15, 1942: British surrendered Singapore. DJI rose 0.01 to 107.31; week later, 106.00.

April 18, 1942: Doolittle's planes raided Japan. DJI rose 0.87 to 96.92; week later, 94.31.

May 1, 1942: Battle of the Coral Sea. DJI rose 0.48 to 98.83; week later, 97.91.

May 6, 1942: Fall of Corregidor. DJI fell 0.58 to 86.71; week later, 97.21.

June 3–6, 1942: Battle of Midway. DJI rose 4.25 to 105.55 in 5 days.

August 7, 1942: Marines landed at Guadalcanal. DJI rose 0.25 to 105.05; week later, 106.15.

November 8, 1942: Allies landed in North Africa. DJI rose 0.38 to November high of 117.30; week later, 115.70.

November 17, 1942: Naval victory in Solomon Islands. DJI fell 1.17 to 114.53; week later, 114.10.

January 14, 1943: Casablanca Conference. DJI rose 0.54 to 120.79; week later, 121.79.

January 27, 1943: First big daylight raid on Emden-Wilhelmshaven. DJI fell 0.23 to 124.08 before moving to month's high of 125.58.

February 2, 1943: Germans surrendered at Stalingrad. DJI rose 0.02 to 125.88; week later, 126.30.

February 9, 1943: Major Japanese resistance ended on Guadalcanal. DJI rose 0.73 to 126.30; week later, 128.31.

May 12, 1943: War ended in Africa. DJI fell 0.12 to 138.24; week later, 139.15.

July 10, 1943: Allies invaded Sicily. DJI rose 0.05 to 144.23; week later, 144.72.

July 27, 1943: Italy reported negotiating for peace. DJI fell 3.32 to 138.75; week later, 135.64.

August 18, 1943: Sicily campaign ended. DJI rose 0.91 to 138.45; week later, 135.90.

September 3, 1943: Italian mainland invaded. DJI rose 0.07 to 137.18; week later, 137.96.

September 8, 1943: Italy surrendered. DJI fell 0.68 to month's low of 136.91; week later, 137.62.

September 10, 1943: Germans seized Rome. DJI rose 0.21 to 137.96; week later, 139.60.

October 1, 1943: Allies captured Naples. DJI rose 0.21 to 140.33, their high for month; week later, 136.74.

October 13, 1943: Italy declared war on Germany. DJI fell 0.13 to 136.48; week later, 138.88.

November 28–December 1, 1943: Teheran Conference. Market mostly on defensive. DJI closed month at low of 129.57 on November 30.

February 3–11, 1944: Yalta Conference. DJI fell 1.67 to 135.41 in 8 days.

June 6, 1944: Allies landed in Normandy. DJI rose 0.59 to 142.21; week later, 145.05.

August 25, 1944: Paris liberated. DJI fell 0.09 to 147.02; week later, 147.16.

October 20, 1944: U.S. landed in Philippines. DJI fell 0.34 to 148.21; week later, 146.29.

October 22–27, 1944: Battle of Leyte Gulf. DJI fell 1.92 to 146.29 in 5 sessions.

December 16, 1944: Battle of Ardennes Bulge. DJI rose 0.25 to 152.53; week later, 150.63.

February 19, 1945: Iwo Jima invaded. DJI rose 0.78 to 159.01; week later, 158.41.

April 1, 1945: Okinawa invaded. DJI rose 1.45 to 155.86; week later, 156.10.

May 2, 1945: Fall of Berlin. DJI fell 0.06 to 165.03; week later, 165.24.

May 6, 1945: Germany surrendered unconditionally. Event already discounted. DJI fell 0.18 to 166.53; week later, 163.45.

July 17–August 2, 1945: Potsdam Conference. Market on defensive. DJI fell 3.72 to 146.77 in 15 sessions.

August 6, 1945: Hiroshima atom-bombed. DJI rose 0.13 to 163.19; week later, 164.11.

August 5, 1945: Nagasaki atom-bombed. Russia declared war on Japan. DJI rose 2.72 to 164.55; week later, 164.38.

August 14, 1945: Japan surrendered. DJI rose 0.68 to 164.79; week later, 163.38.

October 24, 1945: United Nations established. DJI fell 2.43 to 183.72, on account labor situation; week later, 186.60, due to President's wage-price speech.

January 10, 1946: League of Nations dissolved. DJI rose 1.83 to 199.16; week later, 203.49.

February 24, 1948: Communists took over Czechoslovakia. DJI rose 0.20 to 167.80; week later, 168.75.

June 21, 1948: Berlin airlift started. DJI fell 1.94 to 189.71; week later, 187.90 (month's low).

April 4, 1949: Atlantic Pact signed (NATO). DJI fell 0.29 to 176.59; week later, 176.54.

May 12, 1949: Berlin airlift ended. DJI rose 0.30 to 174.70; week later, 174.14.

September 23, 1949: Russia exploded atom bomb. DJI rose 0.47 to 181.30; week later, 182.51.

December 7, 1949: Chinese Nationalists fled to Formosa. DJI fell 0.43 to 194.21; week later, 197.51.

June 25, 1950: Korean War began. DJI fell 10.44 to 213.91 on weekend news; week later, 208.35.

June 30, 1950: U.S. in action in Korea. DJI rose 2.69 to 209.11; week later, 208.59.

September 15, 1950: Marines made Inchon landing. DJI rose 1.37 to 225.85; week later, 226.64.

November 20, 1950: U.S. forces reached Manchurian border. DJI fell 0.11 to 231.53; week later, 234.96.

November 26, 1950: Communist volunteers crossed Yalu River. DJI fell 0.10 to 234.96; week later, 222.33 (December low).

May 27, 1951: Red Chinese absorbed Tibet. DJI rose 1.20 to 247.03; week later, 246.79.

July 10, 1951: Korean peace talks began. DJI fell 0.65 to 250.00; week later, 253.89.

November 11, 1952: U.S. exploded H-bomb. DJI rose 1.00 in next market session to 270.23; week later, 273.47.

June 17, 1953: Communists routed East Berliners. DJI rose 2.86 to 265.74; week later, 267.79.

July 27, 1953: Korean armistice signed. DJI fell 1.30 to 268.46; week later, 276.13.

August 12, 1953: Russia exploded H-bomb. DJI rose 1.12 to 276.42; week later, 271.50.

May 27, 1954: Fall of Dienbienphu. DJI fell 0.74 to 326.37; week later, 271.50.

July 21, 1954: Communists won half of Vietnam at Geneva truce. DJI rose 2.36 to 339.98; week later, 345.11.

September 8, 1954: SEATO agreement in Manila. DJI rose 0.70 to 346.07; week later, 350.63.

January 28, 1955: Eisenhower given emergency powers to protect Formosa and Pescadores. DJI rose 2.08 to 404.68; week later, 409.76.

July 26, 1956: Egypt seized Suez Canal. DJI rose 1.72 to 515.85; week later, 520.95 (August high).

October 23–24, 1956: Russians checked Hungarian revolt. DJI fell 2.60 in 2 days to 482.67; week later, 479.85.

October 29, 1956: Israelis crossed Egyptian border. DJI rose 0.88 to 486.94; week later, 495.37 (November high).

October 31, 1956: France-Britain air-bombed Egyptian installations. DJI fell 6.62 to 479.85; week later, 491.15.

November 5–6, 1956: France-Britain landed troops in Egypt. DJI fell 10.02 from month's high of 495.37 on the 5th to 485.35 on the 9th; week later, 480.67.

November 7, 1956: Cease-fire in Egypt. DJI fell 4.22 to 491.15; week later, 482.36.

July 15, 1958: Marines landed in Lebanon. DJI rose 1.93 to 478.82; week later, 494.89.

January 1, 1959: Batista fled Cuba; Castro took over. DJI rose 3.94 to 587.59; week later, 592.72.

January 10, 1960: U.S. pledged to defend Matsu-Quemoy Islands. DJI fell 8.57 to 667.16; week later, 645.07.

May 1, 1960: Russians shot down U-2 plane. DJI fell 2.09 to 599.61; week later, 607.48.

May 17, 1960: Khrushchev wrecked Paris Summit Conference. DJI rose 4.24 to 621.63; week later, 621.39.

June 29–July 1, 1960: Castro seized U.S. oil refineries. DJI rose 3.84 in 3 days to 641.30; week later, 646.91 (month's high).

November 1, 1960: U.S. pledged to defend Guantanamo. DJI rose 4.88 to 585.24; week later, 602.25.

January 3, 1961: U.S. and Cuba broke relations. DJI fell 5.64 to 610.25; week later, 625.72.

April 17, 1961: Bay of Pigs invasion. DJI rose 3.00 to 696.72 (month's high), but fell 12.48 to 684.24 in next 3 days after invasion failed; week later, 679.54.

August 13, 1961: Communist East Germans built Berlin Wall. DJI fell 3.68 to 718.93; week later, 724.75.

September 1, 1961: Russia broke ban on atomic testing. DJI rose 1.25 to 721.19; week later, 720.91.

October 29, 1961: Russia exploded biggest H-bomb. DJI rose 2.35 to 701.09; week later, 714.60.

January 16, 1962: Dominican Government overthrown. DJI fell 4.21 to 705.29; week later, 698.54.

January 25, 1962: Geneva Conference to end nuclear testing failed. DJI fell 1.65 to 696.52; week later, 702.54.

October 20, 1962: China-India clashed in Himalayas. Market virtually ignored this development, in view of more serious Cuban crisis.

October 22, 1962: JFK ordered sea blockade of Cuba. DJI fell 4.69 to 568.60, thence to new low for month of 558.06 the following day; week later, 588.98.

October 29, 1962: Khrushchev said Cuban missile bases would be removed. DJI rose 10.33 and 9.63 following day to 588.98; week later, 615.75.

November 21, 1962: Blockade of Cuba lifted. DJI rose 4.31 to 637.25; week later, 651.85.

November 2, 1963: South Vietnam Government overthrown. DJI fell 4.51 to 749.22; week later, 753.77.

January 10, 1964: Rioting in Panama Canal Zone. Panama suspended U.S. relations. DJI fell 2.22 to 774.33; week later, 775.69.

January 21, 1964: Geneva disarmament talks resumed. DJI rose 3.41 to 776.44; week later, 787.78 (month's high).

February 6, 1964: Cuba cut off Guantanamo water supply. DJI rose 3.37 to 786.41; week later, 794.42.

February 20, 1964: Malaysia asked British air-aid against Borneo guerrillas. DJI rose 2.08 to 796.99; week later, 797.04.

April 3, 1964: Relations restored with Panama. DJI rose 2.12 to 822.99; week later, 821.75.

May 2, 1964: Aircraft ferry "Card" sunk by saboteurs. DJI rose 6.73 to 823.83; week later, 827.07.

May 14, 1964: McNamara urged more support for South Vietnam. DJI fell 1.33 to 824.45; week later, 819.80.

August 2, 1964: North Vietnam P-T boats attacked U.S. destroyers in Tonkin Gulf. DJI fell 0.75 to 840.35; week later, 829.35.

August 4, 1964: U.S. retaliated against P-T bases after second Tonkin Gulf incident. DJI fell 7.58 to 832.77; week later, 828.08.

August 17, 1964: Indonesian forces reported landing in Malaya. DJI rose 1.40 to 840.21; week later, 837.31.

October 15, 1964: Brezhnev and Kosygin replaced Khrushchev. DJI fell 6.74 to month's low of 868.44; week later, 877.01.

October 16, 1964: Red China exploded first nuclear bomb. DJI rose 5.10 to 873.54; week later, 877.62.

February 8, 1965: Southeast Asia war activity increased. DJI fell 3.68 to 897.89; week later, 885.32.

April 7, 1965: Soviet jets harassed Berlin. DJI rose 1.04 to 892.94; week later, 912.86.

April 28, 1965· Marines sent to Dominican Republic. DJI rose 0.70 to 918.86; week later, 932.22.

May 3, 1965: Paratroops sent to Vietnam. DJI fell 0.20 to 922.11; week later, 931.47.

July 9, 1965: China claimed air-space violation. DJI rose 1.64 to 879.49; week later, 880.43.

July 27, 1965: Jets hit Red missile bases. DJI fell 3.73 to 863.53; week later, 881.20.

August 18, 1965: Marines won first big Vietnam victory. DJI rose 0.11 to 881.85; week later, 879.77.

September 1, 1965: India-Pakistan in undeclared war. DJI rose 0.50 to 893.60; week later, 917.47.

September 16, 1965: China gave India 3 days to raze border bases. DJI rose 8.23 to 931.18; week later, 927.45.

September 22, 1965: India-Pakistan cease-fire. DJI rose 5.10 to 931.62; week later, 932.39.

October 25, 1965: Inter-American force occupied Santo Domingo. DJI fell 4.28 to 948.14; week later, 958.96.

January 31, 1966: LBJ ordered renewed bombing North Vietnam bases. DJI fell 1.84 to 983.51; week later, 989.69.

July 7, 1966: Warsaw Pact nations offered Vietnam volunteers. DJI rose 2.78 to 891.64; week later, 887.80.

September 6, 1966: Gromyko rejected Goldberg's peace proposals. DJI fell 5.35 to 782.34; week later, 795.48.

February 23, 1967: Biggest offensive of Vietnam War. DJI rose 2.67 to 846.77; week later, 846.71.

April 20, 1967: Haiphong bombed first time. DJI rose 4.68 to 878.62; week later, 894.82.

May 18, 1967: Egypt-Israel at swords' points. DJI fell 4.90 to 877.34; week later, 870.71.

May 19, 1967: U.S. invaded DMZ. DJI fell 2.79 to 874.55; week later, 870.32.

May 22, 1967: Egypt closed Gulf of Aqaba. DJI fell 3.50 to 871.05; week later, 864.98.

June 5, 1967: War in Middle East. DJI fell 15.54 to 847.77 (month's low); week later, 878.93.

October 23–24, 1967: Egypt sank Israeli destroyer. Israel bombed Egyptian oil installations. DJI fell 16.99, in 4-day period surrounding these events, to 886.73; week later, 867.08.

December 6, 1967: King Constantine led revolt against Greek junta. DJI rose 4.16 to 892.28; week later, 882.34.

January 22, 1968: U.S. admitted forces crossed into Cambodia. DJI fell 8.61 to 871.71; week later, 863.67, due also to "Pueblo" seizure.

January 24, 1968: North Korea seized "Pueblo." DJI fell 2.54 to 862.23; week later, 855.47.

January 25, 1968: LBJ called up reservists. DJI rose 2.02 to 864.25; week later, 861.36.

January 30, 1968: Viet Cong shelled Saigon; attacked U.S. embassy in Tet offensive. DJI fell 4.10 to 859.97; week later, 861.25.

February 8, 1968: Jets bombed 10 miles from Hanoi. DJI fell 9.60 to 850.32; week later, 839.23.

February 14, 1968: Chinese shot down U.S. plane. DJI rose 5.61 to 837.38; week later, 849.23.

February 21, 1968: Soviet embassy in Washington bombed. DJI rose 6.13 to 849.23; week later, 844.72.

April 8, 1968: North Vietnam agreed to open peace talks. DJI rose 18.61 to 884.42; week later, 910.19.

May 3, 1968: Paris chosen as peace-talk site. DJI rose 1.16 to 919.21; week later, 912.91.

May 9, 1968: Russian troops reported moving on Czechoslovakia. DJI fell 7.51 to 911.35; week later, 903.72.

June 17, 1968: East Germans squeezed Berlin travel. DJI fell 10.17 to 903.45; week later, 901.83.

July 18, 1968: Russia demanded that Czechoslovakia modify democratic reform. DJI fell 3.25 to 917.95; week later, 885.47, due also to enactment of 10% tax surcharge.

July 22, 1968: Czechoslovakia tension mounted. DJI fell 13.60 to 900.32; week later, 883.36.

October 8, 1968: Paris peace-talk break rumored. DJI fell 0.44 to 956.24; week later, 955.31.

October 31, 1968: LBJ suspended North Vietnam bombing. DJI rose 1.31 to 952.39; week later, 950.65.

March 3, 1969: Russians-Chinese clashed. DJI fell 3.62 to 927.30; week later, 932.89.

April 11, 1969: Further Middle East tension. DJI fell 3.75 to 957.86; week later, 959.02.

April 15, 1969: North Korea shot down U.S. plane. DJI fell 0.70 to 931.94; week later, 918.59.

April 22, 1969: U Thant said near state of war existed along Suez. DJI rose 1.08 to 918.59; week later, 934.10.

May 8, 1969: Viet Cong offered peace plan. DJI rose 4.08 to 963.68; week later, 965.16.

July 17, 1969: Peace hopes dashed. DJI rose 3.75 to 853.09; week later, 826.53. Worry about the economy the main bearish factor.

September 9, 1969: Israel in big raid across Suez Canal. DJI rose 3.83 to 815.67; week later, 831.64.

September 29, 1969: Bolivian Government overthrown. DJI fell 6.14 to 818.04; week later, 809.40.

October 14, 1969: Peace hopes renewed. DJI rose 13.13 to 832.43; week later, 846.88.

February 12, 1970: Middle East heated up. DJI fell 1.72 to 755.61; week later, 757.92.

February 24, 1970: Middle East situation worsened. DJI fell 3.04 to 754.42; week later, 787.42.

May 1, 1970: Cambodia a major market depressant. DJI fell 2.44 to 733.63; week later, 717.73.

May 12, 1970: Israel raided Lebanon. DJI fell 5.48 to 704.59; week later, 691.40.

June 8, 1970: North Korea report of sinking U.S. gunboat proven false. DJI rose 5.20 to 700.23; week later, 687.36.

June 30, 1970: U.S. quit Cambodia. DJI rose 0.62 to 683.53; week later, 669.36.

July 23, 1970: Nasser reported more amenable to peace talks. DJI rose 8.01 to 732.68; week later, 734.73.

August 7, 1970: Ninety-day cease-fire in Middle East. DJI rose 2.88 to 725.70; week later, 710.84.

September 8, 1970: Israel threatened to quit peace talks. DJI rose 1.99 to 773.14; week later, 750.55.

September 17, 1970: Viet Cong peace proposals. DJI rose 3.36 to 757.67; week later, 759.31.

September 21, 1970: Jordan vs. guerrillas in civil war. DJI fell 6.57 to 751.92; week later, 758.97.

October 19, 1970: Turmoil in Canada. DJI fell 6.85 to 756.60; week later, 756.43.

October 21, 1970: Rumors of Vietnam cease-fire. DJI rose 0.82 to 759.65.

November 23, 1970: U.S. commandolike raid near Hanoi. DJI rose 5.95 to 767.52; week later, 794.09.

February 4, 1971: Egypt said it would observe month-long cease-fire extension. DJI fell 1.44 to 874.79; week later, 885.34.

February 22, 1971: South Vietnamese drive into Laos stalled. DJI fell 9.58 to 868.98 (month's low); week later, 882.53.

March 3, 1971: Uncertainty over Mid-East cease-fire extension. DJI fell 0.62 to 882.39 (month's low); week later, 895.88.

March 8, 1971: Market worried South Vietnam might invade North Vietnam, bring China into war. DJI rose 0.62 to 898.62; week later, 908.60.

April 1, 1971: Rebels seized East Pakistan city. DJI fell 0.49 to 903.88; week later, 920.39.

April 20, 1971: China to send ping-pong team to U.S. DJI fell 4.43 to 944.42; week later, 947.09.

July 7, 1971: Nixon planned visit to Red China. DJI rose 3.58 to 895.88; week later, 891.21.

October 12, 1971: Nixon to visit Moscow (May, 1972). DJI rose 1.61 to 893.55; week later, 868.43.

December 6, 1971: India-Pakistan War. South Korea proclaimed state of emergency. DJI fell 3.87 to 855.72; week later, 858.79.

December 9, 1971: Pakistan accepted U.N. cease-fire proposal. DJI fell 2.70 to 852.15; week later, 871.39.

December 16, 1971: East Pakistan army surrendered. India set West Pakistan cease-fire. DJI rose 7.63 to 871.39; week later, 881.17.

December 27, 1971: Heavy bombing North Vietnam resumed. DJI rose 0.30 to 881.47; week later, 889.30.

December 30, 1971: Vietnam bombing halted. DJI fell 4.59 to 889.07; week later, 908.49.

PART 4

Theories and the Market

A. THE DOW THEORY

The Dow Theory is a method of forecasting the market's trend direction based on average closing prices of the Dow Jones Industrial and Transportation Averages, together with daily volume on the New York Stock Exchange. It was devised by Charles H. Dow, *Wall Street Journal* founder and father of the famous Averages, but it was improved and developed in a series of editorials written between 1902 and 1929 by William Peter Hamilton, who served under Dow.

The theory holds that three movements of the Averages are simultaneously underway: *The Primary Movement*—broad upward or downward trends, known as bull or bear markets, which may endure for several years; *The Secondary Movement*—a significant decline in a primary bull market, or a primary bear market rally, which generally lasts from 3 weeks to 3 months; *The Tertiary Movement*—daily price fluctuations, which usually are unimportant.

The main crux of the theory is that reliable conclusions cannot be drawn about the market until it has been ascertained that the Industrial and Transportation Averages are moving upward or downward "in gear." Opinions derived from the movement of one average, if unconfirmed by the other, are generally wrong. When successive rallies penetrate preceding high points and ensuing declines hold above preceding

271

lows, the inference is bullish. Conversely, when rallies fail to carry above the old highs and subsequent declines extend below previous lows, the implication is bearish.

As Dow always maintained, "the action of the market itself is the best indication of its future course."

B. YEAR-END RALLY THEORY *

Dow Jones Industrials
(1897–1971)

Year	Xmas Eve	New Year's	Change	Year	Xmas Eve	New Year's	Change
			(P — Plus; M — Minus)				
1897	49.39	49.41	P 0.02	1924	116.74	120.51	P 3.77
1898	60.09	60.52	P 0.43	1925	157.01	156.66	M 0.35
1899	60.57	66.08	P 5.51	1926	160.46	157.20	M 3.26
1900	70.03	70.71	P 0.68	1927	200.30	202.40	P 2.10
1901	61.52	64.56	P 3.04	1928	287.89	300.00	P 12.11
1902	62.61	64.29	P 1.68	1929	234.07	248.48	P 14.41
1903	47.75	49.11	P 1.36	1930	165.20	164.58	M 0.62
1904	68.47	69.61	P 1.14	1931	75.84	77.90	P 2.06
1905	95.05	96.20	P 1.15	1932	57.98	59.93	P 1.95
1906	92.94	94.35	P 1.41	1933	98.04	99.90	P 1.86
1907	58.00	58.75	P 0.75	1934	100.69	104.04	P 3.35
1908	85.68	86.15	P 0.47	1935	141.53	144.13	P 2.60
1909	98.61	99.05	P 0.44	1936	178.60	179.90	P 1.30
1910	81.33	81.36	P 0.03	1937	127.36	120.85	M 6.51
1911	82.11	81.68	M 0.43	1938	151.38	154.76	P 3.38
1912	87.36	87.87	P 0.51	1939	149.85	150.24	P 0.39
1913	78.34	78.78	P 0.44	1940	128.89	131.13	P 2.24
1914	53.17	54.58	P 1.41	1941	106.67	110.96	P 4.29
1915	98.36	99.15	P 0.79	1942	119.27	119.40	P 0.13
1916	94.60	95.00	P 0.40	1943	136.24	135.89	M 0.35
1917	69.29	74.38	P 5.09	1944	150.63	152.32	P 1.69
1918	80.59	82.20	P 1.64	1945	190.67	192.91	P 2.24
1919	103.95	107.23	P 3.28	1946	176.95	177.20	P 0.25
1920	68.91	71.95	P 3.04	1947	180.84	180.56	M 0.28
1921	79.61	81.10	P 1.49	1948	177.42	177.30	M 0.12
1922	98.62	98.73	P 0.11	1949	198.88	200.13	P 1.25
1923	94.42	95.52	P 1.10	1950	231.54	235.41	P 3.87

Year	Xmas Eve	New Year's	Change (P – Plus; M – Minus)		Year	Xmas Eve	New Year's	Change	
1951	265.79	269.23	P	3.44	1962	647.71	652.10	P	4.39
1952	287.37	291.90	P	4.53	1963	756.86	762.95	P	6.09
1953	280.92	280.90	M	0.02	1964	868.16	874.13	P	5.97
1954	397.15	404.39	P	7.24	1965	966.36	969.26	P	2.90
1955	486.59	488.40	P	1.81	1966	799.10	785.69	M	13.41
1956	494.38	499.47	P	5.09	1967	887.37	905.11	P	17.74
1957	429.11	435.69	P	6.58	1968	952.32	943.75	M	8.57
1958	572.73	583.65	P	10.92	1969	794.15	800.36	P	6.21
1959	670.69	679.36	P	8.67	1970	828.38	838.92	P	10.54
1960	613.23	615.89	P	2.66	1971	881.17	890.20	P	9.03
1961	720.87	731.14	P	10.27					

Greatest point gain: 17.74 (1967)   Smallest point gain: .02 (1897)
Greatest point loss: 13.41 (1966)   Smallest point loss: .02 (1953)
Greatest percentage gain: 9.1% (1899)
Greatest percentage loss: 5.1% (1937)

* A theory which holds that the trend of the market is upward between Christmas and New Year's.

C. YEAR-END NUMERAL THEORY *

Dow Jones Industrials' Performance

Year Ending	Closed Up	Closed Down
0	1900, 1950, 1970	1910, 1920, 1930, 1940, 1960
1	1911, 1921, 1951, 1961, 1971	1901, 1931, 1941
2	1912, 1922, 1942, 1952	1902, 1932, 1962
3	1933, 1943, 1963	1903, 1913, 1923, 1953
4	1904, 1924, 1934, 1944, 1954, 1964	1914
5	1905, 1915, 1925, 1935, 1945, 1955, 1965	None
6	1926, 1936, 1956	1906, 1916, 1946, 1966
7	1897, 1927, 1947, 1967	1907, 1917, 1937 1957
8	1898, 1908, 1918, 1928, 1938, 1958, 1968	1948
9	1899, 1909, 1919, 1949, 1959	1929, 1939, 1969

Dow Jones Rail-Trans. Performance

Year Ending	Closed Up	Closed Down
0	1900, 1920, 1950	1910, 1930, 1940, 1960, 1970
1	1901, 1911, 1951, 1961, 1971	1921, 1931, 1941
2	1902, 1912, 1922, 1942, 1952	1932, 1962
3	1933, 1943, 1963	1903, 1913, 1923, 1953
4	1904, 1924, 1944, 1954, 1964	1914, 1934
5	1905, 1915, 1925, 1935, 1945, 1955, 1965	None
6	1926, 1936	1906, 1916, 1946, 1956, 1966
7	1897, 1927, 1947, 1967	1907, 1917, 1937, 1957
8	1898, 1908, 1918, 1928, 1938, 1948, 1958, 1968	None
9	1899, 1909	1919, 1929, 1939, 1949, 1959, 1969

* A theory which holds that specific years are more bullish-bearish than others.

Dow Jones Utilities' Performance *

Year Ending	Closed Up	Closed Down
0	1960, 1970	1930, 1940, 1950
1	1951, 1961, 1971	1931, 1941
2	1942, 1952, 1962	1932
3	1943, 1963	1933, 1953
4	1944, 1954, 1964	1934
5	1935, 1945, 1955	1965
6	1936, 1956	1946, 1966
7	1957	1937, 1947, 1967
8	1938, 1948, 1958	1968
9	1929, 1939, 1949	1959, 1969

* Utility average was not computed until January 1, 1929.

D. JANUARY ACTION DETERMINES THE BALANCE OF YEAR THEORY

January is a key month, according to this theory. The market's action in January determines if the underlying price trend over the next 11 months will be basically bearish or bullish, with a higher or lower close at year's end for the Dow Industrials.

The DJI has advanced 48 times and declined 27 times in January from 1897–1971, inclusive. Thirty-six of these advances and 16 declines extended to December 31 of the same year; this "confirms" the theory of January carry-through strength, or weakness, a total of 52 times in the past 75 years—about 70%.

E. LABOR DAY WEEK THEORY

This theory holds that the action of the Dow Industrials during Labor Day week determines the behavioral pattern of the average over the balance of the month.

The DJI has advanced 35 times and declined 39 times in Labor Day week since 1897. Twenty-five of these advances and 30 declines extended through to month's end. In other words, there have been 55 "confirmations" of Labor Day week action, versus 19 failures, in the past 74 years.*

The evidence indicates that the trend of the Dow immediately following Labor Day has a 75% chance of continuing for at least 3 additional weeks.

* Market was closed in September, 1914, on account of war.

Glossary of Terms

And Interest. Term indicating that accrued interest is to be added to the fixed or quoted price of a bond.

Annunciators. Two large call boards for paging members on the New York Stock Exchange trading floor.

Arbitrage. 1. Buying and selling, at temporarily different prices, two securities which are exchangeable for each other, as under a merger plan. 2. Buying a security or commodity in one market and immediately selling it (or selling it short and then purchasing the same security or commodity) in another market, where the price is temporarily different.

Ascending Tops. A favorable price pattern of higher highs and lows appearing on the chart of an individual stock, or the general market, which shows the highest levels attained during advancing periods extending above the preceding highs, with the lows reached on each decline holding above previous lows.

Balance of Payments. In general, payments made to foreign nations minus total receipts, or vice versa, during a prescribed time period.

Bear. A stock market pessimist, a believer in declining security values, who sells short, i.e., sells what he does not actually possess at the time of sale. If the stock drops in price, as anticipated, his profit is the difference between the higher price at which the short sale was made and the lower price at which it is bought back eventually, or "covered."

Bear Market. A falling market.

Bid and Asked. The highest price that anyone has stated he will pay for a security at a given time, coupled simultaneously with the lowest stated price anyone will accept. Frequently referred to as a quote, or quotation.

278

Bid Price. The highest stated price that anyone will pay for a security, or commodity, at a given moment of time.

Block. A large amount of stock, generally involving at least 10,000 shares.

Blue Chip. The common stock of an established industry leader, whose products or services are widely known and one which has a favorable record of solid performance in good times and bad.

Blue Sky Laws. Laws enacted by various states to protect investors from fraud.

Bond Yields. The income available from a bond bought for investment, to be held to maturity.

Bourse. A stock exchange located in Continental Europe.

Brokerage. Same as "Commission."

Bucket Shops. Dishonest and illegal establishments where bets are made against regular exchange quotations. Orders to buy or sell are not executed; the "bucketeer" merely holds the client's money and bets against him.

Bull. A stock market optimist, who buys stock long in anticipation of rising prices. The opposite of "Bear." Both terms originated on the London Stock Exchange.

Bull Market. A rising market.

Buying Long. Purchasing a security or commodity in anticipation of rising prices. The opposite of "selling short."

Call Loan. A loan which either the borrower or the lender may terminate, or "call," at any time.

Call Money. Borrowed money which is returnable to the lender upon demand.

Call of Stocks, or Call Trading. A system of trading intermittently in stocks by rote, or "call," that began about 1820. In September, 1871, it was superseded by the continuous trading system in use today.

Capital Gains Tax. A federal tax levied upon profits gained from selling a capital asset.

Capitalization. The total amount of a corporation's authorized securities.

Capital Requirements. Rules stipulating the amount of "back up" capital which exchange-member firms must maintain at all times.

Commercial Paper. Short-term notes, bills of exchange, and acceptances arising from industrial, agricultural, or commercial transactions. Attributes include early maturity (3–6 months) and automatic, or self-liquidating, power.

Commission. A broker's fee for buying or selling securities, or commodities, for someone else.

Conglomerate. A multifaceted organization, characterized usually by extensive mergers, or takeovers, in complex deals involving cash and/or securities.

Continuous Market. A market where buyers and sellers are always available during regular business hours.

Corner. A condition brought about intentionally—though sometimes accidentally—when virtually all of the purchasable, or floating, supply of a company's stock is held by an individual, or group, who are thus able to dictate the price. Cornering is a form of manipulation currently outlawed.

Covering Short. "Buying back" a security that was previously sold short.

Curb (The). Abbreviated title for the New York Curb Market Agency formed in 1906 and the New York Curb Market Association formed in 1911. Name changed to New York Curb Exchange in 1929 and to American Stock Exchange, January 5, 1953.

Curbstone Brokers. Nickname for brokers who formerly dealt in securities out of doors, on the streets and curbstones of New York's financial district.

Dear Money. Money which is scarce and available only at high interest rates.

Debenture. An acknowledgment of debt; a promise to pay, which is unsecured and backed solely by a company's general credit.

Demand Deposits. Deposits which may be withdrawn by the depositor at any time.

Depression. Part of a business cycle, characterized by high unemployment, curtailed production, contracting bank credit, general pessimism, low stock prices, and many failures.

Descending Tops. An unfavorable price pattern of lower lows appearing on the chart of an individual stock, or the general market, where the highest level reached during each rallying attempt failed to carry above the previous high, and the lowest level attained on each decline extended below the preceding low.

Discount Rate. The amount charged by Federal Reserve banks to member banks for loans.

Excess Profits Tax. A tax generally enacted during wartime and designed to curb profits derived from heavy consumer spending.

Federal Reserve System. A system of Federal Reserve banks created by the Federal Reserve Act of 1913, which reorganized the nation's banking system.

Financial Fundamentals. Basic business and economic factors, including auto production, rail carloadings, steel output, interest rates, corporate earnings and dividends, et cetera.

Floating Supply. The total amount of stock available for trading and speculation; that which is held usually in anticipation of a quick turnover, as distinguished from stocks bought and held as long-term investments.

Floor Transaction. A purchase or a sale effected actually on the trading floor of an exchange where the security involved is listed.

Give-up. 1. A situation where a floor broker-member of a securities exchange acts for a second member by executing his order to buy or sell with a third member. The first broker gives the second broker's name, rather than his own.

   2. Customer-directed give-ups, where John Q. Public could place an order with Smith & Co. and request that they "give-up" Jones & Co.

for his account with that firm, were banned by the nation's exchanges in December, 1968.

Glamor Stocks. Stocks representing companies which provide a service, or manufacture a product, that is considered exciting and mysterious. Example: products associated with undersea or space exploration.

Go Public. To market an issue of securities publicly for the first time.

Greenbacks. Notes created during the Civil War; so-called because they had green backs.

Holding Company. A company formed primarily for the purpose of owning the securities of corporations it desires to control. A favorite device for concentrating control of large properties in the hands of relatively few.

Institutions (Institutional Investors). Charitable organizations, churches, hospitals, pension funds, savings and commercial banks, life insurance companies, and others, whose securities operations represent an important part of their over-all business, although the organizations themselves are not primarily investment managers.

Intraday. The highest or lowest price level attained by a stock, or the general market, during any particular trading session.

Investment Trust. A company that invests its capital in other companies. An open-end or mutual fund; a closed-end fund.

Jobber. A member of the London Stock Exchange who does not deal with the public but makes a market in securities for fellow members.

Legal Tender. Money legally tenderable in the payment of debts.

Listed Company. A company whose securities have passed the listing requirements of a national stock exchange and has been granted full trading privileges on that exchange.

Lockup Money. Term referring to a note which has been renewed, the date of payment being extended beyond the original date. Since funds represented by the note were undelivered when due, they are withheld, or "locked up," for a further period.

Margin. The amount a client deposits with his broker to cover part of the cost of purchasing a security; the broker furnishes the balance.

Margin Account. An account maintained with a broker for the purpose of dealing in securities on margin, as opposed to buying outright in a cash account.

Market Averages. Barometers of market movements studied by traders and investors to determine the trend direction of the market over the near term, intermediate term, and/or long term.

Market Order. An order which demands an execution at the best price obtainable, as soon as the broker receives it on the trading floor.

Mutual Fund. An investment company, also known as "open-end fund," whose capitalization is not fixed, i.e., more shares can be issued to satisfy the demand. The shares are not exchange-listed and the company stands ready to redeem, or buy them back, at any time.

Nonvoting Stock. Stock in a corporation which does not entitle the owner to a corporate vote.

Odd-lot. An amount of stock, usually representing 1–99 shares, as opposed to a round-lot (100 shares, or any multiple thereof).

Odd-lot Dealers. Exchange members who buy or sell odd, or fractional, lots of stock (usually 1–99 shares) for regular commission brokers.

Odd-lot Differential. Commission received by an odd-lot broker for executing a 1–99 share order.

Off Floor. Term referring to an over-the-counter transaction in an unlisted stock, or the execution of a listed issue that did not take place on a stock exchange trading floor.

One-Eighth Rule. A rule stipulating that stocks may be sold short only under certain price change conditions.

Open-end Fund. Same as "Mutual Fund."

Order Room. A brokerage department responsible for transmitting buy and sell orders, or cancellations thereof, to the trading floor of a stock exchange, and for reporting any executions of same to the person, or organization, who gave the order.

Outstanding Stock. Stock which has actually been issued and sold, as opposed to that which has been authorized.

Overissue. An issue of corporate securities which is more than the amount authorized.

Over-the-Counter. The biggest, broadest, most diverse trading arena in the world. Over five times as many issues are traded there as on all U.S. stock exchanges combined. It is more a "negotiation" market than an "auction" market, as the New York Stock Exchange.

Par Value. 1. The dollar value upon which preferred stock dividends are computed.

   2. The dollar value upon which bond interest is figured.

   3. The face or nominal value imprinted or engraved on a stock certificate, usually $100 per share. Par value and market value are not one and the same.

Pass a Dividend. Failure to pay a dividend which had previously been paid regularly.

Pegged Prices. Prices which rarely change very much from a certain fixed level, because buying or selling pressure is applied intentionally to maintain that level, while the price is "pegged." Term is connected mostly with commodities.

Pool. A form of manipulation currently prohibited, but defined by A. W. Atwood in *The Exchanges and Speculation:* "A number of persons uniting or joining their interests for the purpose of buying or selling, and thus increasing or depressing the price of one or more stocks or commodities."

Posts. Horseshoe-shaped structures on the New York Stock Exchange trading floor, where specific stocks assigned to that location are traded.

Premium. 1. The amount by which a bond or preferred stock sells above its par value.

2. A borrowing charge levied sometimes to make delivery on a short sale.

3. The amount by which the market price of a new issue of securities rises over the original selling price.

4. The redemption price of a security if it exceeds its face value, or market price.

Prime Rate. The lending rate, set generally by big New York City banks, upon which the lending rates of commercial banks throughout the nation are based.

Proxy Fight. A contest between stockholders seeking to control a corporation, in which both parties solicit signed proxy statements representing votes from other stockholders. Proxies are legal documents authorizing one person to act or vote for another.

Puts and Calls. Options or privileges which obligate the writer, or the seller thereof, to accept delivery (put), or to deliver upon demand (call), a certain number of shares of a particular stock at a fixed price within a time period specified by the contract.

Pyramiding. Using "paper profits" (profits gained but not yet realized) as a basis for more margin to finance further purchases, rather than putting up additional cash or securities.

Raid (Bear Raiding). Aggressive selling by professional bear operators, who try to drive stocks downward to levels where they can buy back, or cover, previous short sales at a profit. A form of manipulation currently made impossible by the "One-Eighth Rule" governing short selling.

Redemptions. Shares of a mutual, or open-end, fund which have been redeemed, or bought back, by the fund itself.

Registered Bond. A bond registered in the owner's name.

Registered Representative. Same as Account Executive, Customer's Broker, Customer's Man; a trained person who supervises securities portfolios for clients.

Registered Trader. A broker-member of a stock exchange who, within certain restrictions, is permitted to buy and sell for his own account on the trading floor of that exchange.

Rights. A certificate issued sometimes by a corporation, which gives the owner (usually a stockholder of the company) the privilege or right, ahead of others, to buy new securities of the corporation in proportion to the amount already owned.

Round-lot. Usually 100 shares of stock, or any multiple; with bonds, $1,000 par value.

Seasoned Issues. The securities of well-established corporations which have successfully weathered the tests of time respecting earnings and dividend growth, product acceptance, et cetera.

Seat. A stock exchange membership.

Seat Rights. Rights distributed to 1,100 members of the New York Stock Exchange in February, 1929. The rights gave each member a 25% interest in a new membership, which he could exercise or dispose of by sale or transfer within 3 years.

Secondary Offering, or Distribution. The redistribution of a large block of listed or unlisted stock sometime after it has been sold by the issuing company. The stock is usually offered at a fixed price based on the prevailing market price, and the sale is handled "off floor" by a single firm, or group.

Securities and Exchange Commission. An independent agency of the U.S. Government, whose primary purpose is to protect the investing public against malpractices in the securities markets.

Settlement Date. The date when securities involved in a transaction are to be delivered and paid for, usually 5 full business days after the date of trade.

Shin Plasters. Term referring to depreciated Continental currency in the U.S. after the Revolution. Also, fractional paper currency issued by the Government during the Civil War, while payments in metallic currency were suspended.

Short Account. Virtually the same as "Short Interest."

Short Interest. The aggregate of securities which have been sold short and not yet covered, or bought back, to terminate short selling contracts previously assumed.

Short Position. The market position assumed by those who are pessimistic on security prices.

Selling Short. Selling a security or commodity which is not actually in the seller's possession at the time of sale, and then borrowing it for immediate delivery to the buyer. When the trade is finally consummated, by buying back the security or commodity previously sold short, it is returned to the lender. If, during the interval between selling short and repurchasing, the security or commodity has declined in price the short seller makes a profit. But if it has advanced to a price above that at which the short sale was made, he is liable to incur a loss.

Short-term Profits. The monetary gain derived from selling a security which had been held for less than six months and one day.

Specialist. A stock exchange member whose principal duties include:

    1) Maintaining fair and orderly markets in the stocks in which he specializes;

    2) Acting as a broker's broker on the trading floor of an exchange.

Specie. Metallic, or "hard," money; the opposite of paper, or "soft," money.

Stock Ticker. An instrument which prints the volume and prices of security transactions within minutes after they have taken place on an exchange trading floor.

Stop Order. An order which automatically becomes a market order whenever the price of the stock involved duplicates, or sells through, the price named in the order.

Stop Price. The price at which a stop order automatically becomes a market order.

Support Zone. A price level or area where buying support developed during a previous selling drive.

Ten-share-unit Stocks. Stocks in which the full and accepted unit of trading is 10 shares.

Ticker Lag. When trading volume is so heavy that the ticker cannot print sales fast enough to keep pace with transactions as they occur, the ticker is said to lag and a "late tape" condition exists.

Ticker Tape. A narrow strip, or ribbon, of paper upon which are printed the record and volume of transactions that take place on a stock exchange trading floor.

Tight Money. A condition typified by high interest rates and scarcity of credit.

Topped Out. Phrase referring to a market, or a stock, which carried upward as far as possible before reacting. The topping-out process usually takes place gradually after a long and broad advance.

Transfer Tax. Tax imposed by various states when a security is sold or transferred.

Treasury Bill. A U.S. government obligation, usually maturing in less than one year.

Triple Top, or Bottom. Technical market term meaning that an individual stock, a group of stocks, or the general market has failed on three attempts to penetrate above or below a certain price level.

Undigested Securities. Securities issued beyond the absorptive capacity of the buying public.

Unlisted Privileges. Unlisted securities are those which usually do not have trading privileges on the floor of a stock exchange. The NYSE has no unlisted securities on its trading roster. The ASE still has a few, but since the Securities Exchange Act of 1934 severely restricted such admissions, these unlisted issues really have no "privileges," aside from the fact that they can be traded. They account for slightly less than 4% of total ASE volume.

Volume Discounts. A system giving large investors a commission-price break on trades exceeding a certain dollar amount, or number of shares, involved in the order.

"War Babies." Nickname for the securities of armament-producing companies.

Warrant. A certificate giving the owner the right to buy additional shares of a company's stock at a certain price within a specified time limit, or perpetually.

Went to the Wall. Failed.

When Issued. Term referring to a conditional sale, as when a corporate security has been authorized but not yet actually issued. The buyer or seller of "when issued" stock is not required to pay for or deliver it until a date of settlement is officially announced.

Abbreviations Used

AEC	Atomic Energy Commission
AFL	American Federation of Labor
AP	Associated Press
ASE	American Stock Exchange
AT&T	American Telephone & Telegraph
B&O	Baltimore & Ohio
CIO	Congress of Industrial Organization
DJI	Dow Jones Industrials
DJR	Dow Jones Rails
DJT	Dow Jones Transportation
DJU	Dow Jones Utilities
FCC	Federal Communications Commission
FDR	Franklin Delano Roosevelt
FNMA	Federal National Mortgage Association
FOTLU	Federation of Organized Trades and Labor Unions
FRB	Federal Reserve Board/Federal Reserve Bank
FTC	Federal Trade Commission
GM	General Motors
IBM	International Business Machines
ICC	Interstate Commerce Commission
ICBM	Intercontinental Ballistic Missile

JFK	John Fitzgerald Kennedy
LBJ	Lyndon Baines Johnson
LSE	London Stock Exchange
MIP	Monthly Investment Plan
NASD	National Association of Securities Dealers
NASDAQ	National Association of Securities Dealers Automated Quotations System
NATO	North Atlantic Treaty Organization
NP	Northern Pacific
NRA	National Recovery Administration
NYCE	New York Curb Exchange
NYSE	New York Stock Exchange
OPA	Office of Price Administration
OTC	Over the Counter
RCA	Radio Corporation of America
RFC	Reconstruction Finance Corporation
RFK	Robert Francis Kennedy
SBIC	Small Business Investment Companies
SEATO	Southeast Asia Treaty Organization
SEC	Securities and Exchange Commission
TWA	Trans-World Airways
UAW	United Auto Workers
UMW	United Mine Workers
UN	United Nations
UP	Union Pacific
WPA	Works Progress Administration

Bibliography

American Stock Exchange, Inc. *Amex Databook*. New York: American Stock Exchange, Inc., 1969 and 1971.

Atwood, Albert W. *The Exchanges and Speculation*. New York: D. Appleton & Co., 1922.

Bancroft, Hugh. *The Dow Jones Averages*. New York: Barron's, 1932.

Burton, Theodore E. *Financial Crises*, New York: D. Appleton & Co., 1910.

Clews, Henry. *Twenty Eight Years in Wall Street*. New York: J. S. Ogilvie Publishing Co., 1887.

Colt, C. C. and Keith, N. S. *28 Days—A History of the Banking Crisis*. New York: Greenberg, 1933.

Craf, John R. *Economic Development of the United States*. New York: McGraw-Hill, 1952.

Davis, Forrest. *What Price Wall Street?* New York: William Godwin, Inc., 1932.

Fisher, Irving. *The Stock Market Crash and After*. New York: Macmillan Co., 1930.

Flynn, John T. *Security Speculation*. New York: Harcourt, Brace & Co., 1934.

Fowler, William Worthington. *Ten Years in Wall Street*. Hartford, Conn.: Worthington, Dustin & Co., 1870.

Fuller, Robert H. *Jubilee Jim*. New York: Macmillan Co., 1928.

Gann, William D. *Truth of the Stock Tape*. New York: Financial Guardian Publishing Co., 1923.

Hall, Henry. *How Money Is Made in Security Investments*. New York: De Vinne Press, 1908.

288

Hansl, Proctor W. *Years of Plunder.* New York: Harrison Smith and Robert Haas, 1935.

Hill, Frederick Trevor. *The Story of a Street.* New York: Harper & Brothers, 1908.

Hill, John Jr. *Gold Bricks of Speculation.* Chicago: Lincoln Book Concern, 1904.

Huebner, S. S. *The Stock Market.* New York: D. Appleton & Co., 1922.

Hull, George H. *Industrial Depressions.* New York: Frederick A. Stokes Co., 1911.

Josephson, Matthew. *The Robber Barons.* New York: Harcourt, Brace & Co., 1934.

Medbury, James K. *Men and Mysteries of Wall Street.* Boston: Fields, Osgood & Co., 1870.

Meeker, J. Edward. *Short Selling.* New York: Harper & Bros., 1932.

Munn, Glen G. *Meeting the Bear Market.* New York: Harper & Bros., 1930.

Neill, Humphrey B. *The Inside Story of the Stock Exchange.* New York: B. C. Forbes & Sons, 1950.

New York Stock Exchange, Inc. *Fact Book.* New York: New York Stock Exchange, Inc., various years.

Noyes, Alexander D. *The War Period of American Finance (1908–1925).* New York: G. P. Putnam's Sons, 1926.

Oberholtzer, Ellis Paxson. *Jay Cooke—Financier of the Civil War.* Philadelphia: George W. Jacobs Co., 1907.

Pratt, Sereno S. *The Work of Wall Street.* New York: D. Appleton & Co., 1903.

Rhea, Robert. *The Dow Theory.* New York: Barron's, 1932.

Schabacker, R. W. *Stock Market Theory and Practice.* New York: B. C. Forbes Publishing Co., 1930.

Smith, Matthew Hale. *Bulls and Bears of New York.* Hartford and Chicago: J. B. Burr & Co., 1874.

Sparling, Earl. *Mystery Men of Wall Street.* New York: Greenberg, 1930.

Thom, De Courcy. *A Brief History of Panics.* New York: G. P. Putnam's Sons, 1893.

U.S. Government Printing Office. *A Primer on Money.* Washington, D.C.: U.S. Government, 1964.

Van Antwerp, W. C. *The Stock Exchange from Within.* New York: Doubleday, Page & Co., 1913.

Warshow, Robert Irving. *The Story of Wall Street.* New York: Greenberg, 1929.

White, Horace. *Money and Banking.* Boston: Ginn & Co., 1895.

Winkelman, Barnie F. *Ten Years of Wall Street.* Philadelphia: John C. Winston Co., 1932.

Wyckoff, Richard D. *Wall Street Ventures and Adventures.* New York: Harper & Brothers, 1930.

Index

291

About the Author

Peter Wyckoff was educated at "Le Rosey," Rolle, Switzerland, the Choate School, and Yale and Columbia universities. Now a free lance financial writer, he was formerly a stock broker. His present profession has enabled him to write "The Psychology of Stock Market Timing" and "Dictionary of Stock Market Terms" in addition to the present book. He has been a regular contributor to the *Saturday Review, Forbes, Financial Analyst's Journal, Medical Economics, Trader's Guide, Investor's Future* and other magazines.

Mr. Wyckoff and his wife live in Woodstock, Vermont, in the winter and spend their summers in Bridgewater, Vermont, where he is the proprietor of a small antique shop.